LIES, DAMNED LIES AND HISTORY

A Catalogue of Historical Errors and Misunderstandings

GRAEME DONALD

For Rhona

First published 2009

The History Press
The Mill, Brimscombe Port
Stroud, Gloucestershire, GL5 2QG
www.thehistorypress.co.uk

© Graeme Donald, 2009

The right of Graeme Donald to be identified as the Author
of this work has been asserted in accordance with the
Copyrights, Designs and Patents Act 1988.

British Library Cataloguing in Publication Data.
A catalogue record for this book is available from the British Library.

ISBN 978 0 7524 5233 3

Typesetting and origination by The History Press
Printed in Great Britain

CONTENTS

THE FIRST 1,500 YEARS

THE LAST 510 YEARS

INTRODUCTION

Henry Ford is famed for saying that 'history is bunk', a statement that is something of a curate's egg in that it is right in parts only. Apart from the biased input from the 'history is written by the victors' lobby, the records of our past bear the scars of the interference from others with axes to grind on their spinning agenda. But 'the truth is still out there', as Agent Mulder would say; all you have to do is unearth it.

Some historical myths are home-grown, some are invented by outsiders, some are dreamed up by administrations or prominent individuals desperate to hide the truth of their actions from public view and some are invented by the public themselves, either to exaggerate out of all proportion some minor act of heroism or to hide the enormity of their own excesses from themselves. A fine example of that last category is the Londoners' invention of the 'Blitz Spirit' of Nazi-bombed London when the chirpy Cockneys supposedly met each onslaught with a 'Lorks a-mercy' and a twang of their braces before breaking into a stirring rendition of *Down at the Old Bull and Bush*. This myth of togetherness was invented to gloss over the fact that Londoners showed what they were *really* made of under cover of the blackout; incidents of rape, murder, looting, mugging and the robbing of the dead went through the roof while the public howled for accommodation, capitulation, *anything* to halt the war that 40 per cent believed was 'all about the bloody Jews'.

Nor can the power of cinema be underestimated for it is from the silver screen that we inherit such false notions as witches being burnt at the stake in 'Merrie' England and the indelible image of the American West where it turns out that almost half the of so-called cowboys were non-white and so few could afford sidearms that gunfights were a rarity. You were far more likely to be gunned down in Victorian London than in Dodge City, Tombstone or Abilene.

The power of myth lies in the fact that most invented versions of events present the public with something that is either convenient or simplistic – we wear the white hats and the baddies have black hats, or whatever – or with something that is guaranteed acceptance because it fits with national self-image. While most other nations perceive the British to have been arrogant, self-deluded, rapacious, duplicitous and dictatorial, the British see themselves as stiff upper-lipped defenders of the moral high-ground who meet defeat and victory as the same impostor, to paraphrase Kipling's 'If'. This being the case, the British public were psychologically primed to fall hook, line and sinker for the Dunkirk myth, complete with tales of the guards ignoring the Stukas and strafing Messerschmitts to conduct formation drills on the open beaches while awaiting embarkation. The reality was of course much darker and very different. Troops deserted to go looting and raping in the nearby French towns and villages and many of those who still had weapons threw them away. The withdrawal was a terrible betrayal of the French and the Belgians who were left to face the German advance alone; any of *their* number trying to embark at the beach were met by British guns. And as for the flotilla of plucky civilians popping across the Channel to lend a hand, the Cholmondeley-Warners and Barrington Farquhars of these isles ne'er set sail.

And things are no different in America, where, for example, the Amerindians have been painted as mindless savages to justify the countless broken treaties and massacres and, despite the Hollywood image of the Plains Indians preying on wagon trains, such attacks were few and most often retaliatory with the greatest wagon-train massacre of all time being inflicted not by Indians but by rapacious Mormons. As for Custer's so-called 'Last Stand', this had to be marketed as a perfidious massacre by blood-crazed savages to hide from the public the fact that Custer was a vainglorious idiot who, had he survived, would have been court-marshalled for his stupidity. Ignoring all orders and incoming intelligence, Custer attacked a vastly superior force and had to make a run for it; there was no 'Last Stand', only a runaway scrape during which some evidence points to Custer having shot himself. Faced with no other alternative, the US Army did what it always did with dead idiots and rebranded Custer as a hero.

But there are few real heroes, those perceived as such are almost invariably undeserving individuals who either seek such limelight or have it thrust upon them for reasons of national morale. And, on the other side of the coin, many of those painted as demons were not really that bad. Elizabeth Bathory, aka Countess Dracula, never bathed in blood; Vlad the Impaler was in fact a national hero; 'Bad' King John was a far better ruler than 'Good' King Richard; 'Bloody' Mary killed fewer of her subjects than did 'Good Queen Bess' and the Spanish Inquisition was in reality remarkably tolerant. It is all a question of who gets to write what.

As for Henry Ford and 'history is bunk', well, he never said it, but perhaps he should have.

PRE-HISTORY

CHARIOTS OF IRE

So little is known of Boudicca, Boudicia (d.60 or 61), or whatever you want to call the lady, that it is perhaps not pushing the matter too far to question whether she ever existed outside the minds of a couple of historians writing years after the alleged events. Perhaps they just invented some sort of ferocious bogey-woman under whose umbrella they could cluster a series of events known to have taken place but of which they knew little.

Boudicca – we shall stick with that form for the purposes of this entry – has been so many things to so many people, the first feminist, and so forth, that it is difficult to know where to begin. Always depicted in film as a flame-haired Xena-type with a body like an angry polecat barely contained in leather strappy-bits, the image we all have of her is taken from the over-imaginative statue on Westminster Bridge, this showing a wild-haired battle-vixen clutching her two wronged daughters aboard her scythe-wheeled chariot of war. Let's take that chariot first; no-one with even half a brain would use a chariot in war; the Romans, who knew a thing or two about the efficiencies of slaughter, never used them for anything other than pomp or racing. Battles did not take place on manicured lawns and the wheel/axel-making technology of the time was laughable. A chariot would not have lasted ten minutes on rough terrain and all aboard would have had to hang on for dear life instead of throwing spears or firing arrows with deadly accuracy. At the end of the day, a chariot is useless without its horsepower and that could be taken out at the drop of a hat by archers. As for wheel-scythes, they are pure fiction.

And so to the lady herself. The standard version of the tale is that she was an Iceni queen who took over after her husband, Prasutagus, either died or was poisoned by her, depending on what you read. Not long after this, the Romans announced that they were to annex the kingdom and, when she objected, they gave her a good flogging and raped her two daughters. This alleged brutality turned her into a whirlwind of revenge which engulfed three cities and countless Roman squaddies. But how do we arrive at this yarn with nothing written of such events at the time? We do not even know this woman's name; however you spell the term it is a corruption of 'boudeg', the Brythonic for 'victory' which could instead be a title or a name invented for a fictional character to suit the attributed deeds. It is a bit like the woman in the Bible who supposedly wiped the sweat from Christ's face as he made his way to the killing-ground only to be left with the image of his face on her cloth; she is referred to as Veronica, a name meaning the true image, yet how could her parents have known she would be doing this in later life and christen her accordingly? (The matador's drawing of the cape across the bull's face is also known as a *veronica*, taken from this same legend).

The first reference we have to the alleged Boudicca is in the writings of the Roman Tacitus (56–117) but he was about four years old when Boudicca was inflicting the ravages attributed to her. The only other source is Dio Cassius who, not even born until 164, was even more removed from her supposed time of prominence and likely relied on that same Tacitus as a primary source. Both were writing under the watchful eye of their Roman paymasters so you may draw what conclusions you should from that. All that said and done, the year 60 or 61 most certainly did see an uprising against the Romans with the settlements/cities of Colchester, St Albans and London the subjects of significant attack – even the archaeological evidence bears that out. But was there a Boudicca? At the risk of sounding trite, perhaps people simply got the wrong end of the stick after observing the Iceni horde cheering some priestess who, having issued suitably encouraging prophesies of success, was hailed with cries of Boudeg! Boudeg!

COLOSSUS OF RHODES

The notion that this statue once straddled the entrance to the main harbour of Rhodes is a medieval fantasy which, fuelled by countless paintings and etchings, is pretty much the image held today. In fact, the Colossus stood somewhere to the side of the harbour so it gained admittance to the Seven Wonders of the World club under false pretences.

After the death of Alexander the so-called Great in 323 BC, his over-vaunted empire fell apart like the house of straw it was, leaving his generals grabbing whatever fragments they could before falling to war amongst themselves. Ptolemy got Egypt, and, having cemented a pact with Rhodes, found himself at loggerheads with another of Alexander's heirs, Antigonus Monophthalmus, who, in 305 BC sent his son to lay siege to that island. But junior botched the job and had to flee the next year when Ptolemy turned up to send him packing *sans* half his fleet and all his siege equipment. The Rhodians gathered up all that had been abandoned and held an auction to raise funds for the building of a massive statue of Helios, their sun-god. Completed in 280 BC and made in the main from the re-forged iron and bronze of the abandoned weapons, the finished statue stood about 30 metres high at an unknown location near the harbour entrance – but not for long. Hardly the most durable of the Seven Wonders, it collapsed in the earthquake of 226 BC, snapped off at the knees by the first tremor, and there it lay in pieces for the next 800 years until the Muslim warlord Muawiyah I captured Rhodes in 654 and sold the shattered bits and pieces as scrap to 'a Jew from Emesa'.

CATS, SPATS AND CATACOMBS

Despite its name, the Colosseum was not the largest of the Roman arena or stadia; properly called the Flavian Amphitheatre it was not even referred to by that other name until the year 1000, this 'nickname' inspired by its proximity to the Colossus of Nero, a 40 metre-high statue that was pulled down in the fourth century so that the bronze could be recycled. Although the Flavian could accommodate crowds of about 50,000 it was dwarfed by the Circus Maximus which, on high-days and holidays, held something in the region of 500,000, and it was the specially structured passageways of these two arenas that enabled such massive crowds to exit quickly that gave birth to the myth that the Romans had special rooms where they could throw up between courses to make room for even more food. The much-misunderstood *vomitoria* were, in the case of the Colosseum, the eighty passageways and underpasses through which the entire 50,000 audience of a Colosseum full-house could exit in less than fifteen minutes, this giving the impression that the building was regurgitating its contents back into the city. Rome was certainly a place of excess and many did indeed round off the evening's entertainment doubled up in the shrubbery, but this was never a deliberate ritual in rooms designed for such behaviour. The myth seems to be one of relatively recent origins, first noted in print in Aldous Huxley's *Antic Hay* (1923), a comic novel making reference to massed hurlings in 'the elegant marble *vomitorium* of Petronius Arbiter'. In the relevant entry in the *Oxford English Dictionary*, the proper definition is put forward before the myth is explored. Using Huxley's error as illustration, the text imposes a corrective 'erroneously: A room in which ancient Romans are alleged to have vomited deliberately during feasts'.

And talking of feasts, the Colosseum is best known today as the venue where lions routinely snacked-out on Christians in their thousands. The trouble with that popular image is that it never happened; the whole story was a load of Papal bull calculated to call a halt to the wholesale theft of the masonry, fixtures and fittings by dodgy architects and landscape gardeners who were treating the place like a free-for-all builders' yard. It is clear that even in the Middle Ages the Colosseum meant nothing to Christians, it by then having been used as everything from a fortress to a quarry. Pope Pius V (1566–1572) seems to have been the one to start the ball rolling by declaring that pilgrims to the city should take away with them handfuls of Colosseum sand which, he proclaimed, was impregnated with the blood of countless Christian martyrs – but still no mention of lions. His was very much a minority view and one not shared by the rest of the Vatican hierarchy who continued to sanction varied and secular use of the place. Pope Sixtus V (1585–1590), a confusing name if ever there was one, was prevented only by his own death from turning large sections of the place into a maze of sweatshops to produce woollen goods to flog to the pilgrims. In 1671, Cardinal Altieri announced his intention to turn the place into a bullfighting area. This proved a step too far in the eyes of some, particularly one Carlo Tomassi, who countered Altieri's announcement with a pamphlet hailing the Cardinal's plans a profanation of what should be considered a sanctuary. So successful was the Tomassi campaign that Pope Clement X (1670–1676) eventually had to bow to mounting pressure and order the external arcade to be sealed off and the whole place declared a sanctuary.

The thefts of the Colosseum's very structure ceased overnight as pinching a few stones now became an act of desecration likely to attract the unwelcome attention of clerics with big piles of firewood – for the time being, the place was safe. However, about a century later, by which time the Church had largely lost the power to reduce transgressors to small piles of ash, the theft problem returned – proof-positive that capital punishment does indeed concentrate the minds of the un-godly. To save the place from further desecration Pope Benedict XIV (1740–1758) had Stations of the Cross erected throughout the Colosseum and proclaimed it dedicated to the Christians martyred therein. Everyone jumped on the new bandwagon: artists who plied their trade to the visiting pilgrims immediately began churning out depictions of pious Christians standing calm in their faith before salivating lions and baying crowds of suitably surly pagans. And that was that; thenceforth all and sundry were convinced that Christians were fed to the lions in the Colosseum.

In fact, it is not known if anyone was ever thrown to lions; the arena was all about spectacle and a man-versus-lion bout would not long entertain the crowd. Common criminals and some prisoners of war were pitted against animals, but most such incidents seem to have involved nothing more exotic than wild dogs. Apart from Nero, who most certainly did persecute Christians in his private gardens to entertain his dinner-guests, there does not seem to be any evidence that Christians were routinely singled out for their entertainment value in any arena – suffer they certainly did, but no more than any other minority group. Christians were by no means unique or the preferred dog's dinner as the Romans were quite happy to toss anyone to the dogs for a good laugh. Anyway, in 367 the Emperor Valentinianus banned the use of Christians in the arena, although the embargo did not apply to non-Christians who continued to top the bill in all of the city's arenas. So, far from bearing the main brunt of Roman persecution, Christians in fact got off lightly; the poor old gladiator would have to fight on for another forty years or so.

Since the general concept of the nature and outcome of the gladiatorial games is largely based on films such as *Spartacus* (1960) and *Gladiator* (2000) it is perhaps no surprise that there are more than a few misconceptions attached to the tradition, which was not Roman but Etruscan and, initially at least, never intended for the entertainment of the mob. The custom of voluntary mortal combat was an Etruscan funereal rite intended to provide bodyguards for the departed in the afterlife. As the Harpies played some dirge and sang of immortality, three or perhaps four pairs would fight it out to see who got to go on the trip of a lifetime, so to speak. Although distorted in mythology to creatures of foul unpleasantness, the original Harpy was chosen for her beauty and musical talent, appearing at funerals naked save for a feathered cape representative of the vultures that would devour the corpse and transport the soul into the heavens. Their name was taken from the Greek *harpazein*, to seize or pluck, either in reference to the feeding nature of the birds they represented or for the harps they plucked. Either way, the use of funereal gladiators is first recorded in the Rome of 264 BC when three pairs fought over the grave of Junius Brutus.

Properly called *munera*, such tributes to the dead began as low-key and very private affairs but, with time, they began to get out of hand as the families of the elite vied to hold increasingly impressive funerals; 'your dad only had six pairs fighting on his grave, well, we gave my dad eight' and so forth. Although the numbers inexorably rose, still by the time of the Dictator Julius Caesar (he was never Emperor; Augustus was the first to carry that title) the main focus was on the deceased party with the fights held in their honour. In 65 BC Julius Caesar honoured his father, by then twenty years dead, with a contest between 320 pairs of combatants – he had wanted more, but the Senate, still not over the memory of Spartacus' all-Italian tour of 73 BC, imposed restrictions on the number of slaves and prisoners of war who could be 'tooled-up' at any one time. In 46 BC Caesar again organised such a private function to honour his daughter, Julia, who had died in childbirth eight years before, with protracted and elaborate *munera* played out to a gory conclusion about her tomb. Far from being enjoyed by howling spectators, Caesar's *munera* were criticized for their extravagance and the unacceptable number of deaths involved, and that's not the kind of sentiment one was likely to hear often in ancient Rome.

Throughout the Republic, *munera* were always funded and organized by the family concerned, but the aforementioned rivalry, overlaid by lashings of political ambition, began clouding the original purpose of showing respect for the dead. Augustus, the first Roman Emperor from 27 BC until AD 14, decided to curb the excesses and place all such events under the authority of the Praetors who had their orders to limit such shows to two days a year with no more than sixty pairs at any one event. (This would eventually swell to twelve days a year, still far short of the weekly occurrence of popular imagination). Even as late as the turn of the second century, Tertullian

(160–220) would lament in his *On the Spectacles* (?198): 'this class of entertainment has passed from being a compliment to the dead to being a compliment to the living'.

But human nature is programmed to debase all it creates and so, inevitably, by the rule of Trajan (98–117) military victories and triumphs were celebrated with anything up to 5,000 pairs. By this time *munera* had become the 'Games' and very much the province of the howling mob who sat cheering and jeering at fights every bit as arranged and 'choreographed' as WWE bouts. Throughout the day the crowd was worked by hucksters selling wine, snacks and memorabilia; a day at the arena was no different to a day at a modern football match, apart from the fact that one was far less likely to get killed – at the Colosseum, that is. On the plus side, as far as the combatants were concerned, their lot had dramatically improved. While death was the required outcome at all *munera* this was not so at the Games; top-flight gladiators were far too valuable to be pitted to their death. The top dogs fought no more than a couple of times a year and spent much of the time touring the country putting on shows and inviting the local wannabes to try their hands with wooden swords. Furthermore, not all gladiators were slaves or POWs, many men – and women, for that matter – opted to fight in the arena for the sex and money. Commerce piggy-backing on the reputation of famous sportsmen is nothing new; gladiators ate and drank for free, wherever they went, in establishments happy to offset that cost against the additional trade their celebrity attracted, and clothes, shoe and weapon-makers bid against each other for the honour of kitting out such men for free. And then there was the toga-totty – women of quite elevated status fell over each other in the rush to bed the latest favourite – the gladiators were the football stars of their day.

Sure, some were slaves pressed into such service but if they fought well and survived, for sometimes as little as three years, they were rewarded with their freedom. Many such men, having so won their freedom, opted to stay on in the arena and rack up a fortune. Far from the Hollywood portrayal of gladiatorial contest, these were not undignified *mêlées* glorifying wholesale butchery, there were seven categories of fighter and only certain styles were pitted against each other. The *Retiarius*, for example, who fought with a net and a short trident, could only fight the *Secutor* who was heavily armed and wore a sleek helmet unlikely to become snagged in the net. All gladiators fought in accordance with strict rules enforced by the two referees who had to be present at all times. Much of the training was geared to methods of subduing, not killing, an opponent; defeat through death was far from the norm. A recent study of 200 fights of the first century revealed that only nineteen ended in death and that even in the most violent of these fights simple surrenders outnumbered deaths by 3:1. On average, with a 90 per cent survival rate, the gladiator fared much better then those in the crowd, over half of whom would not, for one reason or another, live to see their twentieth birthday; death was then very much a part of daily life. The only vanquished gladiators who were finished off in the arena had either fought badly or shown signs of cowardice but the notion of thumbs-up signals calling for them to be spared and thumbs down calling for a killing is a very modern invention. Gladiators who had fought well but incurred fatal injuries were removed from the arena to be finished off with a hammer-blow to the head in their quarters so as not to upset the crowd.

Such was the lot of the gladiator – that of the condemned men in the arena was quite another matter. The gladiators fought in the afternoon, but the condemned were the warm-up act put on in the morning with the outcome so predictable that few bothered to attend. Seneca (4 BC – AD 65) noted these to be little more than cheap, mass executions of little finesse or interest: 'The men have no defensive armour. They are exposed to blows at all points, and no one ever strikes in vain... There is no helmet or shield to deflect the weapon. What is the need of defensive armour, or of skill? All these mean delaying death... The spectators demand that the slayer shall face the man who is to slay him in his turn; and they always reserve the latest conqueror for another butchering. The outcome of every fight is death, and the means are fire and sword. This sort of thing even goes on when the arena is empty.' In short, those pitted to their deaths were there for that reason and that alone; no-one expected them to be entertaining.

The final myth surrounding the Christians in Rome is their use of the catacombs as a place to worship or hide from their persecutors. Excavated from soft rock, the catacombs were underground burial chambers, and, for economy of labour and strength of structure, present a maze of narrow tunnels and gangways quite unsuited to any religious gathering; besides, the stench of the rotting corpses would hardly be conducive to communal reverie. As for serving as hiding places for hunted Christians, since the location of all the catacombs was common knowledge; what would be the point? No-one used the catacombs for any other purpose than disposal of the dead.

CLEOPATRA: DRAG QUEEN OF THE NILE

There were many Queen Cleopatras of Egypt, and the term, translating from Greek as flame of the father, was actually a title rather than a name – a bit like 'Caesar' which, incidentally, infiltrated other languages in forms such as Kaiser and Tsar. As far as the West is concerned, the most famous Cleopatra was Thea Phiopater, again from the Greek and translating as 'the Goddess who loves her father', who became Cleopatra VII (69–30 BC) and it must be said that the lady herself was Greek and not Egyptian; she could not even speak the language of the land she ruled.

The dynasty was established by Ptolemy, a general in the army of Alexander, who decided to remain in Egypt and seize power when Alexander died; the tradition of *Cleopatra* as a title was instituted by Ptolemy V, there being some fifteen Cleopatras in all, ours the daughter of Ptolemy XI. Basically, Thea was as Greek as you can get; she spoke Greek; she dressed in the Greek style and generally favoured all aspects of that culture; only on state occasions did she go native – but dressed as a man; Egyptian queens were perceived as men and had to act the part; Thea even had to wear a stick-on beard. Nor was she the erotic vamp of Western imagination; coins dated to but a few years before her death show a face with a sharp and hooked nose, a rather mean little mouth, narrow forehead and a protruding chin; on top of that, her rotting dentures gave her breath that could, by contemporary accounts, fell an ox. Mark Antony, depicted on the other side of these same coins, presents a bull-necked pin-head of a chap with bulging eyes. Quite a pair; and such portrayal must be considered today to have been a trifle flattering as absolute rulers of such times did not appreciate public ridicule or lampoon. Even Plutarch, writing about a century after the Antony–Thea alliance, tactfully pointed out that her physical charms were 'not so remarkable that none could be compared with her ... but the contact of her presence ... was irresistible'. So, while she may not have been drop-dead gorgeous with a body like an angry ferret, she had wit and charm by the bucketful and a fascinating mind; real allure. She was also an extremely astute politician and negotiator, and it was with these attributes that she had first Julius Caesar and then Mark Antony dancing to her tune.

And what of that much-vaunted tender disposition to Mark Antony; this, it seems, is best left on the pages of Shakespeare's play. Whatever else she was, Cleopatra was shrewd and well aware that rulers on the world stage do not have love affairs but power-plays and alliances cemented in bed. After their joint defeat at Actium (31 BC), Cleopatra was quick to realize that all was lost and readily accepted Octavian's proposal to do away with Mark Antony as just one of a list of conditions allowing her to remain on the Egyptian throne but answerable to Rome. She summoned Mark Antony to the mausoleum already built for the pair of them, convinced him she had already taken poison, and then watched him commit suicide before continuing negotiations with Octavian for at least a week, so it was nothing like the star-crossed lovers' death-pact of Shakespeare's imagination. Reading between the lines, Mark Antony appears to have been brave in battle but an otherwise weak and vacillating man who would have been putty in the hands of someone as clever as Thea.

It was only after she learned that Octavian (who would soon become the Emperor Augustus) had no intention of keeping his side of the mooted deal and really planned to take her back to Rome in chains, that she resolved to kill herself. To achieve this, we are supposed to believe, she clasped to her breast a deadly *Naja Haje*, or hooded cobra, the royal snake of Egypt. In reality, Cleopatra resorted to a swift-acting poison she habitually carried with her, usually in a bodkin platted into her hair. Those who found her reported the body free of mark, wound or blemish, and the puncture marks and attendant bruising of a snake bite in an area as tender as the female breast could hardly have gone unnoticed. Besides, she was also noted to be calm and serene in her death, not contorted and covered in her own vomit and waste as she would have been had any cobra been involved.

It seems to have been Octavian himself who inadvertently started all the silly snaky tales. A vain and pompous man, he was determined that Thea's suicide would not rob him of his triumph in Rome and, if he could not parade the real Queen, he would parade her in effigy. For his return to Rome he commissioned a life-size carving of Thea, reclining on a couch, with a cobra coiled about her right bicep and its head and upper body extended across the breast; he was not attempting to indicate the manner of her death, he just wanted to include the most potent symbol of the dynasty he had suppressed.

As for 'Cleopatra's Needle', the pillar of granite standing on London's Victoria Embankment, it is neither the first monument to bear that name nor is it unique, but one of a pair. Europe's first such monument was erected in Paris in the Place de la Concorde in 1833 to mark the spot where Louis XVI and Marie Antoinette were executed in 1793. 'Acquired' by the French from the Temple at Luxor, L'Aiguille de Cleopatre thus predates the British 'acquisition' of their Needle, erected in 1878, by nearly fifty years. The twin of the London obelisk was likewise 'acquired' by William H. Vanderbilt and erected in New York's Central Park in 1881. None have any connection to Thea; all three predating her by a long chalk as the London and New York statues were first erected at Heliopolis *c.* 1500 BC by Thotmes III. As one might well expect, there are many in Egypt, who, having no doubt consulted a good thesaurus, are of the firm opinion that 'stolen' cannot be considered a synonym for 'acquired'.

FACE THAT LAUNCHED A THOUSAND QUIPS

From 1873 until the end of that decade, the world stood agog at a series of finds and announcements from a dodgy archaeologist called Heinrich Schliemann (1822–1890) who claimed to have found the ancient city of Troy in northwest Turkey. Before the world's press he held aloft what he confidently proclaimed to be the Mask of Agamemnon while his wife swanned around bedecked in what he confidently pronounced to be the Jewels of Helen. More finds soon followed and were collectively recognized as Priam's Treasure. It was all true; Helen of Troy; Paris; King Priam; the Trojan War; it had all really happened. From that point – right up to the risible film *Troy* (2004), with assorted hunks and Trojan-totty trying to out-pout each other – interest in the so-called Trojan War stands undiminished as does the general belief that the yarn is actually based on a foundation of truth.

Most of what we know of the Trojan War comes from the writings purported to be those of a chap called Homer who, if he lived at all, flourished some time in the eighth century BC to record in such great detail what had happened in the twelfth century BC. So, given the date of the alleged conflict, the protagonists would not be all

togged up in the shiny armour and finery favoured by the costume
department on the film set of *Troy* – most would have been lucky
to have a goatskin – and the city besieged would not have looked
like a massive stone edifice covering countless acres. Homer's yarn
tells of a Greek army, numbering 110,000, setting out to avenge the
kidnapping of Helen, wife of Menelaus, by Paris, a foppish Trojan
Prince, and besieging said city for ten years. According to most
sources, Helen would have been perhaps twelve or thirteen at the
time and with women in general then regarded in Greece as having
slightly less value that cattle, such abduction is unlikely to have united
all the warring Greek states in her cause. In addition, if every fighting
man in Greece had gone off to Turkey for ten years there would have
been no Greece left to go home to. As for the fabled 'Trojan Horse',
which lives on with us in phraseology and computer-speak for a
type of invading virus, simple maths disproves the possibility of such
a structure.

   According to the legend, the horse contained a war-party of
forty men who would emerge and throw open the gates once the
dumb Trojans had dragged the thing inside. A wooden horse built
to accommodate a single man would have to be about twice the
size of the real thing, so the Greek version would have to have been
100-fold normal size. And how big the gates of Troy for it to pass
through? Some Homer-apologists have ventured to opine that
'horse' could be a misunderstanding of some long-lost designation
for a siege machine or a giant catapult but all such speculation is
unnecessary. All we have is an account of a war that never happened,
written by a man who never existed and an archaeological site hailed
by a con-man to have been the location of all the action. Those who
worked with Schliemann were not shy in telling how most of his
'finds' had either been knocked up by local craftsmen, unearthed in
sites near to, but not at 'Troy' or brought to the dig in packing cases
so that they could be 'found'.

FIVE RING CIRCUS

The modern Olympics were resurrected amidst a shroud of myth
that the Ancient Games were the embodiment of noble and
sportsman-like spirit with nation competing against nation without
fear or favour. Well, we all make mistakes. Also, despite statues of
the French Baron Pierre de Coubertin that are dotted about the

world, proclaiming him the 'Father of the Modern Olympics', de Coubertin borrowed the idea from Dr William Penny Brookes of Much Wenlock in Shropshire whose revival Games began in 1850, forty-six years before the first grand spectacle in Athens in 1896. At first, de Coubertin evaded or fudged his answers to questions as to the part that Brookes had played in the international drive to reinstate the Games but eventually he had to come clean and publicly acknowledge Brookes and his Much Wenlock Games to have been his sole inspiration.

The great focus on the Ancient Olympics has left the impression that these were the only Hellenic Games, whereas they were but one of four and perhaps only the most prominent as their occurrence was used as the marker for the Greek calendar which counted in blocks of four years. Although most now use 'Olympiad' to denote the games themselves, that term properly applies only to the span of four years between each meeting. Using the Olympics as the starting point of the cycle, the other years were marked off by the Nemean Games, the Isthmian Games, the Pythian Games and then back to the Olympics. And it was at the Pythian Games where the laurels were handed out, Olympic winners wore crowns of olive; wild celery at the Nemean and pine leaves at the Isthmian. As for any nobility of competitive spirit, the ancient competitors were just as corrupt and riddled with political intrigue as their modern counterparts; bribes, drugs and bogus claims of nationality were all part of the fun.

Just as there was international outcry in 1984 when the UK 'induced' the South African Zola Budd to assume UK citizenship in an unseemly hurry so that she could run under the Union Jack – thousands of other would-be British citizens were amazed at the speed with which the Foreign Office could act when it wanted to – countless Greek states are on record as having been fined or excluded from the Games for pulling the same sort of trick. Most states were content to bribe foreign athletes to claim birth in another city but with so much money and prestige at stake, there are even examples of one state invading and annexing another to place irrefutable claim over a handful of competitors. Cheating on an individual basis was also rife. If there was no chance of drugging or poisoning the competition, some resorted to sending highly 'athletic' prostitutes to the opposition's tent to 'sap their vital fluids'. Not only is this the origin of the notion that sportsmen should refrain from sex before any major competition but, since it is all pseudo-medical mumbo-jumbo, the would-be cheats were wasting their money. Betting on the results was heavy so, then as now, competitors would set up ring-deals to prearrange the results and then back themselves accordingly. The most famous such event happened at the 112th Olympics when Callipus of Athens bribed his fellow pentathletes to finish in a certain order – all was uncovered and Athens banned from the Games. As for the 'amateur' status of the competitors, that comes down to semantics: competitors and their immediate family were supported by their state throughout their years of training and, while there were no cash prizes *per se*, the rewards were real enough. Not only were there deals to be done for future events, but once home, winners did extremely well out of advertising and sponsorship arrangements – the pentathlon champion drives one of our chariots, or whatever. Also, many of the victors returned home to free villas and olive groves to keep them in comfort for the rest of their days so, make no mistake, these men were the superstars of their day and lived accordingly. As for any nobility of Olympic 'to compete is all' spirit, there were no second prizes; those who let down their team often returned home to be whipped through the streets or even banished.

As for the overall 'spirituality' of the meetings, this too was notably lacking. There was no honouring of the gods and many ancient chroniclers recorded their regret that it was 'that time' again; Elis, where the Olympics were held, was again to be invaded by a horde of ne'er-do-wells, setting up bars, brothels and sideshows to fleece the drunken crowds. The Games attracted tens of thousands to the site, which did not have latrines or other basic facilities to cope with that number of people. Just think Woodstock with no loos, marshals or cleaners and you will arrive at a pretty accurate image of what the place looked like when all the fun was over. And so to the myth of the founding of the modern charade.

As stated at the beginning of this entry, the Olympic revival began not with de Coubertin and Athens but in Much Wenlock's Olympian Society as founded by Dr William Penny Brookes who held his first games in 1850. Having resisted all pressures to restrict entrance to the pupils of public schools or their alumni, as did all other athletic events of the day, Brookes' games were truly egalitarian meetings in which competing was all that mattered; he welcomed Eddie the Eagles before there was an Eddie the Eagle. But this was no penny-ante village affair; it attracted all sort and grades of competitor, including cricket's W.G. Grace who proved a mean hurdler, despite his bulk. Within fifteen years, Brookes had established the National Olympic Association which held its first meeting at Crystal Palace the same year, attracting substantial crowds and international interest. When Athens got wind of these new Olympics, King George I of Greece sent silver medals for the competitors. It was not until 1890 that Brookes invited de Coubertin to the meetings after which the Frenchman scurried off to form the International Olympic Committee in 1894 and managed to push Brookes into the shade by organising the first modern games in 1896 in Athens.

HOLDING THE HOT GATES

Everyone loves a good 'David-and-Goliath' yarn and that telling of a self-sacrificing band of Greeks holding a narrow pass against the might of the Persian horde is a perennial favourite, most recently given a highly camp makeover in the laughably homo-erotic *300* (2006). (Actually, the sword-slash stylization of the numeric title on the posters left this writer puzzled as to why such a film should be called *Zoo*, but there you go). All things considered, Thermopylae is without doubt one of the most evocative and best-known names from the history books of Ancient Greece and one that translates as hot-gates in reference to the sulphur-springs that once bubbled there – the second element on the name is also seen in 'pylon' for their open, gate-like base. Most of what we now hold as the truth of the Greco-Persian confrontation that occurred there in 480 BC comes to us from the writings of Herodotus so it is perhaps little wonder that the present perception is distorted and riddled with exaggeration; after all, this was the 'Father of History' who regaled his readers with expansive accounts of how the denizens of India used trained ants the size of dogs to mine for gold, and other such flights of fancy. Be that as it may, we still retain the abiding image of the 300 Spartans as noble goodies, laying down their lives for others, and the Persians as deviant baddies who arrived with an army the like of which the world had never seen, only for the 300 to hold them at bay in a narrow pass. Not quite.

The Spartans are much over-eulogized, for they were in reality the most savage and brutal of all their fellow states; they railed against the slavery that the Persians might impose and yet built their very nation on such an institution; no Spartan lad could claim to be a man until he had hacked up a defenceless slave in an annual ritual involving old or troublesome slaves being driven out into the hills so that they could be hunted down and killed by those aspiring to manhood – naturally, heads had to be brought back as proof of the deed. This, combined with institutionalized pederasty involving grown men and boys as young as seven years old, made Sparta a somewhat less than appealing place. Western admiration for Sparta, which seems to be as boundless as it is ill-founded, is curiously persistent; while far more civilized peoples, such as the Vikings and the Germanic tribes, are routinely vilified, the Spartans are almost deified despite their producing no art, no writings and no architecture – just death. But of course, they were Greek and there is vested academic interest in sustaining the myth that the Greeks were a philosophical bunch of aesthetes who invented maths, democracy and personal hygiene instead of a squabbling clutch of self-interested and small-minded states put well and truly in the intellectual and scientific shade by India and the Middle East, both streets ahead in all fields.

At the time of writing, *300* (2007) is the latest cinematic shot-in-the-arm for the spurious reputation of this bunch of homicidal paedophiles who would not have been sporting plumed helmets, matching cloaks, brandishing nice shiny weapons and generally strutting about half-naked and body-oiled; this was a culture at the beginning of its iron-age and would have gone to war looking the part. Films such as *300* also perpetuate the myth that the Persians were the aggressor, attacking Greece without reason or warning whereas Xerxes was on a payback call for the Athenian-backed sacking of the Persian city of Sardis in 498 BC. And what of the numbers involved; many sources talk of the Persian Army numbering over 2 million while good old Herodotus is quite specific with 5,283,220, either figure well beyond what any nation on earth could then muster; Xerxes *might* have had a force of about 100,000 at best, divided between a land-army and his navy standing offshore in the Straits of Salamis.

As for the so-called 300, this was only the number of Spartans who turned out for the battle, the overall force numbered a great deal more and, for once, Herodotus is down among the more conservative estimates with a figure of 5,200 – Diodorus Siculus puts their number at 7,400 while Pausanias tops the bill with 11,200. Whatever the real total, the home team was made up of soldiers from about a dozen other nation-states, such as Thebes, and a goodly contingent of Thespians, always keen to act in any theatre of war. Although Leonidas and his Spartans did indeed stay until the bitter end, with the total force by then depleted by casualties, desertions and others dismissed by Leonidas at the eleventh hour, those who made the last stand numbered in the region of 1,400 so it is something of a mystery how the Spartans managed to grab all the glory. Naturally, the story is given additional poignancy with the invention of the evil goatherd, Ephialtes, a sly mutant, of course, who sells the heroes out by telling the enemy of a secret path through the rocks which will allow the Persians to out-flank and destroy the men blocking their way. No good yarn is complete without a Judas and this one carried the additional tang of the suggestion that, without such betrayal, the '300' could have held back the 'millions' indefinitely. Actually, there was no secret path; both sides were well aware of the Anopaia track which is why Leonidas had stationed over 1,000 Phokians there to prevent any encircling movement; when the Persians did try that route the Phokians were quickly overwhelmed but at least managed to send a runner to Leonidas to let him know that he had been out-flanked. At this point Leonidas dismissed the bulk of his force and elected to remain with about 1,400 to give the others time to get clear; whether he actually knew that this was suicide or simply overestimated his chances is down to conjecture but, either way, it was still a brave act.

That the Persians invaded Greece is beyond dispute but exactly what happened and where it happened is less than clear. The Persians are supposed to have lost countless ships in the naval battles at Salamis yet no wrecks can be found in those very diver-friendly waters. At Thermopylae, we are supposed to believe that upwards of 20,000 Persians and over 2,000 Greeks died, the former being buried in mass graves by Xerxes, the rest left to rot. Strange then is it not that archaeologists have not been able to find anything more than arrowheads and spear-tips in numbers suggesting something less than such a concerted military action spanning several days. As for the mass graves of so many men, these too have so far eluded detection. But Thermopylae has been the scene of several conflicts so it is perhaps not that easy to determine which weapon fragments came from which confrontation and who was firing at whom – there were quite a few Greek-on-Greek conflicts at Thermopylae so all involved would have been using similar weapons and arrows.

In 353 BC, Philip II of Macedon was denied the pass and in 279 BC a coalition of Greeks – Aetolians, Boeotians and Athenians – re-grouped to hold the pass against a Gallic army under Brennus who also knew of the so-called 'secret path' and used it to outflank the defenders of the pass who only just managed to escape in boats waiting in the nearby sea. In 191 BC, Antiochus III tried in vain to hold the pass against the Romans and, in more recent times, the Greeks yet again found themselves at Thermopylae, this time trying to hold back 8,000 Turks marching down from Thessaly. The last battle of Thermopylae happened in 1941 with the Australian and New Zealand Army Corps (ANZAC) forces holding back the Germans long enough for the British to evacuate their forces to Crete.

Finally, the modern geography of the place must be addressed, as tourists visiting the site expecting to seek a narrow and rocky stricture are going to be disappointed. Since the 480 BC stand, nature has been at work for 2,500 years leaving the site so dramatically altered by marine erosion and alluvial fan deposit that the sea is 4 miles further out than it was in Leonidas' day. All the modern visitor can see are some rather unimpressive hills with a vast expanse of scrubland stretching from their feet out to the sea. In Leonidas' day there was a coastal road abutting the foot of those hills, running in a narrow cut between the hills and a strip of land before the shore. The hills and that coastal strip did indeed then present a narrow pass which, in several places, was only wide enough to allow the passage of a single cart.

HOT TIME IN THE OLD TOWN TONIGHT

The Great Fire of Rome in AD 64 was certainly a major event and one for which some hold Nero responsible. His plans to remodel the city, with a sumptuous new palace for himself, had been baulked at by the Senate, so the popular conception was that he burned the city to the ground to scotch any further objection. He was certainly mad enough to have done such a thing but all the indications run to the contrary. If not an accident waiting to happen in the prevailing conditions at the time of hot, dry weather and strong winds, then it could indeed have been the Christians, as alleged by Nero.

The fire is known to have started in the shops lining the Circus Maximus and, from there took off like a startled gazelle, moving swiftly through the city to destroy ten of the fourteen districts in its six-day rampage. The first hint of Nero's involvement in any arson comes from the writings of Tacitus who would have been nine years old at the time and had been born into the Roman elite, a stratum of society which not only hated Nero but also lost the most in the fire. Tacitus concentrates on what he claims to have been the implausibility of the fire spreading unaided from the wooden hovels of the poor to the stone-built homes of the rich and razing them so efficiently; gangs of arsonists simply had to have been involved, he reasoned. Leading Italian archaeologist Andrea Carandini, related to the British horror-actor Christopher (Carandini) Lee, tends to agree: 'Everything was destroyed. There was not a single house standing. All the houses [of the aristocracy] were destroyed so they didn't have a proper place to live.' Only the mall in the middle of the Forum remained but that was quickly taken over as a commercial market: 'built on top of aristocratic Rome … so it was, in a way, the end of the power of the aristocracy in Rome.' While all that is undoubtedly true, this only leaves us with a bunch of disgruntled aristos with a grievance but no proof of who started the fire that burned them out.

Although an easy man to hate and thus a pleasure to blame for anything, most of the circumstantial evidence stacks up in Nero's defence. He lost his beloved Domus Transitoria, a massive and palatial residence stretching from the Palatine to the Esqualine, something he would have done his utmost to avoid had he been the puppet-master. True, he wanted to build his new Domus Aurea but the fire broke out over 1 kilometre from the planned site, with no guarantee of it ever reaching that point. Why not simply start it there? Also, the fire broke out just after a full moon which would not have been the best time for gangs of arsonists to prowl the city in plain view of all. Up to 100 fires a day were a normal occurrence in Rome and it seems that this one started as 'just another fire' before being helped along by a concatenation of conspiring factors. The weather had been intolerably hot and dry, hence Nero having escaped to the cool of his villa at Antium (modern Anzio) where myth has him playing his fiddle while the city burned – this would have been a trifle difficult as the violin was centuries away from its invention. In fact, he raced back to the city and made a great show of doing all he could to alleviate the sufferings of the common people, throwing open his own gardens and other residences to accommodate and feed them. Naturally, this could equally have been the actions of a guilty man trying to score brownie points and cover his own guilt, but Nero did not in general give a toss what anyone thought of him, so that would have been way out of character.

All said and done, Tacitus and Carandini are in the minority with few historians today believing the fire to have been Nero's version of urban renewal. Tacitus is right in his assertion that a large proportion of Rome was timber-built but he is wrong to assert that the sturdy homes of the upper-crust should have survived. In 2004 an experiment was conducted in a massive fire chamber with model buildings to scale and the winds, as reported at the time, replicated by blowers. In next to no time the temperature hit 1000°c and the fire spread from the model hovels to those of the stone residences in the Forum with no trouble whatsoever. And, more recent excavations under Professor Clementina Panella of the University of Rome La Sapienza bear out the notion that the fire would have been well up to speed and heat by the time it arrived at the real Forum. Digging down over 20 ft she discovered melted roofing nails, gates and other fixtures and fittings equally tortured by intense heat, as well as collapsed and charred masonry. A fire like that would have been swift-moving and driven by the south-easterly winds mentioned by all contemporary accounts. Tacitus describes the fire moving simultaneously north up the Palatine and south up the Aventine Hill but this does not suggest the arson he is so anxious to hang around Nero's neck, rather a fire behaving consistently with creating its own up-draughts and fanning out along any available route in its desperate search for oxygen. In addition there is another academic in the arena who is convinced that Nero was quite right to blame the Christians who, if not wholly responsible for starting the initial fire, most likely gave it a helping hand by starting others.

Having spent years examining various ancient texts and Christian paraphernalia, Professor Gerhard Baudy of Germany's University of Knostanz asserts that in the days leading up to the fire Christian activists were circulating pamphlets predicting the destruction of the city by fire in accordance with the ancient prophecy that such an event would happen to coincide with the rising of Sirius, the Dog Star, which did indeed rise on the night of the fire. (The rising of Sirius frequently coincides with the onset of excessively hot and arid days in the Mediterranean, hence 'dog-days' describing such conditions). Baudy believes that the Christians were determined to make that prophecy come true by whatever means necessary to highlight the validity of their faith and the evil embodied by the Rome that so persecuted them. Who knows; but get the blame they most certainly did. In the aftermath of the fire, the displaced were entertained by Christians being clad in still-bloodied animal skins and thrown to wild dogs while they ate their free meals in Nero's gardens which were illuminated by the gentle light emanating from crucified Christians smeared in tar and set alight, the original Roman candle.

LET WHAT PEOPLE GO?

Even those who consider the Bible to stand anywhere between unreliable and a catalogue of myths and fairytales happily accept as fact that, at some time, the so-called Children of Israel were held in slavery in Egypt for a considerable period of time – perhaps as long as 400 years. Back in 1977, Menahem Begin, then Prime Minister of Israel, caused a political storm on a visit to that country by casually observing in an 'as-everybody-knows' voice: 'Of course, *we* built the Pyramids'. More recently, throughout the American Presidencies of both George Snr and George 'Dubya' Bush the standing joke on Capitol Hill held that neither man would succeed in their Middle East peace-initiatives because the last time the Israelis listened to a bush they spent forty years in the wilderness. Trite, perhaps, but it does underline the broad acceptance of the whole tradition as fact, whereas the Israelites were never in Ancient Egypt.

Eric H. Cline PhD, Professor of Ancient History, Archaeology and Anthropology, Chair of the Department of Classical and Semitic Languages and Literature at George Washington University and a man who has conducted several high-profile 'digs' in Israel, has firmly disproved any notion of prolonged or even temporary captivity. Such a host of people, a number approaching 3 million, quitting Egypt for forty years habitation in the desert, would, he calculated, have presented a column 150 miles long if they marched ten abreast; even if they bunched up to a column a quarter of a mile wide they would still be tailing back about 30 miles. When the food, fuel and water requirements are factored in everything goes off the chart. Israeli Army quartermasters reckon for that particular climate, 3 million people and their livestock would need 1,500 tons of food, 11 million gallons of water and 4,000 tons of wood for fuel per day – remember, it gets pretty damned cold in the desert at night. When camped, that number of people would cover about 25 square miles yet no trace has ever been found to indicate even a fraction of that number sustaining a presence in the desert – and plenty have looked – even one-day's latrine production of 3 million people would be hard to miss.

There are plenty of other statistical fish to shoot in this barrel, but the main nail in this particular coffin is the fact that there is no trace of Israelite influence in the early Egyptian language or vice-versa. In every incidence of one nation enslaving another culture, this always happens. Nor is there anything to suggest any crossover influence of customs, cooking methods, fashion, hair-braiding techniques, sports or martial activities, these also being consistent factors of prolonged interaction through slavery, trade or even protracted conflict between free nations. Yet nothing exists from four centuries of close interaction on such a large scale and no single mention can be found of such enslavement in Egyptian records or imagery. Despite archaeologists from a dozen nations digging up half of Egypt over the years and stealing countless treasures, not one single item suggesting Israelite influence has been found from a 400-year, 3 million-strong Israelite presence in that land. With the population of Egypt at the time itself only being around 3 million, one has to ask why a people enjoying numerical parity would tolerate slavery. Where is there any mention of rebellion? Apart from the fact that the Egypt of the time could have in no way afforded to keep and feed so many slaves, it is a simple matter of fact that the Pyramids were built by the Egyptians themselves, with free labour who would not have let the taint of a foreigner anywhere near a task of such religious importance. It never happened.

LITTLE-BOOTS AND SADDLES

The main problem with Caligula (AD 12–41) is that of all the Roman Emperors he has such a bad reputation that any accusation may be made with complete confidence of it being accepted as fact, including the notion that he appointed his horse to the office of Consul.

Properly named Gaius – 'Caligula' was a childhood nickname meaning little-boots and born of the fact that the troops he loved to hang around with made him his own pair of mini *caligae* or marching boots – it is beyond dispute that he was, like all Roman Emperors, a power-crazed despot who let no-one stand between him and what he wanted. The little we know of his reign comes from only six sources of varying reliability, with most of the tales of deranged depravity and homicidal paranoia being more modern embellishments of a few unsubstantiated snippets of salacious gossip recorded by only two of those sources, Seneca the Younger and Philo of Alexandria who knew the man personally. Tacitus and Josephus, who were writing not long after his death, and Suetonius and Dio, the real gossip-mongers, published their character assassinations across a time span ranging from AD 120 to AD 240. It must always be kept in mind that this was not a time when historians earned a living from their efforts but wrote under the sponsorship of a paymaster who made it clear from the outset how the commissioned work should present certain characters or predecessors. Most significantly with Caligula, the later the works were published the more salacious they became, yet none of the newly alleged crimes rested on any foundation that can be found in earlier works. In short, they were pure invention. By the time of Robert Graves' *I Claudius* (1934) and *Caligula* (1938, first performed 1945), by Albert Camus, the man is already a monster; fast-forward to more recent publications, such as *Blond's Roman Emperors* (1994) by Anthony Blond and the ridiculous soft porn-flick, *Caligula* (1980) and the image of Caligula is so over-egged that we are left with a sexually incontinent psycho hang-gliding over the abyss.

Although all six ancient sources were, for various reasons, hostile to Caligula, none is a patch on those modern hatchet-jobs which, failing to find what they needed in the six original sources, invented stories off their own bats by trawling many ancient sources for inspiration in apocrypha told about other Imperial bad-asses, such as Nero or Commodus, and hung the charges round Caligula's neck. Yes, he was murderous but so too were all the other Emperors and some a great deal more dangerous than him; yes, he was incapable of keeping it in his toga but he was only in his twenties at the outset of his reign; modern rock stars are no different when offered all on a plate and they only have their entourage of groupies to abuse – Caligula had an entire empire. As for his alleged incestuous inclinations, Josephus hints, without any corroboration or reference to a previous source, that there was something going on between Caligula and one of his three sisters. Suetonius and Dio, writing decades later, pick up on this and announce, out of the blue, that he was routinely boffing all three of them. By the time that Camus, Graves and Hollywood have added their pennyworth, Caligula is a non-stop sex-machine of such twisted psyche that when he gets one sister, Drusilla, pregnant he hacks out the child himself and eats it, before branching out into necrophilia, giving her corpse a rousing '*bon-voyage*' in his own inimitable way. Modern imagination also suggests that he routinely, when in a prankish mood, sat naked on the Imperial throne, indulging in some frantic *agito ergo cum* to embarrass assorted dignitaries anxious to discuss matters of state. He did no such thing.

Graves has him murdering his own father at the tender age of eight and smothering the ailing Tiberius to hasten his end – he did neither. Camus has him murdering his second wife with his bare hands, but she survives him, although only for a matter of hours until the assassins who finished off Caligula caught up with her too. He did indeed bump off several members of his own family and execute more than a few high-rankers he suspected of conspiracy but this was so routine among Roman Imperials that it borders on the mundane.

Finally, we come to his famous 'my little pony' complex which supposedly culminated in the appointment of his favourite horse, Incitatus, to the office of Consul or Senator, depending on which version one reads. Suetonius alone (later copied by Dio) only alleges that Caligula joked of appointing the horse a Consul but this was enough for the modern myth-makers; Graves has him making the horse a Senator and Lloyd C. Douglas' 1942 book *The Robe* (made into a film in 1953) has Incitatus appointed Consul. Not content with this, the 1980 porno-*Caligula* has the man establishing such a 'stable relationship' with his four-legged friend that the Imperial throat kept 'getting more than a little hoarse'. With such license taken with the known facts of Caligula's life it is likely fair to say that he is now beyond any serious biographical salvation.

REVERENDING STORY

Assuming for one moment that the Gospels are the historical accounts which many purport them to be, these texts are responsible for many contradictions and also the sources for most of the myths and misconceptions surrounding the birth and death of Jesus. This is mainly due to the fact that all four Gospels were, at their very inception, forgeries which later forgers have played about with to impart 'spin' in one direction or another. There is no intention to offend by using the word 'forgery' but the accepted dating of the writings calls for such terminology. All four texts had to have been penned after the destruction of the Temple of Solomon in AD 70 and Mark is acknowledged to be the earliest, written sometime in the late AD 70s, next is Matthew in the mid to late AD 80s, then Luke in the 90s and last the so-called 'eye-witness' gospel by John which dates from the early second century. So, unless those four men, drawn in the main from the common herd, not only beat the appalling literacy rate of the day as well as somehow managing to exceed the average life span by a century and a bit, these accounts of the alleged events had to have been written by persons unknown who put the work out as if written by actual disciples, to give their work a bit of instant credibility, and that, by any yardstick you choose to use, constitutes forgery.

Mark and John ignore the subject and manner of the birth altogether, this significant in itself, and the two accounts, nailed clumsily onto the front of the originals of Matthew and Luke, argue with each other every step of the way. The impetus for all the text-twisting was the fact that in the first and second centuries, when these books were penned by whoever, there were four main, wholly separate and dissembling Christian communities. Two of these were Jewish-Christian and, quite content with the concept of a Christ of Davidic descent, set about fabricating genealogies to back up that lie, never imagining for one minute that others would put forward a Jesus of divine paternity and parthenogenetic birth to make the Bible argue with itself from cover to cover. These other two camps were not only hell-bent on a divine Jesus but, determined not to be outshone by other cults and religions, went overboard with virgins, angelic warnings, wicked kings, shooting stars and stable births.

That the Davidic camp had a hand in the texts is more than obvious; there are countless references to Jesus as the descendant of David: *Matt.,* 9: 27: 'Thou Son of David, have mercy on us.' *Rom.,* 1: 3: 'his son, Jesus Christ, Our Lord, who was made of the seed of David' and so forth. To back up claims of Davidic descent, the forgers invented contradictory genealogies; in *Matt.,* 1:14–15 Joseph is the son of Jacob, son of Matthan, son of Eleazar, whereas *Luke* maintains him to be 'son of Heli, son of Matthat, son of Levi'.

Both concocted genealogies are quite astounding in that they diverge immediately after David (*c.*1000 BC) and do not meet up again until Joseph. Furthermore, Luke's genealogy (3: 23-31) purports there to be forty-one generations between David and Jesus while Matthew allows for only twenty-seven. If one takes *Matthew* as a whole, including its clumsy nativity account claiming divine origins, one is bound to question why the book doggedly constructs an ancestry back to a man who is not, in the divine concept scale, the father. To further complicate the issue, the Vatican possesses an ancient manuscript which states that 'Jacob begat Joseph, and Joseph begat Jesus'. Naturally, this is not something they reproduce on postcards for the devout tourist to mail home.

All this confusion and contradiction stems from the fact that there were screeds of texts to choose from to make up the 'official' Bible and those who made this selection, over perhaps 300 years, did so with an agenda and went on a pick-and-mix exercise, only selecting writings that matched or approximated the matrix they had in mind. Unfortunately, no one single person ever oversaw this exercise or sat down and read the end result from stem to stern to make sure that the collars matched the cuffs throughout.

Mark obviously has no use for a Davidic Jesus, the author even lapsing to polemics against the concept. But, if *Mark* is so happy with the divine Jesus, how come the text ridicules the same idea at 3: 21. Jesus is described as being at the temple and infuriating the elders by pronouncing himself to be The Son of Man and therefore of Divine origin. The aforementioned verse in the New International Version relates that: 'When his family heard of this they set out to take charge of him, for they said, "He is out of his mind."' This is a strange reaction indeed from his 'mother and brothers', (more of the brothers later), especially Mary who, if there was a divine conception, would more than anyone be aware of such fact and have expected no less from her son.

And so to Bethlehem. There is no earthly reason for Jesus to have been born anywhere other than Nazareth, there being countless references to the man as Jesus gen-Nazareth; even the Vatican seemed to be hedging its bets in 2007 when it rather pointedly set up its nativity tableau in Nazareth for the first time. But there were, of course, unearthly reasons demanding the birth be moved about 80 miles cross-country to Bethlehem; the ancient prophesies foretold that the Messiah would be born in that city and that his name would be Immanuel so Matthew and Luke had to turn history on its ear to shift the birth-scene to bolster their claim for Jesus to be the long-awaited Messiah.

According to *Matthew*, Jesus' parents were resident in Bethlehem in a house at the time of the delivery, and notes nothing remarkable or unusual surrounding the event. This 'forger' now has the problem of shifting the family back to Nazareth where they belong, this accomplished by the invention of the 'Slaughter of the Innocents' by Herod and the introduction of a couple of angels sent to tip the family off that it was time for a sharp exit. Strangely, no-one other than *Matthew* thought this act of wholesale infanticide worth mentioning; no other gospel writer or any other contemporary historian even hints at such an occurrence. In short, *Matthew* is re-working what was even then a tired old chestnut telling of a king forewarned of the birth of his own usurper and trying to out-flank fate by killing all the children of a certain age to make sure he got the right one. The mythology of every nation teems with such examples.

Luke gets even more inventive; his Joseph and Mary are living peacefully in Nazareth but, while Mary was pregnant, had to go into Bethlehem to be counted in the Roman census 'of all the world' which took place during the reign of King Herod. Everyone, *Luke* maintains, had to return to the city of their lineage to be counted; Joseph was of the House of David (really?); Bethlehem was the City of David, ergo Joseph and Mary must go to Bethlehem and that, while there, 'the days were accomplished that she should be delivered'. This may sound all very neat but Roman census-taking methods are well-recorded and, quite sensibly, required everyone to stay put or at least keep travel to a minimum while the officers toured the land making the count. Imagine the chaos caused by the entire country going walkabout; cross-tribe-married families splitting up and heading off in different directions for weeks on end; whole cities becoming inundated with temporary influx; crops, livestock and houses being left empty at the mercy of bandits? In short, it never happened and this 'forger' is also quite obviously ignorant of the fact that it was Herod himself who was responsible for the collection of Judean taxation and thus not subject to Roman censuses. No Roman census was carried out in Judea during the reign of Herod and at no time was there a single census taken by the Romans of the whole world as known to them. There was a census conducted by the Governor Quirinus throughout the territories abutting Judea and apologists say that the writer of *Luke* simply got confused – but that census was conduced in AD 6 and Herod is known to have died in 4 BC so the Gospels cannot have it both ways with a ten-year gap. The family cannot have been marching for days to take part in some imaginary census while simultaneously fleeing the homicidal rage of a king ten years dead.

In the preceding paragraph it is mentioned that *Luke* stated that while in the city 'the days were accomplished that she should be delivered' which hardly sounds like the last-minute, gut-clutching rush across the desert of popular imagination. Nor, according to any text in the Bible, was there any recalcitrant inn-keeper; no mention of any stable and, as for any stellar-led deputation from parts afar, these men were not kings nor even wise men but Magi, members of a Persian cult of mystic astrologers much famed for their tricks and illusions, hence 'magic', properly the skills of the Magi. According to the texts, having seen a strange star rise in the east, this deputation, number unknown but certainly a lot more than three, set off *west* to Bethlehem to inquire at the court of Herod as to the location of the birth – at no time in this week-long journey did they again see the star. After making their inquiries *chez* Herod – thus tipping him off that it was time to kill all male offspring up to the age of two – they are told that the ancient prophesies state quite clearly that the Messiah will be born in Bethlehem. It is on this last leg of their quest that they again see the star but, as Bethlehem was and still is visible from the ruins of Herod's stronghold and as the Magi were aware of their destination, it is fair to say that at no time in their travels were they led by a star. The age-limit imposed on the slaughter is telling of the time lag between the birth of Jesus and the arrival of the Magi who are said to have visited 'the child' Jesus in 'the house', they having missed the nativity by that amount of time. This is recognized by the Church which celebrates the visitation of the Magi as a separate event on 6 January with Epiphany.

The only mention of the location of the birth can be found in the original Greek version of *Luke* which sites the event in a *kataluma*, a term denoting a functions room, a spare room in a private residence or some kind of temporary shelter, such as a tent or a cave, set aside as guest accommodation. Paid accommodation in an inn would be termed a *pandocheion*. Of all these alternatives the cave is the most likely option; many homes in such times and climes were little more than bricked up caves, ideal in that they would have been easy to heat in the winter and cool in the summer. Even posh people with a nice home had a cave for animals and guests, this blending of the two functions not to be taken as any kind of insult to either group and, while there is indeed mention in *Luke* of a manger, this should in no way be taken as any indication of stabling, which only very rich homes had as separate facilities. Even the up-market Billy-two-caves would have to bring the animals into the house at night leaving a manger a normal feature of most middle-class homes. Nor was such a peculiarity of the East; in England it was the norm in rural homes until perhaps the seventeenth century which is why the space under the stairs is still called the cubby-hole, this originally being cubby-hold, the small corral for the young and the weak to find protection through the night. That same Greek version of *Luke* places the Last Supper in a *kataluma* yet no-one has so far suggested that Jesus and his Disciples gathered in a stable for a meal. Either way, it was over a cave that Constantine built the Bethlehem Church of the Nativity.

Quite understandably most hold the image of Jesus as an only child despite the New Testament being littered with references to the man as 'Mary's first-born', this placing considerable strain on the concept of the ever-Virgin Mary. According to the Bible he had four brothers – James, Joses, Simeon and Jude – and two sisters, names unknown. Nor would Mary have been the woman portrayed in iconography for she was herself but a child. The original Aramaic texts denote her '*almah*', a girl of marriageable age, which in those days meant about ten or eleven; had she been a mature woman, who was also a virgin, then the term '*bethulah*' would have been the word to use. By the time these original texts were being translated into Greek the virgin-birth yarn had the upper hand so '*almah*' was deliberately mistranslated as '*parthenos*'. Naturally, no Church likes to highlight this aspect of the impregnation and iconography sticks religiously to churning out daubings of the infant Jesus being cared for by a woman in her late twenties or early thirties, but such child-bride scandal is not unique to Christianity. The Islamic Prophet Muhammad took for his second wife a girl called Aisha who was six, but he held off consummation until she was nine.

As for Jesus the carpenter, this too is a misunderstanding born of deliberate mistranslation. The original texts term him '*tektron*', someone who worked with their hands, a builder or general handyman, and despite the significance of Jesus as a carpenter in Christian tradition and iconography there is but one reference to him following that trade (*Mark*, 6:3) and again, there was clear and deliberate thinking behind the mistranslation. Many Eastern faiths then believed the world created by Tvashtri, the divine carpenter, and, ever-anxious to be as user-friendly to as many other faiths as possible, the early Church marketed their Jesus as either a carpenter himself or the carpenter's son. On to Golgotha.

First it is important to understand the actual cause of death on the cross which was not shock, heat exhaustion or blood loss, as is generally imagined, but asphyxia. Even the fourteenth edition of *Encyclopaedia Britannica*, in circulation until 1973, states: 'Death, apparently caused by exhaustion or heart failure, could be hastened by shattering the legs with an iron club, but the medical reasons for death are not fully understood.' The Romans knew full well what caused death and they intended it to be a long time coming.

Crucifixion was not only a grim method of execution but also intended to serve as a salutary warning to all and sundry that retribution from Rome was both ruthless and extremely unpleasant. A competent officer in charge of a crucifixion could keep a victim alive for about three days. With nails being both expensive and wholly unnecessary to the procedure most victims were simply bound to the cross by the wrists and ankles. After hanging by the arms for a short time, violent cramps beset the chest making breathing extremely difficult and painful through pressure exerted on the diaphragm, forcing the victim to alternate the strain between the arms and the legs until too tired to continue the procedure. Anyone left hanging by the arms, whatever the method of fixing, will soon die.

Basically the drill was as follows; first thing in the morning the execution squad had to sign out all necessary equipment from stores with the uprights of the crosses being taken straight to the killing-ground and locked into position; the cross-members were taken to wherever the condemned were being held. Next – and this depended on the mood of the mob, the nature of the offence or the whim of the authorities – the condemned might be scourged. The maximum number of lashes allowed under Sadducean law was thirty-nine so as to fall short of forty, the mystic and cabalistic number. Any man who had been scourged was not expected to carry his cross-member to the killing-ground as he would no longer be capable. In these cases a surrogate was picked from the crowd under pain of death for refusal and, in the case of Jesus, we are told that a Cyrenean named Simon stepped forward as a volunteer.

Once at the execution ground those already tied to their cross-members were hoisted onto the uprights before their feet were positioned on a small ledge and then tied in place. Although quite unnecessary to the procedure and its inevitable outcome, nails were sometimes used for additional dramatic effect but iconography showing the hands and feet so secured is way wide of the mark. When they were used, nails were always driven in through the wrists, never through the hands which would simply tear through under the victim's own weight. The officer in charge had to drive the nail in through the wrist and watch for the involuntary clench of the fist which indicated the nail had pierced the median nerve; if no such clenching occurred then the nail had to be withdrawn and struck through again until properly positioned. None of the Gospels mention nails. Only then could the cross-member, complete with attached victim, be hoisted up and secured to the top of upright to produce the tau, or 'T' shaped cross. The Romans never used the so-called Latin cross as favoured in iconography as it was too difficult to assemble with a victim hanging on the cross-member and the upright would have to be made of extra-thick timber to take the deep joint, and heavy timber was at a premium.

But the nailing of the feet does not jibe with the purpose of the grim spectacle designed to keep victims alive for as long as possible, the end only coming when they could no longer take the weight on their legs, something they could not even attempt with feet shattered by the thumping great spikes that passed for Roman nails. The uprights were slotted to take a small seat, should the presiding officer feel any of his charges were flagging too fast and in need of a rest. Victims were kept fed and watered to a minimum and, if bribed, the guards would offer the condemned a stick with a sponge soaked in vinegar into which had been dissolved assorted soporific herbs and opium. All four gospels mention the offering of vinegar to Jesus on the cross with Matthew, Mark and John noting that it was immediately after this that he gave up the spirit, the implications of that being perhaps quite significant. Either way, whoever wrote the lines suggested in each case that the sponge was proffered in derision instead of cool water suggesting that the writers were obviously ignorant of the drill.

When it came time to ring down the curtain on the whole grizzly event, the officer smashed everyone's legs with a hammer. Not only would this hasten the end but the Romans knew that 'resurrection' could occur amongst crucifixion victims; the dead were taken down and thrown into an open pit to be eaten by feral animals and it was not unknown for some to come round in the cold night air and walk away to safety, something they could not do with shattered legs. So, why didn't the guards smash Jesus' legs; why did he die so quickly on the cross and so soon after getting that vinegar; how come he managed to 'cry out in a loud voice' at the end when those dying of suffocation cannot even manage a whisper and why does the Bible assert him to have been alive up until he was taken down from the cross?

The usual answer to the first question is that Jesus was so obviously dead that the guards felt no need to bother with this finesse – but this runs counter to the reason for the leg-smashing in the first place. The other justification for this gross dereliction of duty was the fulfilment of the prophecy that not one bone in Christ's body would be broken – but why should a squad of brutish legionnaires care two figs about any prophecy concerning a man they themselves had hung on a cross? The only thing that would convince a Roman soldier to skip that part of the routine would have been a hefty bribe from the victim's family and friends.

We can conjecture with reasonable certainty that Jesus was offered the soporific sponge on the tip of a spear. The gospels (*Matt.*, 7:48; *Mark*, 15:36; *Luke*, 23: 36; *John*, 19:29) state the sponge to have been proffered on a piece of reed, John specifying hyssop, but this is impossible as hyssop does not grow in the Middle East and, even if it did, the plant has a very bendy stem which would render it quite unsuitable for such a purpose; when translating texts out of the Greek, *hyssopos* must have been confused with *hyssos*, a short spear. The significance of the sponge is that the squad were open to bribery – and those who accept a small bribe will be open to a large one – large enough to permit the fudging of the execution and the removal of an apparently dead body which was in fact alive but in a drug-induced coma.

Certain effects of opium are so pronounced that a heavily-dosed person will appear dead despite fairly close inspection. The presence of an alkaloid called papaverine ensures total muscle relaxation while other properties of the drug dramatically reduce the heart rate and drop respiration to a point where a mirror is needed to be sure this function is present. In short, a good dose of Palestine opium would have made Jesus appear dead to the world he had come to save and oblivious to any pain caused by the odd prodding with a spear – an action which itself pokes a massive hole in claims of resurrection. No doubt unintentionally, the Bible gives several strong pointers to Jesus having survived the cross.

Firstly there is the short duration of his torment – either three hours or six hours, depending on which Gospel account is favoured – this prompting Pilate himself to express surprise at the rapidity of Jesus' death and ask if all went as it should; the two thieves put up at the same time as Jesus were still going strong and lucid enough to carry on a conversation as to the nature of Jesus' supernatural status. Next we have the clear statement that Jesus cried out at the very end – but those in the final stages of asphyxia are not capable of a full-throated cry, each word discernible by those standing some way distant. And now to the most significant of all questions, that raised by the spear thrust. Corpses do not bleed or issue forth any other fluids when breached, cut or stabbed, so why, according to the Bible, did the wound bring forth blood and water?

The first problem we have with the involvement of the spear is that in the Greek translation of the Gospels the inflicted wound was merely a *nyssein*, a light scratch, not the gaping wound of later imagination. Those who translated the Greek into Latin and later to English started to talk, as does *John*, 19:34, of a spear that pierced the side of Jesus. This deliberately distorted translation was likely inspired by the desire of the writer to present irrefutable 'proof' of the cessation of life and thus make the alleged resurrection all the more impressive. But why would a Roman squaddie attempt to ensure death by a light tickle to the side; surely he would simply shove the spear straight through the chest and go for the heart. If anything, side-tickling with a spear sounds more like a bribed soldier indulging in a bit of gallery-playing for any too-watchful observer. It is perhaps unfair to drag the Turin Shroud into the argument but many who adhere to the traditional death-and-resurrection account also point to the shroud as confirmation of those 'facts'. But it would seem that whoever knocked up the shroud was equally unaware that corpses do not bleed and that the original account of the spear thrust mentioned a mere scratch rather than a gaping wound. After nine hours on a cross in the sun any blood on the skin would have dried to a veritable crust, and we know it was sunny because the Bible says it became dark and overcast at the moment of alleged death. Yet the shroud is stained head to foot with blood, most importantly from a rivulet running from a serious wound in the side to collect under the back. So, if the Turin Shroud is genuine then whoever was wrapped up in it was alive at the time.

Most puzzling of all are the facts that, prior to any English versions of the Bible, there is no mention of Jesus having been killed on a cross of any kind and that the Latin cross as a religious symbol long predates the advent of Christianity. It is also telling that early Christians were offended by the symbol because of all its pagan associations. The third-century Church Father, Minucius Felix, (200–240) wrote : 'You it is, ye Pagans, who are the most likely people to adore wooden crosses … for what else are your ensigns, flags and standards but crosses gilt and beautiful, Your victorious trophies not only represent a simple cross but a cross with a man on it.' The pre-English Greek texts say instead that Jesus dies on a *stauros*, meaning an upright stake or, at a stretch, a tree. The Romans quite often used trees as tools of executions, simply because they were handy and saved the use of heavy lumber which was at a premium. If this was the case for Jesus then it would explain the otherwise puzzling contradictions found at *Acts*, 5:30: 'Jesus, whom ye slew and hanged on a tree' and, again, at 10:39, which talk of Jesus in the: 'land of the Jews, and in Jerusalem, whom they slew and hanged in a tree'; it was common then for the condemned to be simply killed and tossed into the upper branches of a tree to be picked clean by the vultures. Either way, both statements in *Acts* are quite clear that Jesus was first killed and then put into the tree; it does not in any way say that he was put onto a tree, beam or pole *to* be killed. Unfortunately for Christians, this leaves them with a divinity cursed by their own Bible; *Galatians* 3:13 reads: 'Christ has redeemed us from the curse of the law, being made a curse for us: for it is written, Cursed is everyone that hangeth on a tree'.

Making a final return to the troublesome spear-thrust, here is a rather nice etymological hand-me-down from that alleged incident that gives its name to the modern domestic lounge. A tremendous cult grew around the spear-wielder who was named Longinus, the Latin for the kind of spear he would have being carrying. Early iconography depicted Longinus slumped against his spear at the foot of the cross causing his name to be used of any slacker or idler. The verbal 'lounge' is noted from 1508 with the noun appearing in the early nineteenth century to describe a lazy spell before the 1880s when the word transferred to any room where people could relax.

SAPPHIC LORE AND LESBIAN RULE

The basics are so well known – Sappho was a gay poet who presided over a coterie of similarly inclined young ladies on the Isle of Lesbos, hence 'lesbian' – that they hardly need repeating here; except to say that none of it is true.

Born some time around 620 BC and fading from sight by 570 BC, so little is known of the woman herself and so little of her work survives, it is remarkable that anyone found sufficient foundation for even a hint of homosexuality; all we have left is one complete work, *Hymn to Aphrodite*, and a few fragments of other works, titles unknown, which are purported to be hers. On the other side of the coin she is recorded as being married with a daughter and, according to one, no doubt apocryphal, tradition, ending her own life by hurling herself into the sea over unrequited love of a ferryman called Phaon. Of the very few contemporary references to her, Alcaeus of Mytilene says she was 'violet-haired, pure and honey-smiling' and the later, in the second century AD Maximus of Tyre wrote that her relationships with the women in her school were on a parallel with those between Socrates and his students: 'What else was the love of the Lesbian woman except Socrates' art of love? For they seem to me to have practised love each in their own way, she that of women, he that of men. For they say that both loved many and were captivated by all things beautiful. What Alcibiades and Charmides and Phaedrus were to him, Gyrinna and Atthis and Anactoria were to the Lesbian.' The nature of the relationships between Socrates and his students was famously outlined in a piece by Plato from which derives the term 'platonic'.

Sappho was without doubt one of the greatest of the Greek lyric poets and obviously a woman of great passions and great depth of feeling, if a trifle theatrical, so the reading of what little remains of her work must be done with that in mind, along with the fact that both sexes then waxed lyrical about the intensity of the bonds of friendship in terms that few today would consider using to their best friend for fear of misunderstanding. One only has to go back to Victorian times to find writings from prominent men and women, both waxing purple about a particular friendship in terms that today would have eyebrows formed to a quizzical arch. Sure; if one sets out to read the extant scraps of Sappho's work with the mind-set to find suggestion of homosexuality then it can be found, but then the modern 'thought police' have likewise established that there is a homo-erotic leitmotif running through the tales of Noddy and Big Ears. Most significantly of all is that there was no sexual connotation attached to either 'Sapphic' or 'Lesbian' until the late nineteenth century and the ever-increasing number of ladies' salons established as centres of higher education, formed in emulation of the 'finishing school' over which Sappho herself was imagined to have presided.

On the positive side, these 'Sapphic' salons actually gave rise to the formal finishing school, as found halfway up any good Swiss mountain, but on the negative, these 'petticoateries' attracted great suspicion in a social climate receptive to Nietzsche the Nutty Professor opining that any woman aspiring to education had to have something seriously wrong with her genitals and sexuality. The ever-present 'if-she-won't-sleep-with-me-then-she-must-be-a-lesbian' brigade did their two-times table to come up with five which, from the 1890s onwards, sidetracked both 'sapphic' and 'lesbian' to the role they fulfil in the language today. There was also unintentional impetus imparted in this new linguistic spin by a misunderstanding in the general mind of the anciently established use of 'lesbian' to mean pliable and bendable, in both the physical and moral sense, this in turn stemming from equally laughable misunderstandings of 'Lesbian rule'. Far from denoting some jack-booting 'lesbocracy', overseen by Sappho, this instead denoted a flexible masons' measure, invented on Lesbos, to allow Lesbian masons to measure around corners.

Finally we come to that greatest of all Victorian velvet-tipping myths, the widespread belief that there has never been any legislation against female homosexuality because no-one had the nerve to brief Queen Victoria about the exact nature of the activities to be proscribed by any such addition to the statute book. Rubbish; Victoria had nothing to do with the drafting of any legislation nor did she hold the power to pick and choose which laws were passed and which not.

This myth centres on the Labouchere Amendment which was rushed through at the last minute to append the Criminal Law Amendment Act of 1885. This infamous amendment provided for two years of hard labour for any man caught engaged in 'gross indecency' with another man without detailing exactly what constituted 'gross indecency'; basically, any action deemed grossly indecent by any judge or jury was enough to have you banged up; Oscar Wilde was the first to be imprisoned under this Amendment. But the reason the amendment only covered men was in fact more insulting to women than their inclusion; it simply didn't matter what women did so long as it didn't have an impact on men. Also, if the pleasures of the lesbian underground became highlighted by any ban it might attract more women to explore that avenue, especially if they were in a less-than-rewarding marriage at the time – lesbian activity was not even listed as grounds for divorce. On the subject of the 'Victorian morals' to which so many today desire that we return, history tells a different story; Victorian London was a moral sewer and one of the issues addressed in that Criminal Law Amendment Act of 1885 was the raising of the age of consent for girls from twelve to sixteen. With birth records among the poor being scanty at best, paedophilia was widespread and tolerated, as long as there was someone on hand to swear blind that some eight-year-old girl was in fact twelve and a bit small for her age, Bob was the relative of your choice.

SPARTACUS, THE GAY BLADE

Poor old Spartacus (109–71 BC), vilified until the middle of the eighteenth century, transformed into a symbol of people-power by nineteenth-century Communists only to be turned into the greatest gay icon of all time by Michael 'Dimples' Douglas cavorting about the screen in various stages of undress in Stanley Kubrick's eponymous film of 1960. Throughout this homo-heroic romp, Spartacus is made to mouth-off about the dignity of man; the evils of slavery, the inhumanity of men being goaded to fight to the death in the arena like animals and so on, whereas the real Spartacus was nothing like that. He didn't give a monkey's about slaves and the plight of humanity under the Roman yoke; all he wanted was his own freedom and enough money to live it up somewhere beyond the reach of Rome – with his own coterie of slaves running around at *his* beck and call.

Up until Bernard-Joseph Saurin's *Spartacus* (1760), first performed in Paris before touring Europe, all accounts of the chap had been unfavourable to say the least; he and his raggle-taggle army were not thought of as 'Robin Hood' characters, cheered on and loved by all, but rightly feared for the brutal horde of murderous, thieving rapists that they were. Spartacus was simply a man of his time and thus no better or worse that any other iron-age bandit leader, and no better or worse than the Romans he initially and willingly served with. It is said that he was Thracian, and thus from modern Bulgaria, but 'Thracian' could also denote a style of gladiatorial fighting, so it is impossible to tell from any contextual reference whether the use of the term in relation to him should be taken as an indicator of nationality or not. He had served as a mercenary in the Roman Army and, for some transgression or other, ended up in a gladiatorial school in Capua where, in 73 BC, he and the rest of the arena-bait broke out to raid settlements in the immediate area, their numbers increased by the slaves from the households they slaughtered. At this early stage, Spartacus was joint leader with Gauls, Crixus and Oenomaus but, after the death of the latter and the reluctance of the former to ride under Spartacus' ascending star as the rebellion progressed and spread, he was indeed left in full control. Initially regarded as nothing more than a local problem and one of little significance, the size of the Gladiators' Army grew until Rome felt obliged to dispatch a force of 3,000 to nip the insurgency in the bud but the Romans, thinking they had nothing to deal with but a rabble, sent out raw recruits and untested militia under the equally unseasoned command of one Clodius Glaberer.

In the meantime, and unbeknown to the Romans, their objective had swelled in number to something around the 30,000 mark and, equally unbeknown to the advancing Romans, was the fact that one of the rebel leaders was a time-served legionnaire with a good grounding in Roman fighting methods and standard tactics. The Gladiators' Army was by now camped on the slopes of Mount Vesuvius so the rather doltish Glaber deployed his men about the base of the mountain, near the only road leading to the crest and sat back and waited for something to happen. It did; the Gladiators cut vines and abseiled down a cliff at night to eradicate the entire Roman force as it slept in camp. From here Spartacus & co moved north with some vague objective of escaping the wrath of Rome by crossing over the Alps but they had so much fun looting the length of Italy and trashing every force that Rome sent against them, that when they got there Spartacus was easily convinced by Crixus to turn round, go back through Italy again like a dose of salts and then to abandon their army to its fate and escape by sea to live the life of Reilly. Obviously a caring, sharing commander.

So, within arm's reach of the freedom most believe to have been the man's heartfelt yearning, Spartacus pulled a u-turn and went on the rampage again, proving once more that he was just another happy-go-lucky thug. Now at the head of an army 120,000 strong, he and Crixus, whose name translated from his native tongue as 'Curly', had a ball, murdering and pillaging everything in their path. They demolished all formal opposition, even resorting to crucifying captured solders or using prisoners of war in their own gladiatorial games to while away blank spots in their busy schedule. However the cracks were beginning to show and Crixus eventually broke away with about 20,000 men to go on a spree of his own, but was soon cornered and wiped out by a force under Lucius Gellius Publicola. Lack of purpose and discipline among the rabble was the Romans' main advantage and these independent ventures continued to compromise the fighting integrity of the main force as their worst nightmare closed in on them – Crassus. A dangerous and ambitious man, determined to make political capital out of Spartacus' destruction, Crassus, with a battle-hardened force, pursued the rabble into the foot of Italy where Spartacus would strike a 'deal' that showed the measure of the man. He hired Sicilian pirates to transport him, his chosen companions and all their booty to safety by sea, leaving the rest to Crassus' tender mercies. But the fool paid the pirates upfront and was then surprised when they failed to turn up. Hello! Pirates! Apologists maintain that this deal was for the transport of all but where in the hell would a bunch of pirates get sufficient shipping to evacuate 120,000 people and all their belongings? Now trapped on the peninsula, Spartacus could only sit and watch as Crassus built 32 miles of defensive walls and ditches, from coast to coast, to trap and starve him into submission. As his supplies dwindled, Spartacus now had no option but to fight his way out, which he did, breaching the defences in a sudden night-attack, and once again started north towards Lucania without any real plan or objective. With Crassus on his tail and a second army under Pompey due to arrive any day, squabbling again depleted the main force with Ganicus and Cestus, two other Gaulish sub-commanders, peeling off to go a-raiding. Their force was surprised asleep at Lucanian Lake with losses of over 12,000. It was now only a question of time, and the main column was brought to battle at Petelia and wiped out. Spartacus, having spotted Crassus in the field, made a valiant attempt to cut him down and damn near made it, before, wounded, he was overwhelmed and hacked down. So, no 'I'm Spartacus!' moment for him.

UP YOURS, PAL

Shakespeare has done more than most to foster the notion that Julius Caesar (100 – 44 BC) was bumped off in the capitol but before addressing the real location of the assassination it is perhaps worth disposing of the equally erroneous notion that he was a Roman Emperor. Although repeatedly elected dictator of Rome he never held the title of emperor for the simple reason that the Empire itself was not established until 27 BC, some seventeen years after his death. Augustus (63 BC – AD 14) was the first of that peculiar breed.

The one thing Shakespeare did get right in his eponymous romp was that Calpurnia, Caesar's wife, had become decidedly twitchy by the time that the Ides of March rolled around; she, and plenty of others, knew full well that trouble was afoot. Caesar, too, cannot have been unaware that his enemies were circling so it is something of a mystery that he went out alone that day; some have even suggested that he went willingly to his death instead of waiting for his increasingly poor health to grind him down. Who knows, but he was actually killed at the foot of a statue of Pompey in a room sometimes used as a meeting-place by the Senate. As for uttering the immortal '*Et tu, Brute?*' it is doubtful that he said any such thing. When writing of the murder, a short time afterwards, Seutonius noted: 'Caesar did not utter a sound after Casca's blow had drawn a groan from him' and Casca struck first. Actually, some maintain that in the Latin of the day such construction would have held a literal meaning of 'You too, Brutus', as in 'Up yours, Brutus!'

THE FIRST 1,500 YEARS

ATTILA'S HUNEYMOON

Despite the penchant of film directors to cast actors of Schwartze-neggerian proportions in the role of Attila (d.453) the man himself was far from the brick-built barbarian of modern imagination. Quite the reverse; he was, by all surviving accounts, a stunted little chap with a barrel-chest, a turned-up snout of a nose, deep-seated eyes and a broad, flat forehead because he was, of course, of Chinese stock, not German. The Huns were warlike nomads driven out of north west China and Mongolia to drift west and into Europe where they arrived some time in the fourth century, but this was not the first contact between Europe and China. Long before Marco Polo was spinning his lies of his own visit, the Romans had established trade links with western China and Chinese silks became fairly common in Rome from the first century BC onwards. It seems that there were Romans in China by that time and not all of them were there of their own volition.

After his campaign against Spartacus in 71 BC, Crassus sought other victories, finally being defeated and killed by the Parthians and their Hunnish allies at the Battle of Carrhae in 53 BC, in what is now modern Turkey. Thousands of Romans were captured and some taken home to China by the Huns to promote one of the most intriguing anthropological mysteries concerning the denizens of the remote village of Liqian in north-western China where the occurrence of tall blond-haired 'Chinese' with blue or green eyes and aquiline noses is hard to miss. The local tradition tells of 145 Romans brought back by the Huns, and records do show that when the Chinese went up against that Hunnish stronghold they found it built very much like a Roman log-piled fort with the occupants forming a phalanx to fight. At the time of writing, DNA tests are being carried out to see if reality matches tradition.

Either way, come the fifth century the Huns were under Attila and all over Europe like a bad suit. His invasion of Italy produced two things, the city of Venice and the myth that Pope Leo I rode out of

Rome alone on a donkey, with a noose around his neck indicating his own willingness to die for his flock, and confronted the Barbarian, demanding in the name of the cross that he down-tools and desist from attacking and sacking the city. Venice first.

When Attila began his all-Italian tour in 452 AD, many of the residents of Padua, Aquileia, Altino and what is now Portogruaro thought it best to flee into the marshes where Attila's cavalry would be hard pressed to follow and, deciding that better wet than dead, they stayed and devised methods of building on reed-rafts to establish what would become the 'Queen of the Adriatic'. Interestingly enough, when the first European explorers of South America saw the native houses built on stilts out over the cool rivers they thought it reminiscent of their city and so called the area Venezuela, or 'like Venice'. And as for the Pope-on-a-rope ploy, this never happened as some sources declare Leo I to have already fled the twin dangers of attack and the plague that had already arrived in the city before Attila got anywhere near. Others say that there was a meeting of sorts with the Pope forming part of the reception committee which, using the plague as a powerful bargaining chip, came to an agreement of a knock-down price to pay Attila not to attack. Either way, with his own army depleted by plague, Attila decided, with or without a pay-off, to avoid Rome like the ... well, the plague. And, after all that, the so-called Scourge of Rome died a few months later, not on the battlefield, but in bed on his honeymoon, after taking the incautious step of marrying a nineteen-year-old Germanic girl named Ildico – he should have known better.

Common to the Huns, Goths, Vizigoths and Vandals and indeed most early cultures, was a quaint pre-nup agreement whereby the bridge and groom acknowledged their intention to quaff a daily amount of honey-mead throughout the first month (a word that originally presented as 'moonth') of their marriage to sustain them through the protracted bouts of carnal callisthenics prone to occur at such times, hence 'honeymoon'. Attila tarried long at his own wedding feast, knocking back such alarming quantities of the stuff that, legend has it, he galloped off into history, well and truly laid low by a slip of a girl. More realistic research reveals that he suffered some sort of catastrophic haemorrhage, drowning in his own blood, and that this was induced by some sort of poison administered with or without his bride's connivance. As for the muddle between these Chinese nomads and the use of 'Hun' for the Germans, this is a comparatively recent confusion and one for which we must thank

Kaiser Wilhelm II (1859–1941) and his intrusion into China, to take the Hun full-cycle.

During the so-called 'Boxer' rebellion of 1900, all European legations holed-up in their own compounds and waited for relief columns to be sent by their respective countries: France, Japan, America, Great Britain and Germany. The only casualty of any importance had been the German minister hacked to death in the street. Addressing the German contingent of the relief force before it set out from Bremerhaven on 27 July 1900, Wilhelm informed the detachment that when it got to China it should get stuck in like a rat up a down-pipe and kill all the opposition. 'When you come upon the enemy smite him. No quarter will be given; no prisoners will be taken; let all who fall into your hands be at your mercy. Just as the Huns of 1,000 years ago, under the leadership of Attila, gained a reputation by which they still live in historical tradition, so may the name of Germany be known in such a manner in China that no Chinaman will ever again dare to look askance at a German'. This sort of talk was not thought of as helpful by anyone else, leading to Wilhelm being lampooned with several cartoons showing German soldiers half-and-halved with Mongolian warriors, the image being an easy morph in that both wore spiked headgear. Basically, had Wilhelm picked the name of any other horde known for its brutality, then that name would today be the nickname of the Germans because of that silly speech.

At the beginning of the previous paragraph the Boxer Rebellion was referred to as the 'so-called' and that is because the Europeans messed up their Mandarin pictograms – an easy thing to do. A splinter group from the ancient White Lotus Sect, the I-He-Tuan, the Righteous and Harmonious Band, as it was properly known, was a radical and xenophobic movement formed to rid the country of all the foreign interference in Chinese affairs, but the Europeans they so hated mistranslated the pictogram as *I-He-Ch'uan*, the Righteous and Harmonious Hand/Fist and, because of the martial arts skills of these men, misnamed them the boxers.

'BAD' KING JOHN SEALS HIS OWN FATE

Magna Carta, as 'signed' by King John (1167–1216) at Runnymede in 1215, is popularly believed to be a document ensuring the legal protection of the common man and one of the main foundations of modern democracy, yet little of this holds up to examination.

King John, who was nowhere near as bad as his brother, Richard I (1157–1199), was at loggerheads with the Barons who wished to curb his powers while ensuring the continuance of their own rights to trample over the common man and tax him to the eyeballs. It was with this self-interest in mind that they forced John to attach his seal – he could not write – to the Articles of the Barons at Runnymede, the text of which would form the basis of Magna Carta, which the King was likewise forced to seal on 15 June 1215. None of the 63 Articles concerned themselves one iota with the plight of the common man and only three are still held valid today; Article 61, for example, ensured the establishment of a committee of twenty-five Barons who could at any time meet to overrule the will of the King to the point or armed rebellion and seizure of Crown property.

The much-vaunted Article 39, which provided that no free man should be arrested without due cause or denied a trial by a jury of his peers, only applied to the Barons, Church officials, merchants and other 'free men' who made up a scant 25 per cent of the population; the other 75 per cent of the nation, those who really needed such protection, were excluded; the notion of Johnnie Swineherd invoking such rights would have turned the Barons apoplectic. All they wanted to ensure was that they could only be held to account by their own kind who could be relied on to look kindly upon each other's transgressions as a mutual back-scratching legal nicety. It would be a century and a half before these rights were extended to those in need of them; not until 1354 and by command of Edward III, was the wording altered to 'no man of what estate or condition that he be' so it is he and not the Barons of John that we have to thank. Also, there was little new or exciting in the document, the Barons were only trying to get the King to formally acknowledge that which before had been implicit and, as such, the vast majority of the text was lifted wholesale from the older Charter of Liberties, which was issued voluntarily by Henry I in 1100 to detail the legal restraints on the Crown and the limits of his own control and jurisdiction over the nobility.

At the end of the day, the document now regarded as Magna Carta is not that sealed by John in 1215 because as soon as he was out of the Barons' clutches he ran simpering to the Pope to have the document declared null and void as he had only enacted it under duress which, to be fair, was correct. Innocent III agreed and, on 24 August, issued a Papal Bull declaring the Charter null and void.

But it wouldn't go away; there was another Charter of 1225 and another still in 1297; it is this latest version which has passed through to us. Nor is there one definitive Charter; dozens of copies were churned out at the same time. Durham Cathedral has a copy of the 1216 version, the 1217 version and the 1225 version, and many other churches and institutions hold authentic copies – the Bodleian Library has four. Even the Australians have one; in 1952, King's School, Bruton, presumably in need of some readies, flogged their copy to the Australian Government for a mere £12,500; it currently stands valued at about A$20 million, so a good deal done by those down under!

Obviously, in time the right to trial by a jury of peers filtered down to the great unwashed but this was not without its legal complications. The concept was adopted in many European countries, including Germany, where in 1499 this produced a fine legal conundrum. No matter how ridiculous it sounds today, medieval trials of animals were common throughout Medieval Europe and, in 1499, a German bear was arrested for causing affray and terrorizing several villages on the fringe of the Black Forest. In an ill-advised attempt to highlight the stupidity of the impending trial, the defence lawyer insisted on his client's right to a jury of his peers resulting in the judge ordering the rounding up of a jury of local dancing and otherwise performing bears. But as soon as the jury was ushered in the trouble began. One particularly truculent juror made a lunge for the prosecution council who died of his wounds the next day and, inspired by their colleague's example, the rest of the jurors cut loose, either fighting among themselves or savaging the peasantry who had come to see the fun. In the confusion, the defendant escaped, never to be seen again. Animal trials went on until well into the eighteenth century and those interested to read further on such lunacy only need google the subject to see how the law really can be an ass.

It is also fair to say that the main purpose of the Charter – to bring the Crown under the power of the law – has yet to be seen; that too was scotched by the jury-of-peers clause. The Crown has no peers; the present incumbent could, with impunity, appear on the balcony of Buckingham Palace and spray the adoring crowds with an Uzi, knowing herself to be beyond prosecution. Apart from her lack of peers, cases are pressed by the Crown Prosecution Services, in the name of the Queen, so it would be a legal nightmare for her to prosecute herself. On the other hand, the right of the Barons to resort to trial by 'those who understood them best' persisted until the twentieth century with the Peers of the Realm clinging onto the right to be tried by their chums in the House of Lords. The last two infamous such cases involved members of the Russell clan, a family whose arrogance seems to have known no bounds. In 1901, the same year that he was issued with the UK's first vehicle registration plate of A1, John Francis, 2nd Earl Russell, elder brother of the philosopher Bertrand Russell, elected to be tried for his bigamy in the House of Lords rather than risk the full weight of the law as would be faced by any commoner. A campaigner of reform of the divorce laws, Russell seems to have been somewhat cavalier in his own approach to such matters and presented his chums with something of a problem in that the case against him was watertight; he was a bang-to-rights bigamist. In the end, they found him guilty on the condition that he served no more than three months, instead of the five years he would have got in the Old Bailey, on the grounds that the 'torture' of his first marriage had been punishment enough.

The Russells were back before the House of Lords in 1935 when Edward Southwell Russell, 26th Baron de Clifford, a keen supporter of the British Union of Fascists under Mosley and an avid campaigner for the imposition of road speed limits and a driving test, sought the sanctuary of the Lords after his arrest on 15 August 1935 for killing a man in a head-on collision while driving his sports car up the wrong side of the road. He was acquitted. But the public had by now had its fill of such spectacle and, sensitive to the new mood of post-war Britain, the House of Lords itself put a stop to their abuse of Article 39 of the Magna Carta.

BATHORY BATH-NIGHT

Otherwise known as Countess Elizabeth Nadasdy (1560–1614) or in more recent times as Countess Dracula, Bathory was the lady commonly believed to have bathed nightly in the blood of virgins to retain her great beauty. Between 1600 and 1610 the Hungarian harpy and her minions are alleged today to have murdered over 600 virgins from the villages surrounding her castle which, given the population levels of rural Hungary at such a time, does seems a mite ambitious.

Apart from the remaining records of her trial and the accusations laid, the main problems with this legend are the social conditions of the day and basic human biology. With the average life-expectancy in the early 1600s being around the thirty-five to forty mark people married very young and, if they had the time for a mid-life crisis, they would have to indulge that fiction in their late teens. Even in comparatively enlightened nineteenth-century Britain, the marriageable age for girls was twelve (Bathory herself was betrothed to Nadasdy by the age of eleven) with betrothals allowed at the tender age of eight. Consequently fully-grown, adult virgins were mighty thin on the ground in Bathory's day. A fully-grown adult would yield perhaps a gallon of her unusual bathwater and a twelve-year-old perhaps half that. A decent bath would call for something in the region of, say, 30 gallons which would require sixty or so twelve-year-old girls rendering half a gallon each. Next there is the obvious problem of coagulation; draining that number of victims into the one bath would have called for great speed and concentration of labour to preclude the blood from the first having long coagulated before the last had been added; factor in the number of assistants required to contain and process that number of girls in the one, supposedly very large bathing chamber and the problems spiral out of all control. Moreover, her 600 alleged victims would only provide for perhaps ten baths; to bath nightly over that period of ten years she would have had to round up something in the region of 250,000 virgins. The ridiculous tale concludes with the escape of one girl to raise the alarm – like no-one else has noticed the other 249,999 are missing – this leading to Bathory's trial and downfall but, because she was of noble blood, she could not be executed and so was walled up in a room in her gory castle to starve to death. The truth tells a different story.

Not only was Bathory enormously wealthy and influential in her own right but when Nadasdy died she took control of all his estates to boot; she was also unusually well-educated for her time – she was fluent in both Latin and German at a time when most of the Hungarian nobility could barely write their own names – and was also headstrong and independent. As if that was not enough, she would not be cowed or 'know her place' in what was a very male-dominated society, this making her many enemies determined to have her stripped of her wealth and position and marginalized. Prime movers in this charade were King Matthias II of Hungary and his Prime Minister, Guyorgy Thurzo, who was also Bathory's cousin. Perhaps unwisely, Bathory was constantly pestering the morally and financially bankrupt Matthias for payment of his debts to the Bathory estates – something over 17,000 guilden – and Thurzo too owed her more than he had hope of repaying; he had already tried to wipe out these debts with a cynical proposal of marriage only to have her laugh in his face, so no friend of hers he. Matthias ordered Thurzo to sort her out but to tread carefully as she was far too powerful and had too many allies throughout Hungary and Poland (ruled by King Stephen Bathory) for her to be dealt with too harshly. Having laid his plans, Thurzo arrested her on 29 December 1610.

Keeping her under house arrest, Thurzo took away several of her household and tortured them until they agreed to everything he alleged. Having been deprived of assorted bodily parts and tasted the delights of Thurzo's firepit, all 'witnesses' were agreed that Bathory was indeed a witch who practiced the dark arts in her castle, these frequently involving the torture and murder of young girls on her satanic altar. Feeling confident, Thurzo went to trial on 2 January 1611 but made a hash of things and had to call a halt to his own proceedings. Come the second trial of 7 January he had miraculously found a catalogue of Bathory's crimes in her own handwriting, the scribble bearing no resemblance to the numerous examples of her own hand on other contemporary documents. For added safety, the trial was conducted in Latin, with the 'witnesses', bound and gagged, being prodded when it was time for them to nod or shake their heads. Bathory herself never stood trial; rightfully holding the whole sorry charade in contempt, she refused to enter any plea and did not attend either of the so-called trials.

Naturally, Thurzo and Matthias had their way and Bathory was found guilty; the bulk of her lands and wealth falling forfeit to be divvied up among the interested parties and the still-gagged witnesses taken out for immediate execution, just to keep things neat and tidy. Knowing he had gone as far as he dared, and indeed as far as was necessary, Thurzo did not have Bathory walled up to starve to death but allowed her to remain at her castle at Cachtice in the Carpathian mountains providing she kept her mouth shut and didn't make any waves. Here she remained, dying of natural causes just over four years later. But, no matter how outlandish the charges laid against her by Thurzo, there was no mention of any gory bathing habits and certainly no mention of any blood-guzzling vampiric rituals;

even Thurzo was not that imaginative. The popular and highly lurid perception of Bathory's idea of a good time would not emerge for another century when a dotty Jesuit called Laszlo Turoczi produced *A Short Description of Hungary together with its Kings* (1729). Determined to make his tome a bit of a page-turner, Turoczi dreamed up the virgin-bathing bit on his own and if ever there was proof required of the old adage maintaining that a good lie will be halfway around the world before truth has got its boots on, then this is it. Despite being nothing more than a wronged woman, shafted in a kangaroo court full of men after her money, Bathory seems destined to drag the ridiculous epithet of Countess Dracula through eternity.

BLOODY MARY AND EXECUTIONS

It does seem rather unfair to saddle Queen Mary (1516-1558) with 'Bloody' for although persecution of Protestants undoubtedly took place during her five-year reign, the executions numbered about 300. This works out to less than sixty a year which, for a monarch of that era, embarking upon a programme of religious suppression, would indicate a considerable degree of self-restraint rather than blood-lust. Her thuggish father, Henry VIII, inflicted a great many more religious killings during his rapacious Dissolution of the Monasteries (1536–1541), this augmented by perhaps 100,000 secular executions during his paranoid purges ranging from 1513 to 1547. Elizabeth I burned just as many Catholics as Mary had Protestants but she comes out of history smelling of Tudor roses. The trouble with Mary was that she was not a particularly likeable person nor popular with the people; her marriage to Philip II of Spain was repugnant to her subjects who also blamed her for the loss of Calais; had she not been given this sobriquet then she would have doubtless ended up with another equally unpleasant.

THE DOVE WAS A HAWK

It has oft been said that had Columbus been married he would never have discovered America: 'You're going where; to do what? And I suppose she gave you all those ships for nothing?' But the continuation of such old jokes and America's obsession with its Columbus Day only goes to show just how deeply entrenched is the myth that he *did* discover America in 1492.

The first notion to dispel is the persistent myth that all opposition to Columbus' proposed venture was rooted in the fact that most then thought the world flat and that, if he sailed as far as he was suggesting, then he would simply fall off the edge. No-one had believed the earth to be anything other than round since Aristotle (384–322 BC) had proved the fact beyond dispute; besides, the navigation systems used in Columbus' day relied on calculations cross-relating stellar plotting to the curvature of the earth. Opposition to his venture came in the main from the Council of Salamanca, set up by King Ferdinand of Spain to double-check the viability of the proposal as many of Columbus' assertions clashed with intelligence Ferdinand was getting from Bristol, but more of that later. The Salamancan savants agreed the feasibility of the proposed venture but with the over-rider that Columbus had greatly underestimated the expanse of the ocean and, as things turned out, they were right.

All the flat-earth nonsense was invented wholecloth by the American writer, Washington Irving (1783–1859), and given wide circulation by the international success of his *The Life and Voyages of Christopher Columbus* (1828) which, by the end of that century, ran to 175 editions. Not content with a simple lie, Irving over-egged his pudding with bogus quotes and an entirely false account of the dispute with the Salamancan Council, these men presented as a bunch of blockheaded clerics spouting fundamentalist garbage. So successful was Irving in this falsification of events that the imagined confrontation of reason and religion became for years a much-quoted example of ecclesiastics stupidly blocking the advance of science; it was even bandied about in the Darwin debate of 1860.

The trouble with Columbus was that he thought the world to be about half the size it really is and, as the real purpose of his voyage was to find an alternative route to India, when he got to the Americas on 12 October 1492, that is where he thought he was and so called the locals 'Indians'. (The addition of 'Red' would come later through some tribes' use of red ochre body-paint) And so began the atrocities. Children in America are still taught such a sanitized account of the activities of this money-grubbing and genocidal maniac that it would be laughable were the facts not so grim. Although there are numerous internet sites branding him a murderous rapist it cannot be stated with any certainty that he personally murdered or raped anyone, but he certainly allowed it to happen with monotonous regularity under his command. He was there for gold and slaves and did not give a damn how these two products were 'harvested'. The rape and murder carried out by his entourage beggars belief; any Indians unwilling or unable to render the demanded gold-tribute had their hand cut off and were left to bleed to death in front of their fellows, *pour encourager les autres*. The horrors inflicted are too many and varied to dwell upon here; those interested to read how Columbus & co moved from village to village, behaving like some extended Manson Family, will find all they need with a google of 'Columbus' sins' or 'Columbus' crimes'. Here we shall content ourselves with the example of Haiti and its population of perhaps 500,000 Arawaks; within two years of his arrival that population had been depleted by half, either through slaughter or shipment to Spain in chains. (Columbus himself would later be shipped home in chains after all got sick to the back teeth with him). By 1515 there were less than 50,000 Arawak on the island and by 1530 a mere 500 were left alive. There is today considerable opposition throughout the Americas to the celebration of Columbus Day on 12 October and, far from being bleeding-heart political correctness, this opposition is very broad and has been on the wax since the mid-1800s when American historical societies revealed in detail for the first time the full extent of the death and destruction that Columbus had visited on the indigenous peoples who were now expected to line up and wave flags in honour of their ancestors' killer. Venezuela has actually renamed 12 October as the Day of Indigenous Resistance. But, for all that fuss on Columbus Day, did he 'discover' America? No!

The first Europeans to find America were Siberians who simply wandered across the ice-bridge to Alaska some 15,000 years ago and settled down to become Columbus' 'Indians'. Next came the Vikings; Biarni Heriulfson shipped out of Norway *c.* 985 to visit his parents in Iceland but when he got there he found out they had moved to Greenland (perhaps they were trying to tell him something); it was en route to that god-forsaken land that he was blown off course to spot the mainland of North America. Although he did not land he told others of his discovery and over the next fifteen years or so, many Viking ships visited the American mainland, which is more than Columbus ever did. His first landing was in the Bahamas, then the Virgin Islands and Puerto Rico and Central America, so why such a fuss is made of the man in the United States is nothing short of a mystery.

The first Viking to get to North America and establish a settlement was Eric the Red in 986 who set up a settlement on what is now Greenland before sailing home to encourage others to follow him back. Changes in global weather patterns gave rise to the myth that Eric only told his mates back in the Fjords that the place was called Greenland in order to con them into following him back to what is now a bit of a frozen wasteland, but in Eric's day Greenland was exactly that; lush and verdant. Next came Leif, son of Eric the Red, who in 1000 actually established a thriving community on a part of the American mainland he called Vinland. In the 1960s a Viking settlement was excavated at L'Anse aux Meadows, in modern Newfoundland, and proclaimed by some to be Leif's community. Others dispute this and believe Vinland to have been much further south and in what is now New England. Either way, it was the Vikings who discovered mainland America, not Columbus who restricted his rapacious activities to offshore islands, never imagining for one minute what lay within his avaricious grasp. Although it will never replace Columbus Day, in 1964 the United States Congress finally bowed to pressure and proclaimed 9 October to be Leif Ericsson Day.

As to the origin of the name of that landmass, this is equally disputed. The standard theory is that the continent is named after Amerigo Vespucci but this should be hotly contested, if only on the grounds that this would make the naming unique in all history as the first and only instance of any new land or discovery of any kind being named from someone's Christian name. Hudson Bay is not Henry Bay; Tasmania is not Able-Land nor was Rhodesia named Cecilia, although, to be fair, that would have been quite funny given the sexual proclivities of Cecil Rhodes himself. No; if the Americas were named after Vespucci we would today be talking about Vespuccia. The earliest known map using 'America' is the *Cosmographiae Introductio* as published in April 1507 by the German cartographers Martin Waldseemuller (1470–1522) and Matthiar Ringmann (1482–1511), they dedicating their first edition to Vespucci. Only on this map does Waldseemuller suggest that the New World be named America after his hero: 'But now these parts [Europe, Asia and Africa, the three continents of the Ptolemaic geography] have been extensively explored and a fourth part has been discovered by Americus Vespuccius [a Latin form of Vespucci's name], as will be seen in the appendix: I do not see what right any one would have to object to calling this part after Americus, who discovered it and who is a man of intelligence, [and so to name it] *Amerige*, that is, the Land of Americus, or *America*: since both Europa and Asia got their names from women.' It seems that Waldseemuller had received correspondence from his hero, Vespucci, in which the latter called the Terra Nova 'America' and, adding two and two to come up with the perennially troublesome five, presumed Vespucci to be laying claim to the discovery/exploration of that land and stamping his name on it. Any such eponymous etymology is baulked by the fact that 'America' would have to be structured on a feminized form of Vespucci's Christian name and, most significantly, neither Waldseemuller nor Ringmann ever used that name again; in later editions of the *Cosmographiae* and in all other maps they reverted to 'Terra Nova'.

More likely is the claim put forward on behalf of the Welsh-born Bristol merchant, Richard Amerike (1445–1503) who was the main sponsor of the voyages that John Cabot made to the New World – the first in 1497 to establish a British claim to what is now Canada, and another in 1498, this latter still beating Vespucci to the New World by a clear year. Historians have long suspected that, years before Columbus set sail, Bristolian merchants were dealing in salted cod from the other side of the Atlantic and letters found in various archives indicate that as early as the 1470s Amerike was funding the exploration of Newfoundland and its fishing grounds; one letter of 1481 shows he was shipping salt as a fish-preservative to his associates in a part of the New World referred to as Brassyle. None of these New World ventures evaded the gaze of Spanish eyes in England, particularly Pedro de Ayala, a London-based envoy, who was assiduously keeping Ferdinand and Isabella up to speed. Documents discovered in Westminster Abbey indicate that Columbus knew all about the Bristol successes too so, instead of being some king of far-sighted vision, he was just a grubby little opportunist out to steal Amerike's limelight; and in that he was spectacularly successful. To return to the general perception of Columbus having to pester the Spanish royals and convince an unbelieving Church of the feasibility of his proposed venture, it is evident that all parties were spoofing each other; there is no record of any of the parties concerned so much as mentioning Amerike and the Bristol/New World trade even though it is now firmly established that all concerned knew every detail. Columbus would have been reluctant to back up his case by telling Ferdinand that some chap from Bristol had already been there and worn the t-shirt in case the king saw no kudos in coming second and pulled out. Ferdinand too kept his cards close to his chest and probably did not want to risk Columbus losing interest for the same reasons and so failed to mention the intelligence he was receiving from de Ayala, while the Church was aware that Ferdinand and Columbus each knew independently of the Bristolian journeys because they had their own spies as well.

So, there it is; in the 1930s some Vikophiles tried to convince everyone of a rather tortured link to Ap Eric (the Red) or Amt-Eric, both meaning the Land of Eric but the smart money is on Dick Amerike and his salty cod pieces; rather intriguingly, the Amerike family crest is structured in manner of the Stars and Stripes but, given even the Massachusetts-based American Flag Research Centre's reluctant admittance that the inspiration for the design is unknown, this can only be happy coincidence; can't it?

EMBROIDERING THE TRUTH

The so-called Bayeux Tapestry had nothing to do with the French town, it is not a tapestry and all the arrow-in-the-eye guff surrounding the death of Harold is later invention. Apart from that, everything is fine.

The tradition in France is that the work was commissioned by Queen Mathilde, wife of William the Conqueror, and carried out by her own fair hand and those of her ladies-in-waiting, but it was more likely to have been the idea of Bishop Odo, William's thuggish half-brother. There is in fact nothing to indicate a French hand involved; the kind of stitch-work and the colours of the vegetable dyes employed would point towards Anglo-Saxon input, this is reflected in the style of Latin used in the text as well. All the indications are that the needlework was executed in England, most likely somewhere in Odo's personal power-base of Kent. The work is actually an embroidered scroll, not a tapestry, and the only reason the name of Bayeux got in on the act is that this is where it surfaced in the eighteenth century when it was found bundled up in some storeroom in Bayeux Cathedral, itself built by Odo. Nor does it seem to have been held in high esteem by the 'Bayeuxans' who, during some battle or other, dragged it out of the Cathedral to line an ammunition wagon which doubtless would have been the end of the embroidery had not a local lawyer saved the relic from such fate by proffering his own bed sheets for the job.

Obviously, taking the scroll as a historical document is to go skating on very thin ice; a yob like Odo would only have commissioned something depicting full justification for the Norman invasion of England. The scroll begins with the heirless Edward the Confessor sending his trusted Earl, Harold Godwinson, over to Normandy to invite William to ascend the throne of England upon his, Edward's, death. After a few depictions of manly deeds and adventure of both Harold and William, the scroll shows Harold informing William of Edward's wishes and Harold swearing on a holy reliquary to support William in that succession. Of course, Edward dies on 5 January 1066; Harold accepts the throne, in violation of his alleged sacred oath of support to William, and is crowned, with perhaps indecent haste, on 6 January in Westminster Abbey's first ever coronation. William, brooding on the other side of the Channel, plots his invasion and sets sail for England on 27 September. The two armies face off for the so-called Battle of Hastings on 14 October and Harold gets something in his eye – maybe. Actually, the battle did not take place at Hastings but some 6 miles away at what is now called Senlac Hill. At the time it was called Santlache, or Sandy-Stream, but the victorious Normans punned this to Sanguelac, Blood-Lake, which, in time, was modified to the present name.

Before looking at the arrow-in-the-eye panel, there is another little-known mystery of the scroll. One of the early panels shows an unnamed priest reaching out to either touch or slap a woman's face; she is identified in the attendant text as Aelfgyva, sometimes referred to as the Mysterious Lady of the Bayeux Tapestry. Below them is a naked man brandishing a penis of considerable proportion and in a state of some arousal, all of which would suggest that the overall imagery referred to a scandal of the day that was so well known as to need no explanation. That is as may be but no record of any scandal fitting the figures can be traced; it is the norm for this scene, or at least the priapic flasher, to be omitted from reproductions. And so to Harold and the manner of his death.

The relevant scene is well known; there is a standing figure, apparently shot through the right eye with an arrow, to the right is a falling figure being hacked down by a Norman horseman and above the lot is inscribed 'King Harold – he is slain'. This is fine as far as it goes, but the standing figure's arrow seems to be a later addition; initially, that standing man was holding a spear in his right hand angled down at about 45 degrees. Later stitching modified the shaft to the arrow in the eye leaving a man who must have been shot by an archer lying on the ground in front of him to achieve such an angle of penetration. Extensive etchings of the embroidery were made by Bernard de Montfaucon in 1729 and he included no arrow. This would jibe with the tradition and the artistic devices of the time with the dead or dying always shown prone or falling, not just standing upright as that man. Just to confuse matters further, the figure to the right, shown falling, did at one time have an arrow in his eye but the stitching has been removed. But the thinking behind the arrow is perhaps clearer; it was then the just end of those who broke an oath to have their eyes put out and, as far as the French were concerned, that was Harold's major crime and the putting out of one or both his eyes was his just desserts.

The most recent mystery attached to the scroll has also been solved with the vindication of the nineteenth-century English author, Anna Eliza Stothard, whose life was overshadowed by the shame of being accused of hacking a piece out of the 'tapestry' while her husband, Charles, made copies of various sections for the London Society of Antiquaries in 1816. After the pair left, curators found a few bits missing from the scroll and, unable to believe a man of Stothard's academic standing capable of such vandalism, blamed his wife. The largest of the missing pieces turned up in the Victoria and Albert Museum, not being returned to Bayeux until 1872 when the V&A needed permission to make another copy and the French made it clear that the return of the fragment was a non-negotiable condition of permission. Michael Lewis of the British Museum has dug further into the matter and the provenance of that fragment to establish that it was in fact Charles and not Anna who nicked a few bits for keepsakes. And he did not long evade the retribution of Bayeux; on 28 May 1821 Charles was painting a replica of a stained glass window in the church at Bere Ferrers near Yelverton in Devon and made the mistake of standing back to admire his work, forgetting he was up on some scaffolding. He is buried in that same churchyard.

GALILEO

Although Galileo (1564–1642) did face the Inquisition – twice – he was not harmed in any way or imprisoned; quite the contrary, each time he was summoned he was put up in fancy apartments, allowed to visit whoever he liked and even went to a few parties up at the

Vatican. Far from the popular image of a bunch of frothy-mouthed fundamentalists baying for blood, the Inquisition was desperately trying to extricate itself from an uncomfortable position into which it had been manoeuvred by Galileo's numerous enemies – neither the Inquisition nor the Vatican in general sought a scrap with science, they were pushed into it, mainly by Galileo himself.

Galileo was definitely an astronomer with attitude; rather than engage in cogent debate with those opposed to his views and opinions, he publicly lampooned and lambasted them which, in academic circles, has never been the way to make friends and influence people. (Especially when one is in the wrong, as was Galileo when he publicly ridiculed Kepler for suggesting that the moon influenced the tides). Galileo's advocacy of the Copernican theories – including the notion that the earth moves round the sun rather than standing regally static at the centre of the universe – placed him in direct conflict with the old-school, mainstream Aristotelian teachings and those who espoused them. The beginning of Galileo's end came in 1609 when he built himself a telescope to better observe the planets. He did not invent the telescope, as is so often asserted, but built one to specifications published the year before by an otherwise obscure Dutch optical engineer called Hans Lippershey (1570–1619). His observation of Venus cemented his ideas as the planet sometimes presented itself as a crescent whereas if the earth stood still and all planets revolved about it then Venus could never present itself as anything other than a disc. He published his findings in 1610 as *The Starry Messenger* and was roundly applauded. He was even invited to demonstrate his telescope and findings to the Pope's own astronomers who were happy to openly confirm that he was right. And if Galileo had resisted the urge to crow at the Aristotelian lobby all would have been well, but he couldn't and it wasn't.

His continual goading of the Jesuit science-lobby in the Vatican drew him enemies from many quarters and his first run-in with the Inquisition was, as with other misfortunes in his life, due entirely to his belligerence and inability to let sleeping dogs do what they do best. The first major shot across his bow was fired from the pulpit of a rabid Dominican called Tommaso Caccini who publicly denounced Galileo as a 'practitioner of diabolic arts' and 'an enemy of true religion'. The next day, Caccini's fellow-conspirator, Niccolae Lorini, sent a letter to the Holy Office, demanding that Galileo be charged with heresy, backing up his request with doctored copies of letters Galileo had sent to Archbishop Piero Dini. This clumsy frame was quashed when the original copy of that letter was sent to the Holy Office, they immediately dropping the case and warning Lorini never to darken their door again. Not knowing when to quit, Caccini went to Rome himself, armed with other botched 'evidence' against Galileo and presented it to the Inquisition. Never the bunch of idiots they are popularly held to have been, the Inquisitors saw through the smoke and, realizing that they were being manoeuvred like a pawn in some academic vendetta, threw out the case and also cautioned Caccini that he was treading on very thin ice. And that would have been the end of the matter had Galileo not leapt in with his size tens.

Injured pride and a lust for revenge and vindication drove the fool to send a copy of his newly published *Treatise on the Tides* to Cardinal Orsini with the request that it be forwarded to Pope Paul V. This was his book that, ridiculing Kepler's suggestion that the moon had anything to do with the tides, suggested instead that it was the movement of the earth itself which sloshed the oceans about like water in a bathtub … ho-hum. Anyway, this was a step too far, leaving Paul V determined to ask the Inquisition to rule for once and for all whether Copernican theories were heretical and thus stop all the squabbling. It must be remembered that this was the early 1600s, not to be judged by today's standards and knowledge. It is all too easy, with educated hindsight, to see the Vatican as a bunch of dolts unable to see the obvious truth staring them in the face, but there was not then a single scrap of proof that Copernicus was right; all was theory. That Copernican/static earth debate is perhaps best compared today to a couple of physicists arguing the true nature of quarks and constantly turning to a non-scientific 'referee' to say which was right. To the seventeenth-century homo-in-the-via, and to a large extent most of the Vatican, it really did not matter a damn; all that then mattered was what was heretical and what was not.

After due consideration, the Inquisition ruled that, without any firm supporting evidence, the Copernican theories could not be regarded as factual and, because they also ran contrary to the Bible, they were also heretical. Of the many myths arising from this hearing is the notion that the Inquisition also banned Copernicus' *On the Revolution of the Spheres*; they did not, they only ordered that further publication be suspended until about a dozen-or-so affirmations of its absolute truth had been removed from the text. So, instead of receiving the validation he sought, Galileo shot himself in the foot. But he was not charged retrospectively with heresy – the Inquisition had neither the power nor the desire to do so – he was only cautioned that now the ruling was in place he must refrain from any public promotion of those theories. To protect the reputations of all involved, Galileo's friend, Cardinal Robert Bellarmino, present throughout the hearing, issued Galileo with papers certifying that he had not been charged for any sin or transgression by the Inquisition but that he should thenceforth abandon all public and private considerations of said theories. It should also be repeated that at no time was Galileo in prison but in fact accommodated in a rather swanky villa from which he was free to roam as he pleased.

Free to go, Galileo returned to Florence but in 1623, when his old chum Cardinal Maffeo Barberini became Pope Urban VIII, the old dog again grabbed his bone and headed for Rome to pressure his friend into rescinding the 1616 ban. Unwilling to execute such a u-turn, Urban offered his friend the compromise of Papal permission to write about both the Ptolemaic and the Copernican theories, with the proviso that he did so even-handedly and that unless he had any concrete proof of the Copernican system he presented it only as a hypothetical mathematical construct. Galileo agreed and scurried off to betray his friend in a most unforgivable way. When his subsequent *Dialogue Concerning the Two Chief World Systems* (1632) was published it was blatantly clear to all that Galileo was not only sticking up two fingers at the Inquisition but that he had lampooned his friend into the bargain by having the Papal standpoint spouted from the mouth of an idiotic character called Simplicio. Rightly feeling completely betrayed and held up to public ridicule, Urban needed no urging to hand the matter back to the Inquisition which immediately issued a summons for Galileo to present himself before it. Yet again, he was housed in luxurious accommodation and allowed to wander free; at no time in his entire life was he imprisoned or tortured by the Inquisition.

Desperate to avoid embroilment in any scientific battle that might leave them with collectively well-egged faces, the Vatican and the Inquisition went through all manner of machinations to avoid, yet again, charging the old fool with heresy; he was only charged with having broken the conditions imposed on him by the 1616 ruling; contempt of court, if you like. But Galileo's enemies were circling and knew which of his buttons to push. It was suggested to the Inquisition that in 1616, not only had Galileo promised to recant any support for Copernicus but that he had agreed to work under licence from the Vatican on the condition that he never again so much as speak or write the name Copernicus. To back up this spurious claim, the following forgery, dated 26 February 1616, was miraculously 'found' in the records:

> In the Palace and residence of Cardinal Bellarmino, Galileo being called and being in the presence of the Cardinal and of the Reverend Father Michelangelo Seghizzi of Lodi, of the Order of Preachers, Commissary General of the Holy Office, the Cardinal admonished the said Galileo of the error of the above-mentioned opinion and warned him to abandon it; and immediately and without delay, the said Cardinal being still present, the said Commissary gave Galileo a precept and ordered him in the name of His Holiness the Pope and the whole body of the Holy Office to the effect that the said opinion that the Sun is the centre of the universal and the Earth moves must be entirely abandoned, nor might he from then on in any way hold, teach or defend it by word or in writing, otherwise the Holy Office would proceed against him.

Everybody knew that this was a forgery and if the silly old goat had concentrated his defence on attacking that target then most consider that he would have walked free. Instead, cranked up by his smirking enemies, Galileo's inflated ego came to the fore and, ignoring his supporters nearly breaking their necks by head-banging violently in the direction of the letter, he launched himself on the full seas of a doomed and untenable defence of *Dialogue*. Convinced he could talk his way out of anything, Galileo tried to defend the book as a refutation of Copernicus saying:

> I did not consider that in writing it I was acting contrary to, far less disobeying, the command not to hold, defend, or teach that opinion, but rather that I was refuting the opinion… I have neither maintained nor defended in that book the opinion that the Earth moves and that the Sun is stationary but have rather demonstrated the opposite of the Copernican opinion and shown that the arguments of Copernicus are weak and inconclusive.

So, far from the popular perception of Galileo sticking to his guns and uttering the later-invented '*Eppur si muove!*', 'Nevertheless, it [the earth] moves!' in defiance of his accusers, Galileo tried to weasel-out and ended up shooting himself in both feet. Left with no room to manoeuvre, the Inquisition had no option but to hedge its bets and find him guilty of being 'suspect of heresy' and hand down a formal prison sentence of indefinite period, which was hurriedly commuted to house-arrest. For six days Galileo remained a guest of the Tuscan Embassy while arrangements were made for him to be bundled off into the 'custody' of his old friend, Archbishop Piccolomini of Sienna and, after a short stay with him, Galileo was allowed to slip quietly back to his villa in Florence.

With Galileo out of the way, life returned to normal but it must be said that Galileo was a devout Catholic and the Vatican stance was nowhere near as entrenched as popularly believed. The Vatican was as prepared to move with the times as any, once there was proof instead of conjecture, as can be seen by the following, written by Cardinal Bellarmino after all the dust had settled:

> If there were a true demonstration that the sun was in the centre of the universe and the earth in the third sphere, and that the sun did not travel around the earth but the earth circled the sun, then it would be necessary to proceed with great caution in explaining the passages of Scripture which seemed contrary, and we would rather have to say that we did not understand them than to say that something was false which has been demonstrated. But I do not believe that there is any such demonstration; none has been shown to me. It is not the same thing to show that the appearances are saved by assuming that the sun really is in the centre and the earth in the heavens. I believe that the first demonstration might exist, but I have grave doubts about the second, and in a case of doubt, one may not depart from the Scriptures as explained by the holy Fathers.

If it matters, the passages in the Bible that caused all the fuss in the first place are the account in *Joshua* of the sun being brought to a halt and *Psalm 19* which also states the sun to be in motion.

As for Galileo conducting any experiment involving the dropping of a cannonball and a pebble from the leaning tower of Pisa, this is a confused yarn to say the least. It was not Galileo who set out to prove that two falling objects of differing weight would hit the ground in unison as he had already established this by maths and the rolling of differently weighted balls down a measured incline. It was a group of his Aristotelean detractors who conducted the experiment in an attempt to prove Galileo wrong and their ancient mentor right when he said that the heavier the object the faster the fall. As it happens, the experiment was re-enacted on the moon by Dave Scott, commander of the *Apollo 15* mission, and not by Neil Armstrong as sometimes asserted. On 2 August 1971 in the airless atmosphere on the moon he let fall a hammer and a feather, both of which bit the moon dust at the same time.

Galileo, the astronomer and savant died in 1642 but did not get to his final resting place until 1737. While the body was in transit to the Church of Santa Croce in Florence, an admirer hacked three shrivelled fingers from the corpse to cherish as keepsakes; two are now in private collections and the third, his middle finger, is proudly displayed by Florence's Museum of the History of Science, pointing to the heavens in what appears to be a defiantly crude gesture of which Galileo would be inordinately proud.

A HOT TIME IN THE OLD CROWN TONIGHT

To the endless glee of generations of smutty-minded schoolboys, the English King Edward II (1284–1327?) is generally supposed to have been killed by a red-hot poker being shoved up his backside, the location of this incident being Berkeley Castle in 1327. Perhaps.

Edward's reign was marked by endless and largely pointless conflict with the Barons, his disastrous marriage to Isabella, the She-Wolf of France (1295–1358), and the collective resentment of the king's closeness to his favourite, Piers Gaveston (1284-1312). The matter of Edward's sexuality will be addressed later but it is worth pointing out here that there is not one scrap of evidence to back up the general belief that he was gay and Gaveston his lover. In the hotbed of court intrigue the king sleeping with another man could not have remained long hidden and there is no mention of any such goings-on at the time. James I was definitely gay, resulting in countless references to his predilections at the time, so why not with Edward? Anyway, in 1325, Isabella's brother, King Charles IV of France, reclaimed all of the English Crown's possessions in France and Isabella, in the company of Roger Mortimer (1287–1330), was sent home to negotiate some sort of settlement. Instead of attending to that, she and Mortimer became lovers and co-conspirators in a plan to invade England and oust Edward. They landed on the Suffolk coast with a modest army of mercenaries on 21 September 1326 and so many rallied to their banner that Edward was deposed and thrown in prison within a couple of months. This much is known; now for the shady areas.

After all the political manoeuvrings had run their course and the ink dried on the papers, Edward was transferred to Gloucestershire's Berkeley Castle, the place where earlier disgruntled Barons had gathered in 1215 before nipping down to Runnymede to force King John to acknowledge the Magna Carta. By now, the young Edward III (1312–1377) was on the throne, he the son of Edward and Isabella, but very much under the thumb of his mother and Mortimer. Although this unappetising pair had the lad under control, Edward II remained a problem; that they wanted him out of circulation is beyond doubt, the only question is whether they had him killed or just spirited away to be kept on ice in case they were ever in need of a high-ranking 'get out of jail free' card. The standard version of events tells that on the night of 11 October 1327 assassins were sent by Isabella and Mortimer to Berkeley Castle where they tied Edward face-down to his bed and shoved a metal tube up his backside to allow a hot poker to be inserted without leaving any tell-tale burn marks. But no-one at the time had a clue what had happened to Edward; all the hot-poker stuff came much later, possibly as an implied punishment for his alleged sexual preference. Those writing at the time conjectured suffocation or strangulation, while others contend that he did not die in Berkeley Castle at all.

Despite the popular and modern conspiracy that no-one famous ever actually dies but takes advantage of some mishap to slip away to a quiet life in Cleethorpes, or wherever, there does seem to be some substance to the notion that Edward escaped Berkeley and that those entrusted with keeping him there were sufficiently in fear of their lives as to rustle up a surrogate stiff and proclaim him dead. They didn't call Isabella the She-Wolf without cause. A letter announcing Edward's death, but giving no cause, was sent from Berkeley Castle to Isabella and Edward III at Lincoln with a public announcement following on 29 September, just before Parliament went into recess. Three weeks later Lord Berkeley led the funeral procession into London but no-one was allowed to view the body which had been encased in heavily waxed cerecloth, by then set like iron, and encased in two locked coffins. This was the first time ever that a carved effigy of any monarch was paraded instead of his body open on a bier and, shortly after the funeral, rumours of Edward's escape began to circulate and be accepted by the likes of the Earl of Kent, the Archbishop of York and the Bishop of London.

That Earl of Kent, Edmund Woodstock or Edmund Plantagenet, was also Edward II's half brother and was executed on 19 March 1330 – about two-and-a-half years after the alleged death of Edward II – for conspiring to effect the release of his semi-sibling from Corfe Castle in Ireland. So, either Kent was a raving lunatic – which by all accounts he was not – or there was more than a smattering of truth to the rumours. And if Kent was barking then so too were the following because they were all later implicated as being involved to one degree or another in the plan to return Edward II to the throne. There was Sir Edward de Monthermer, son of Joan of Acre; William, Abbot of Langdon; Richard Bliton, Confessor to the younger of the two Despensers; the Bishop of London; Lady Vescy; Simon de Swanland; Hamo de Chigwell, former Mayor of London; the unfortunately named Sir Fulk Fitz Warin; Sir John Pecche, notable in that he had been Constable of Corfe Castle until September 1329; Lord Beaumont and Sir William de la Zouch who at various stages in his life held such offices as Lord Privy Seal, Lord High Treasurer and Archbishop of York – it was also his family name responsible for the peculiar Leicestershire toponym of Ashby de la Zouch. He was also Mortimer's cousin – were all these and as many more all barking mad or deluded too?

At Kent's kangaroo trial, in which the charges were not read out – how can you prosecute someone for conspiring to rescue a dead man – Mortimer was the self-appointed prosecutor and made several odd statements, including: 'that you [Kent] are his [Edward III's] deadly enemy and a traitor and also a common enemy to the realm; and that have been about many a day to make privily deliverance of Sir Edward [II], sometime King of England, your brother, who was put down out of his royalty by common assent of all the lords of England, and in impairing of our lord the king's estate, and also of his realm'. No mention of his being dead. Everyone at the trial appears to have been talking of someone still alive. Condemned to immediate death, Kent had to wait around for five hours as no executioner could be found to carry out what was an extremely unpopular sentence; eventually a condemned murderer stepped forward to do the job in return for a pardon.

But the first tangible evidence to support the notion that Kent & co were on the right track emerged in 1877 when a French archivist discovered the file-copy of a letter sent from Papal Notary, Manuele de Fieschi, to Edward III informing him that his father was alive and living in Europe. Conservative historians immediately declared this to be a forgery and, when later science was up to the job of accurately dating the letter to 1336, that same lobby retreated to the last ditch of maintaining that although the letter was genuine the contents must be false.

In short, Fieshi told Edward III that his father had escaped Berkeley Castle, killing the gatekeeper in the process and it was this body that was sent to London. According to the rest of the letter, Edward II went to Ireland, thence through the Lowlands and France to Italy where he lived in seclusion in a succession of monasteries and religious retreats. It is also known that when Edward III visited Cologne in 1338, he was presented with 'William of Wales' (Edward II was born in Caernarvon and the first to carry the title of Prince of Wales, a title to which he might naturally revert after abdication) who claimed, with impunity, to be the new king's father – false pretence to monarchy then carried the death penalty. We know that this was not the fate of the claimant as he was again in Edward III's company at Antwerp later the same year. Edward II supposedly ended his days somewhere near Milan and there is an intriguing traditional tale in the nearby town of Cecima that their empty medieval tomb was that of an English king whose body was repatriated by his son.

And there is much more that is odd; Berkeley and Sir John Maltravers, jointly responsible for Edward II's safety while in their custody, were never charged with any crime or dereliction of duty and, when later questioned by Parliament about the ex-king's death, Berkeley said an extraordinary thing: '*nec unquam scivit de morte sua usque in presenti parlimento isto*', or, that he did not even know of Edward's death until this present Parliament (of 1330). Obviously there is more to the disappearance of Edward II than meets the eye and those interested in digging further could do no better than to visit the official site of leading historian Dr Ian Mortimer, and pick out his essay entitled 'The Uncertain Death of Edward II'.

Whether Edward II died at Berkeley Castle or not, the poker yarn was invented years after the alleged event and touted as a fitting end in view of his homosexuality; although, as I have said, there is not a shred of evidence to suggest that Edward batted for the other team. It is true that he had his favourites but so too did all the kings; Isabella certainly resented the time he spent with his friends instead of paying court to her but at the time of their marriage Edward was in his mid-twenties and she a foot-stamping petulanta of twelve; it would be more worrying if he had preferred to be closeted with a twelve-year-old girl than be with his peers. Those who sought to muddy the waters with tales of Edward's homosexuality queered their own pitch with lies and inaccuracies. When the married couple returned to England early in 1308 she is recorded by some as having been revolted by her husband rushing to fawn over Piers Gaveston, but Edward and Isabella arrived home in separate boats which landed at different points, neither of which was attended by Gaveston. The barons, whose suspicion and jealousy of Gaveston's position would culminate in his murder in 1312, and Isabella's desire to formalise her position with Mortimer, with whom she was by now embarked on a full-blown affair, meant that all concerned had a vested interest in coming up with a valid reason for getting rid of Edward II – branding him gay was as good as anything. But not only were both married – I know, so was Oscar Wilde – but both of these men had numerous heterosexual affairs with Edward known to have fathered at least one illegitimate son. Much of the hypothesizing about Edward's sexuality is likely based on misinterpretations of the traditions of the time which included something called 'Wedded Brotherhood', a sort of up-market blood-brothers ritual, complete with a Church ceremony and a blessing that mirrored the marriage ceremony. Such ritual was common throughout Europe with some churches having specific liturgy for such Adelphopoiesis, the making of brothers, as it was known. Another English king, Edmund Ironside, was so 'wedded' to his eleventh-century adversary, Cnut, to seal their truce, but the tradition faded from use and general memory by the late 1600s leaving modern readers of certain tracts thinking the worst. The last such bonding recorded is that of Sir Thomas Baines and Sir John Finch whose lifelong friendship and platonic devotion is commemorated by their joint tomb in Christ's College, Cambridge after their closely timed deaths in 1682.

So, rituals and traditions must be seen in their chronological context – much the same accusation is made of Richard I as the result of a similar misunderstanding. In 1187 he is recorded as spending the night in bed with King Philip II of France which modern readers, perhaps naturally, take as proof-positive of his and Philip's homosexual inclinations; because of this one single mention Richard I is frequently included in the lists of famous homosexuals.

But the two monarchs had just come to some fairly far-ranging agreements and, to proclaim their political unity to their respective entourages, they spent the day eating off the same plate, drinking from the same chalice and spending the night in the same bed; a bit strange by today's standards, but that is all there was to the ritual; public proclamation of unity – your honour!

JOAN – THE AUNTIE-POPE

The yarn about a ninth-century female Pope is a myth that will not lie down and die. As recently as 1996 the 'factional' novel, *Pope Joan* by Donna Woolfolk Cross was published, selling millions throughout Europe and America, this being made into a film in 2009. The story goes that, some time around 855, the Papal throne was ascended by a woman in drag who reigned for about two-and-a-half years before her deception was revealed by her going into labour in the street, somewhere between the Coliseum and St Clement's Church, during the Easter Papal procession making its way from St Peter's Basilica to that of St John Lateran. (Although the former is the better known it is not the main church of Rome, it is in fact the lesser-known latter which is designated Mother and Head of all Churches in the City and the World). Not wishing to be thought misogynistic, the assembled Cardinals tied her to the back of her horse to be dragged through the streets to her death before, holding onto their mitres, they trampled her baby into the cobblestones. A charming and cautionary tale, but all is myth; for a start, the Papal Easter Parade did not follow that route.

The first sight of any female Pope is found in the writings of Martin Polonus, a pretty reliable thirteenth-century Dominican historian, but few believe the relevant passage to be original; most see it as a later insert. It must be remembered that medieval monks were the photocopiers of their time, all copying each others' work (hence 'copious') and always adding bits here and there to cater to the whims and fancies of whoever was paying for the finished tome. Once a genuine error or a malicious spoof got into the mix it was doomed to centuries of meticulous repetition. The greatest nail in the myth of Pope Joan, apart from the fact that the dates in the Papal lineage do not allow for any such tenure, is that no contemporary chronicler mentions such a terrible and public spectacle as her brutal end. Sure, there are *apparent* mentions in reproductions of ninth- and tenth-century writings but all these are forgeries inserted years later after the myth of Pope Joan had taken hold.

The longest gap between any deposed/murdered/deceased pope and his successor did indeed occur in 855 after Leo IV died leaving behind him a most unseemly squabble over the papal throne. The prime candidate was Hadrian, Cardinal Priest of St Marco, but he had the wisdom to turn the job down flat. Second choice was Benedict who was briefly enthroned before a mob of militant bishops and clerics dragged him off to prison to clear the way for Anastasius, an overly ambitious back-stabber who had been anathematized and exiled by Leo IV. Anastasius ruled briefly and unofficially until he and his supporters realized that his position was quite untenable. Thus, Benedict was released, dusted down and popped quickly into the throne as if nothing had happened. All this was a mere glitch running from 17 July 855 until 29 September the same year. So, we have Leo IV (847–855), Benedict III (855–857), and Nicholas I (858–867) who leave no room at all for any otho-'doxie'. Furthermore, no proponent of the myth has so far put forward a plausible background for the woman they say served as Pope John VIII; it is hardly the sort of job one falls into; no-one, man or woman, could have simply wandered in off the street and casually announced interest in becoming the Pope. Even back then, with some decidedly dodgy Popes running the Vatican, proposed candidates needed some sort of track-record and supporters, yet no credible explanation is forthcoming for Joan/John's presence in the Vatican in the first place. The stories began circulating in the thirteenth century, over 500 years after the alleged events, and it was not until the fourteenth century that the name was uniformly touted as Joan, prior to this various names were attributed, usually Agnes or Gilberta.

Supporters of the myth point out, quite correctly, that all papal processions shun a tiny set of streets between the Colosseum and St Clement's Church which does indeed include a Vicus Papissa, but, alas for those who choose to believe, this is the Street of Mrs Pape, not the Street of the Female Pope. Either way, the avoidance of this small enclave does seem to be a case of the myth back-feeding into Vatican tradition. Another Vatican oddity, leapt upon with glee, is the existence of a couple of admittedly strangely-shaped perforated marble throne-like chairs, the seats of which have a keyhole shaped cut-away – the infamous *Sedia Stercoraria*. Defenders of the myth hail these chairs to have played a peculiar role in post-Joan Papal elections to ensure that no woman ever again perpetrated such fraud. After the selection process and the voting, the Pope-elect had to sit on one of these chairs in the buff while a viewing party retired to the room below which had a hole cut in the ceiling. In full view of this committee, a young cleric – no doubt a pretty one – had to approach the Pope and grab his papal appendages and shout out, if satisfied as to the matter: '*Testiculos habet et bene pendente*', or 'he has testicles and they hang well', this pronouncement no doubt of great relief to all concerned. The only trouble with this part of the yarn is that the name of the chairs translates as the dung-chairs and they predate the alleged time of Joan by centuries; in fact they predate the advent of the Catholic Church itself. They are nothing more than commodes.

As for the impetus behind the ever-persistent myth of a female Pope, that may be nothing more sinister that an unexplained inclusion in the early medieval Tarot, a card called La Papessa, this being enough to start people weaving yarns about such a person. Not surprisingly, most such rumour came from the newly formed Protestants, all young and gobby about their unedifying diet of Worms, and determined to strike at the very heart of the opposition with the misogynistic Vatican's own worst nightmare; a woman Pope. Not only did this hit all the right buttons but it harked back to the scandal of the Vatican's pornocracy which reached its height at about the same time as the propagandists pitched the rule of their fictitious Joan. The scandal was still a sore point on the Hill as the Papal court watched the rise of Protestantism with absolute horror.

At the centre of the scandal lay, literally and metaphorically, the women of the incredibly wealthy and powerful Theophylact family who controlled the papal throne with their thighs for nigh-on half a century, after Theodora had her evil way with the weak vacillating Pope Sergius who did her bidding throughout his reign from 904–911. She and her equally 'enthusiastic' daughters, Theodora and Marozia made the Borgias look like a bunch of amateurs; the illegitimate son, grandson and great-grandson of Marozia all took their turns on the Papal throne; a unique achievement for any family in Vatican history. All three women in their time carried by Papal decree the title of Setnatrix and Patricia of Rome and this 'Rule of Harlots', as it became known, took the Vatican a long time to live down. As for the nut-clutching ceremony, that too had foundation in reality.

In Rome, as indeed in other early cultures, solemn statement was given with clutched testicles, castration being the penalty for telling porkies. Perjurers were so modified before being sewn up in a sack with a couple of wild dogs and thrown off the Tarpian Rock. Draconian, perhaps, but the repeat rate on perjury in Roman courts was extremely low. Not only did this interesting little ritual produce terms such as 'testify' and 'testimony' but it, and its corollary, the gripping of the testicles of the superior to whom oath of allegiance was being sworn, infiltrated the early Roman Church, much to the amusement of outsiders. The inspiration for the Church's ritual came from no less a source than the Bible and *Genesis* 24:2 which reads: 'And Abraham said unto his eldest servant of his house, that ruled over all that he had, put, I pray thee, thy hand under my thigh and I will make you swear by the Lord, the God of Heaven, and the God of the earth, that thou shalt not take a wife unto my son of the daughters of the Canaanites among whom I dwell'. Again, in *Genesis* 47:29, Joseph is required to do likewise to his own father and swear not to bury him in Egyptian soil. While not at every occurrence of the word in the Old Testament – oops, there we go again – 'thigh' appears frequently as a euphemism for 'penis'; lots of talk of various characters' children detailed as being 'of their thigh', to differentiate from adopted or otherwise. With a misguided enthusiasm for Biblical tradition the early Roman Church embraced this form of oath-taking, much to its later chagrin.

LONDON'S BURNING

The Great Fire of London burned for four and a half days and laid waste an incredible 436 acres, taking with it 13,200 houses, the old St Paul's Cathedral, 86 lesser churches, 6 chapels, the Guild Hall, the Royal Exchange, the Customs House, 148 hospitals, asylums and lazarettos, countless libraries and other municipal buildings of note, 52 Company Halls, 3 of the city gates, 4 stone bridges and several prisons including Newgate and Fleet. The two main myths attached to the fire, which left 90 per cent of Londoners homeless, are that it only claimed a handful of lives and that it purged the city of the plague; neither is true.

According to myth the death toll of the fire was a scant four; Alice, the simple-minded serving-girl in the Farynor's bakery where the fire is said to have started on the night of 2 September 1666; an unnamed woman who, with a misplaced trust in the Lord wisely unshared by those she besought to follow her, took refuge in the old St Paul's just before it exploded in a fire ball; an old man who ignored instructions not to return to his burning home to retrieve some bedding, and Paul Lowell, a watch-maker of Shoe Lane who, dismissing the fire as nothing out of the ordinary and the dangers exaggerated, announced his intention to remain in his house 'until it do fall in on top of me', which the building obligingly did. Some accounts claim the death toll to number six, but this includes two drunks who, reluctant to quit their deserted local until it was actually on fire, ran out and fell into the Thames to drown. But deaths of the poor did not warrant counting in such times and a more realistic figure would be perhaps 8,000 or 10,000, the remains of whom were never found as the temperatures in the fire-storms approached those achieved by a modern crematorium. Steel lying on the wharfs was later found to have melted as had the massive city gates, this indicating temperatures approaching 3,000°f. Although not a direct result of the fire, anything up to 20,000 people died from cholera and other diseases which flourished in the unsanitary and over-crowded camps set up to accommodate the teeming homeless.

The frequently proffered explanation to bolster the low death toll myth cites the plague having arrived the year before to deplete the city's population to such a degree that the fire was left raging through a ghost town and, while there is an element of truth in this, the figures do not stack up in total support. When the plague was first recognised during the week commencing 6 June 1665 there were forty-three noted deaths, with the city's population in the region of 600,000. The weekly toll climbed to a peak of 7,165 in the week commencing 19 September before tailing off again to around the fifty per week mark by the January of 1666. In all, there were some 70,000 recorded deaths so it is perhaps safe to assume that the real total would have been something more like 100,000. True, those would could afford it or had estates in the country did indeed flee the pestilence but the vast majority of Londoners simply didn't have anywhere else to go and just had to sit tight and take their chances. When the Great Fire erupted, there were still about 400,000 people in the city. As for the myth that the fire purged the plague, this too is untenable; while the devastation was epic, over four-fifths of the city was untouched, including the sprawling slums that were the plague's strongholds. Besides, the plague evaporated from most other European cities at about the same time without the need for other capitols to be razed.

When the smoke cleared the rumours began: it was all the work of Papist terrorists; it was a guerrilla action mounted by disaffected ex-Cromwellian officers; it was… etc… etc. Keen to avert riots and reprisals, the authorities welcomed the enthusiastically volunteered confession of guilt proffered by the clearly mad Robert Hubert of Rouen (he was French, perfect) and strung him up at Tyburn despite overwhelming proof that he had been at sea on a Swedish ship when the fire started – he didn't even dock in London until two days after it was all over. But his death seemed to cheer everyone up and attention turned to the re-building of the city, with one of the men involved seeing a new opportunity raised by the fire – the property insurance business.

Son of the piously named PraiseGod Barebones, after whom the Cromwellian Barebones Parliament had been named, Nicholas Barebones, who made a considerable fortune from the extensive rebuilding of the city, launched the first property fire insurance company. He had actually been christened If-Jesus-Christ-Had-Not-Died-For-Thee-Thou-Would-Be-Damned Barebones but rightly thought that Nicholas would be less of a hindrance when it came to signing papers. Given the impetus for this new venture, which opened for business on Threadneedle Street on 13 May 1680, he called his brainchild the Phoenix Insurance Company proving that he, like most others, totally misunderstood the legend of said mythical creature. The legend of the phoenix held that after living for 500 years the one-and-only bird died in its own self-built funeral pyre to make way for another and wholly separate phoenix to be born elsewhere. But no matter, Barebones' venture was a roaring success with others jumping on his bandwagon. Each client received a plaque to fix to the side of the insured building and each insurance company had its own fire brigade which would only respond to its own clients' fires. This system persisted until quite recently with the last insurance-company run brigade being that of the Norwich Union in Worcester which was only merged with the regular service in 1929.

A MAN FOR NO TREASONS

Thomas Becket (1118–1170) may have had French parents – the oft-told tale of his mother being a Saracen princess is just that, an oft-told tale – but at no time did his name include the French 'a' as is still commonly inserted for no good reason. Writing in the seventeenth century, the historian John Strype took the trouble to note in his biography of *Thomas Cranmer* (1694) 'It is a small error, but being so oft repeated deserveth to be observed into corrected. The name of that archbishop was Thomas Becket. If the vulgar did formerly, as it doth now, call him "Thomas à Becket" their mistake is not to be followed by learned men.' How the 'a' invaded the name is a mystery, as despite that French parentage, no contemporary reference to him as such can be found; indeed, most of his contemporaries called him Thomas of London. Like any man in such high position, he had enemies and perhaps it was they who, to highlight and deride his foreign heritage, included the French designation in mockery thereof. This would explain why writers of his time avoided it, they being reluctant to demean their work with court-circle slurs.

The traditional explanation of the circumstances leading up to Becket's murder also rings false. Re-told in countless plays and films, the story goes that Henry II wished out loud to be rid of 'this turbulent priest' and four knights, who just happened to be hanging about in earshot, took this lament to be a strong royal hint that they should pop off down to Canterbury and total the Bish. Henry then trowels on the 'Oh-God-shock-horror-what-have-I-said-and-brought-about' routine and, in between theatrical bouts of teeth-gnashing and loud lamentation, finds time to organise the escape of those very four men he without doubt sent out to do the job. The myth also tells that Henry took to the road as a penitent, touring every monastery in the land so he could be flogged by the occupants of each. So much for the myth.

Becket had only just returned from a six-year exile in France after fleeing the king's wrath and in fear of his life; in fact, so turbulent was the relationship between the two once-friends that people had coined 'to play Hal and Tommy' for any argumentative situation, this truncating to 'play Hal' before corrupting to 'play hell'. Not long before Becket's departure for the safety of France, Henry had decreed castration for any cleric who sided with Becket in any of their many disputes. In *History of England*, the respected Scottish historian and philosopher, David Hume (1711–1776) records that this did not deter all of Becket's supporters. The king 'ordered the whole of them to be castrated, and caused all their testicles to be brought to him on a platter.' Now wasn't that a tasty dish to set before the king; but as Hume himself observed somewhat philosophically: 'Of the pain and danger they, the monks, might justly complain, yet since they had vowed chastity, he [Henry] deprived them of a superfluous pleasure.' The really important thing about this is that it proves beyond doubt that Henry and Thomas were most certainly at loggerheads come 1170.

As soon as Becket returned from France he was, once again, in direct conflict with Henry and thus a prime candidate for 'removal' but it is modern myth that the king loudly bemoaned 'Will no-one rid me of this turbulent priest?' According to Edward Grim's *The Life of Thomas Becket* (1180), the cry of exasperation was: 'What miserable drones and traitors have I nourished and brought up in my household, who let their lord be treated with such shameful contempt by a low-born cleric?' Not even a half-wit would have interpreted that as a royal decree for assassination; more likely is it that the four approached the king and asked him exactly what it was that he wanted to happen and then went out and did his express bidding. Why else were none of the four punished or even rebuked but instead shuffled off the scene until all the fuss died down? This is the clearest indication of all that Henry ordered Becket's death and promised the four assassins immunity whatever the outcome. Reginald FitzUrse disappeared to Ireland where he is said to have established the MacMohan clan; FitzUrse meaning son of the bear and MacMohan the same, Hugh de Morville and William de Tracy took themselves off to the Holy Lands for a spot of crusading and Richard le Breton opted for a life of low-profile retirement on the Isle of Jersey. His most famous descendant, Emilie Charlotte Le Breton, would take to the stage under the name of Lillie Langtry, aka the Jersey Lily.

Back at the ranch, Henry's hand-wringing and protestations continued in their abject failure to convince anyone of his remorse but the fuss was not long endured nor the Church long troubled by the murder; Becket was canonized in 1173 and Henry absolved for the murder of a saint in the July of the next year; well, no point in crying over spilt milk. The new saint's shrine at Canterbury became the must-have badge of all serious pilgrims whose stream of patronage started up a whole new industry selling the very last word in pilgrim-chic – the gauvardine. Basically the Old French for 'pilgrim' this was an extremely hardwearing and waterproofed garment which proclaimed the wearer to be no fair-weather walker but a hardy year-rounder. By the sixteenth century this term had modified to 'gabardine' and shifted more to the type of material used in the make-up rather than the garment itself. There was also a roaring trade in tiny vials of Becket's blood – god knows how the monks kept a straight face over that one as they shifted gallons of the stuff which was but very expensive pig's blood – and the 'I've seen the shrine' badges as flogged by the custodian of the shrine itself. Becket was big money. Canterbury was still popular with early eighteenth-century pilgrims who rode down from London at an easy pace that became known as a 'Canterbury gallop', or 'canter' as it is now. As for poor old Becket he was not long at rest before he was disturbed by another Henry.

Having split from Rome over Papal disapproval of his spouse-recycling programme, the Welsh thug, Henry Twdyr, or Henry VIII as he is better known, got the Abbey-habit in 1536 and began the systematic Dissolution of the Monasteries which included the destruction of all saints' shrines, Becket's included. While he did steal the considerable wealth the shrine had generated over the previous 500 years and order the shrine smashed and the bones dispersed, it is but persistent myth that, in a syphilis-fuelled bout of lunacy, he had the bones piled up in the Star Chamber to stand trial for treason against Henry II. The story goes that, having conducted an abysmal self-defence, the pile of bones was found guilty and burnt in the courtyard outside.

PLAGUE'S PROGRESS

There is much confusion surrounding the various plagues that ravaged Europe and England and Wales throughout the Middle Ages and the last one that struck in 1665, just before the Great Fire of London. The exact nature of these attacks has long been argued to no great satisfaction – were they all a recurrence of the same pestilence, a modified version of the same, or were they bubonic, pneumonic, haemorrhagic or even a strain of anthrax. The broadly accepted explanation – that they were all incidents of bubonic plague, transmitted by the rat-flea – is about the only theory that does *not* hold water; the rats, it seems, have been getting bad press. Although the emotive 'Black Death' was not even coined until the early nineteenth century, we shall use that term here as a convenience with readers bearing in mind that role of the rat-flea in the transmission of bubonic plague was not even recognised until 1894. In fact, according to Dr James Wood PhD of Pennsylvania State University, an anthropologist and demographer specialising in the spread of epidemics, bubonic plague itself cannot be reliably traced to any time before the late eighteenth century; doubtless it existed before that point but no-one knows just how far it goes back.

There are a number of problems with the bubonic/rat-flea premise; first there is the alarming speed with which the Black Death always raced across Europe, not only did it move on a broad front at the rate of perhaps 10 to 15 miles per week, but it also threw 'spikes', erupting in sporadic locations many miles ahead of that front. Despite modern transport and people being far more mobile today, modern outbreaks of bubonic plague, fortunately, have trouble advancing more than 15 or 20 miles per year, killing a mere 3 per cent (with treatment) of those in its path. How could this possibly be the same beast that moved 100 times faster and killed 40 per cent of those in its path? Next there is the puzzling immunity which arose in resistance to those outbreaks of Black Death: at times when it struck year after year, which was not uncommon, the mortality rate would fall from 40 per cent to perhaps 4 per cent, eventually only attacking children without any acquired immunity. No-one today shows any signs of developing immunity after surviving their first encounter with bubonic plague. Finally there is the question raised by the rats and the fleas themselves: how was the Black Death just as widespread and just as deadly in countries like Iceland, where there were no rats until the nineteenth century, and how was the Black Death just as 'active' in climates outside the temperature/humidity tolerance of said fleas which can only exist and breed within certain parameters. There is also the question raised by the tradition of the Derbyshire village of Eyam, of which more later, and the manner in which they maintain that the plague came a-calling.

None of this is wild conjecture nor is it anything new; since the 1980s there has been a steadily increasing lobby of academics questioning the very nature of the Black Death, much to the ire of the traditionalist Bubonics, if we might call them that for convenience. The first significant shot across their collective bows came from a well-respected British zoologist called Dr Graham Twigg and his *The Black Death: A Biological Reappraisal* (1984) in which he considers anthrax to be the culprit. Others, such as medical statisticians Susan Shaw and Christopher Duncan of the University of Liverpool, would follow with their *The Biology of Plagues* (2005), in which they conjecture a haemorrhagic virus, pointing to the wealth of evidence indicating human-to-human infection, while bubonic plague is only communicated by the rat-flea to humans on an individual basis. There was also *The Black Death Transformed* (2002) by Samuel Kline Cohn, Professor of Medieval History at Glasgow University but all those with the temerity to question the Bubonics are dismissed by them as 'Plague Deniers', deliberately coined to resonate with 'Holocaust Deniers'. Not only is this a rather unpleasant coinage but is also wildly inaccurate: none of the 'Deniers' have ever denied that the Black Death turned up with monotonous regularity, they only question the nature of the contagion. Some even suggest that it was a one-off infective that burnt itself out in 1670, never to be seen again.

Let us assume for a moment that the agent was indeed bubonic and ponder the issues which that raises. The vector is the rat-flea which only moves from its chosen host after stupidly infecting and killing its own 'home'. When the rat population is seriously depleted by such means, the rat-fleas move to their next option of cats and dogs; only when these too drop in number do the fleas resort to humans. Naturally, this would mean a massive decrease in the populations of rats, cats and dogs prior to any incident of bubonic plague yet none of the chroniclers, from the fourteenth century to the seventeenth century, mention towns or cities being knee-deep in dead rats, cats and dogs just before every outbreak. It is worth mentioning here that the best thing a city can do, once bubonic plague has come to visit, is to import as many rats as possible and turn them loose to give the fleas somewhere to go – sounds silly but it works. Next, a comparison between the known symptoms and manifestations of bubonic plague and those repeatedly noted during attacks of the Black Death. Modern bubonic infection presents buboes in the groin only; fleas rarely bite humans any higher up the body than the ankle and the nearest lymph nodes to receive the infection are in the groin. Medieval chroniclers talk of buboes all over the victims' bodies, even behind the ears, which never happens with bubonic infection.

Medieval medics also recorded weeping sores and abscesses, atypical of bubonic infection, and black pustules, again atypical of bubonic infection but quite typical of anthrax, hence its name as taken from the Latin for coal and thus a sister-word of 'anthracite'.

Next, the speed of the pandemic spread. Rats tend to stay put once they have found somewhere suitable, only moving on a matter of perhaps a mile when conditions and food supply no longer suit. This explains the slow progress of modern outbreaks of bubonic plague but hardly jibes with the speed of progress of the Black Death; that kind of dispersal would call for a veritable carpet of racing-rodents running full pelt and non-stop across Europe, hurling their fleas like biological paw-grenades at the occupants of every settlement they sped through. And, if rat-carried, how did the Black Death cross the Alps, the Pyrenees, and make the long cold journey to rat-free Iceland and Greenland? It is easy to say 'on a ship' but with the length of such voyages in such times and the known incubation/kill-time of bubonic plague being well established, there would be records of ships full of dead rats and equally dead sailors washing up along the shores of Europe, yet there are no such accounts. If rat-carried, why did the Black Death always fan out along trade routes and why did quarantine seem to work? Surely, if the vector was the rat then quarantining any already-infected victim would have had no effect at all since bubonic plague cannot be transmitted from one person to another. That being the case, how come the mortality among doctors and clerics tending the sick was so extraordinarily high? And what of the rat-flea itself? These flourish in high humidity and at temperatures between 50°F and 78°F yet when Professor Cohn examined all the outbreaks of the Black Death and cross referenced them to local climate and conditions, they largely coincided with conditions so hostile to the rat-flea that numbers should have been at their nadir.

All 'Deniers' point to Eyam in Derbyshire as proof in a microcosm. Some time towards the end of August, the local tailor, George Vicars, received a delivery of cloth from London and was dead by 7 September. Those who favour the anthrax theory are quick to point out, quite rightly, that the spores can remain active in infected wool, cloth and other animal products for years. Whatever the nature of the Black Death's arrival in Eyam, Vicars had already passed it on to several others before dying – again, not a characteristic of bubonic plague. The tradition goes that the doughty villagers, under the guidance of their rector, the Revd. William Mompesson (1639-1709),

observed a protracted and self-imposed quarantine to halt the progress
of the plague and prevent it spreading to the surrounding villages.
According to the tradition, all stayed put to take their chances with
food and other necessities being brought to pick-up points by people
from the villages they were trying to save, these people collecting
payment from vinegar dips to avoid infection. The quarantine lasted
fourteen months after which only eighty-three of the original 350
remained alive. Now, had the visiting infection really been bubonic
then quarantine would have been absolutely useless, unless imposed
upon the rats. It is perhaps unkind to pick on the Eyam tradition
but it should be said that there is no contemporary documentation
to back up the tale and a captive population of 350 would not
long hold the attention of a single infective, certainly not for
fourteen months. It is also known that several families did indeed flee
the area with Mompesson himself packing his two children off to
Sheffield. And then there is that worrying vinegar dip which crops
up in all such tales. People simply did not know about germs, bacteria
and viruses in such times; it was not until Louis Pasteur's experiments
of the 1870s that medical circles accepted the germ-theory; prior
to that everyone thought sickness was caused by bad air (mal-aria)
and smells. Even Florence Nightingale laughed her lamp out at the
mere suggestion that sickness was caused by tiny creepie-crawlies
that invaded the body in their thousands and marched around inside
doing harm. So how come the Eyamites were two centuries ahead of
medical knowledge with their germ-killing vinegar dip?

Eyam has also done much to 'encourage' the notion that the
children's chant of 'Ring-a-Ring o' Roses' was made up in that
village by children watching the deadly drama unfold about them.
Used by extension as the title of the play, *The Roses of Eyam*,
the public have been hood-winked into thinking the rhyme a
gruesome plague-chant with the title referring to blotches that
encircled the body or the neck with violent sneezing besetting
the sufferers just before 'They all fell down'. Nice try but no
cigar. No-one in the 1665 outbreak mentioned circles of rose-red
blotches; violent sneezing was not any indication of infection or
final stages and, most damning of all, the rhyme was unknown
before the 1880s and, according to the *Oxford Dictionary of Nursery
Rhymes*, an English variant of a rhyme popular in New England
which seems to have crossed the Atlantic. This same Eyam/
rhyme/sneezing/death yarn has also given rise to the equally

popular notion that the tradition of saying 'Bless you!' to someone sneezing is born of the same link in that this could indicate the onset of the Black Death. Again, no cigar; plague victims did not sneeze and the tradition is linked instead to the once widespread belief that a person's spirit and breath were somehow linked and that a violent sneeze might 'evict' the soul, hence the blessing. This belief was by no means restricted to Europe; in the Hindu culture it is common for sneezers to clap their hands loudly in front of their own mouths to frighten any escaping spirit back into their body and the Inuit 'kiss' is not a nose-rub but a gentle exchange of spirit-breath through their noses.

Another town to leave its name in the history books because of the Black Death was Taranto in Italy. This was not the only place where the inhabitants went in for wild 'whirling-dervish' type dancing to ward off the disease but it was the only town where they went in for the practice with such verve and vigour that the inhabitants evolved the ritual into a recognised style – the Tarantella. Like Eyam, the inhabitants of Taranto aimed for the tourist-trade and, long after the Black Death disappeared from the face of the earth in 1670, people made pilgrimages to the town to witness what was claimed to have kept the Black Death at bay. Some have claimed that the dance evolved from a frenzy brought on by bites from the local variant of the tarantula spider, which was in fact the European wolf-spider, but this is not so; contrary to general opinion the bite of the tarantula is a tad painful but by no means harmful to humans. Both the dance and the spider take their names, quite independently, from Taranto. Another Italian plague-myth claims that all Venetian gondolas were ordered to be painted black for the shipment of victims of the Black Death; this is indeed what all the tourists are told by their guides but the truth is more mundane. The City Magistrates passed a Sumptuary Tax on 18 April 1633 demanding a levy for each extra colour a gondola carried, not only on its shell but on its canopies. Things had got a little out of hand in that department with many private gondolas looking like floating juke-boxes. As all upon production were painted with pitch, most opted to just leave it at that and avoid the tax.

After the passing of the Black Death the face of rural Europe was changed forever. With the labour-force so dramatically depleted, those who remained could demand increasingly higher wages leaving the landlord-farmers the unappetising option of either paying up or watching their crops rot in the fields. With so many of the landlord-farmers themselves dead, the land parcels became dramatically larger as those who survived snapped up the land of the deceased, grubbed up the dividing tree-lines and hedge-rows to produce much larger fields and the 'patchwork countryside' thought so natural today. Having to work such massive areas with reduced labour, the rural economy drove the technological revolution for mechanization that brought forth the likes of Jethro Tull whose machines would further change the face of the rural Britain forever. According to Susan Shaw and Christopher Duncan's *The Biology of Plagues*, about 10 per cent of us also have to thank the residual immunity against the Black Death that lives on in the population for resistance to HIV. So, not all bad.

THE PLAY THAT DARE NOT SPEAK ITS NAME

Only in Shakespeare's play does Macbeth (d. 1057), (properly MacBethad), murder his cousin, Duncan, as he lies in his bed. In reality Duncan fell to Macbeth in open combat in 1040 on a battlefield near Elgin.

Macbeth was nothing like the conniving usurper of Shakespeare's imagination, both he and Duncan held valid claims to the throne through their respective maternal lineage, but Macbeth carried the day after a fair fight. He ruled Scotland for about fourteen years, and he ruled justly with the equally maligned Lady Macbeth at his side; Gruach, by all accounts a kind and compassionate woman who never provoked anyone's murder, is equally ill-served by the evil reputation hung about her neck by the same inaccurate and slanderous play. The pair did much to encourage Christianity and he even attended a Papal Jubilee in Rome, arriving there with a flotilla of Viking longships rowed by god-fearing Norsemen. This is how his fellows and subjects perceived the matter, for Macbeth was buried with full honours on the Isle of Iona, the resting place for all lawful kings, and no usurper would have found his way there.

Of course, the most oft-heard misquotation from Shakespeare's slander is 'Lead on MacDuff', this is invariably employed as a humorous entreaty for another to proceed. But the line is 'Lay on

MacDuff' and is uttered prior to combat by Macbeth telling the
other man to strike out as hard as he can 'And damn'd be him that
first cries Hold, enough!' Basically it is a command to fight to the
death, not go first through a door.

POCAHONTAS – MIDDLESEX GIRL

There are innumerable myths attached to this woman's life and
loves, all of which were woven by white men apparently trying to
project the concept of a noble savage saved by Western civilization
and Christianity.

She was in fact married twice in her short life, but neither time
to the settler John Smith who seems to have invented the tale of
her having saved him from being killed by her vengeful father. At
the time he pitches said events Pocahontas was not yet twelve and
thus a mite young (not to mention female) to interfere in tribal
affairs. Actually, her name was Matoaka – Pocahontas, meaning
'playful thing', was her father's pet-name for her. Her father is
frequently but erroneously referred to as Powhatan, this in fact being
the tribal title of the man properly called Wahunsunacawh. Smith
did not think to mention Pocahontas risking her own life to save
his until ten years after the alleged event and, since he had previously
vaunted a strikingly similar tale of his life being saved by a
beautiful Turkish girl after his capture by such people in Hungary in
1602, it is safe to dismiss any such yarns as one of his recurring fantasies.

Her first marriage, aged perhaps fourteen, was tribal and to
someone called Kocoum of whom nothing else is known, but
presumably he died or otherwise disappeared. Despite an uneasy
truce between Wahunsunacawh and the Jamestown settlers there
were repeated incidents prompting the latter to kidnap and hold the
young Algonquian princess to ransom. Wahunsunacawh refused to
pay so she remained a captive pawn in the ensuing negotiations and
machinations. Forcibly instructed in Christianity in preparation for a
political marriage to benefit the colony, the young prisoner had little
choice in the matter and, baptized as Rebecca, she married settler
John Rolfe in the April of 1614. While hardly the loving union of
Disney-inspired imagination, the marriage did produce a period of
peace between the settlers and the locals.

Immediately impregnated to leave her no option of returning
to her own people, she gave birth to a son, Thomas, in the

January of the following year and stayed with Rolfe on his Virginia plantation until 1616 when they both set sail with him for England to launch a PR exercise for the Virginia Company, anxious to promote further colonization. The couple lived in Brentford, Middlesex for several months where the poor girl, not yet twenty-two, contracted smallpox. She died en route to the return trans-Atlantic transport and was buried at Gravesend in Kent on 21 March 1617. Rolfe returned to America to be killed by her kinsmen a few years later.

It is popularly held that the area to the north of London's Ludgate Hill, known as La Belle Sauvage or The Bell Savage, is so named in commemoration of Pocahontas' visit to the capital; not only does chronology dispute this but the true origin lies in the fact that the site once accommodated a well-known inn run by Isobel Savage, known to all as Belle, who punned her pub-sign with a bell and a fierce-looking native.

PUBLIC ENEMA No 1

One of the great images of general history is that of Martin Luther (1483–1546) kicking off the Protestant Reformation by nailing his famous ninety-five points to the doors of All Saints' Catholic Church in his home town of Wittenberg on 31 October 1517. This image is still very big in Protestant circles and framed copies of old etchings showing a barefoot and pious Luther hammering at said doors are a big seller, so it must be true. Unfortunately not. Luther never nailed anything to any church doors and he was hardly the barefoot and pious type, in fact, he was neither nice nor even big in the Christian-spirit department.

The main point in Luther's list of grievances was the Catholic selling of Indulgences, a tasteful little scheme allowing anyone with the money to buy themselves a sort of stairway to heaven. The Confession box bought you forgiveness but the rules said that, once dead, you had to spend the requisite time in the staging-house of Purgatory to properly purge your sins before entering Heaven-proper. Not only did all men have their price but so too did their deeds with a strictly controlled sliding scale of sin-costs to cover all eventualities; by the time Luther had penned his 95-pronged attack, things had got so out of hand that there was even a pay-now-sin-later scheme for recidivists planning for the future – I'll take two rapes and one murder to go, please! But Luther did not nail anything to any door; he sent copies to a carefully selected few, including the Archbishop of Mainz, this the most important recipient in that here was the seat of the Chancellor of the Holy Roman Empire, a misnomer if ever there was one as it was neither Holy, nor Roman, nor an Empire. Anyway, having run his mail-shot, Luther sat back and waited for the fireworks, and fireworks there were. Our own Henry VIII responded with such a stinging attack on Luther that a delighted Pope Leo X awarded him the title of Defender of the Faith, the Catholic faith that is, this title being revoked after Henry split from Rome to set up the Church of England. Although Parliament hurriedly re-conferred the title, there are many who hold that they had not the power to do so and that neither Henry nor any of his successors, including the present Elizabeth II, have the right to proclaim themselves as such. But the Reformation was underway and the rest, as they say, is history.

As for Luther himself, those who desire to present him as a kindly old theologian are playing fast and loose with the known facts; the only egalitarian thing about Luther was the equal spread of his hatreds and prejudices; he was racist, misogynistic, misanthropic, xenophobic and reserved a special dislike for the poor. His opinion of the down-trodden is best illustrated by his response to the German Peasants' War of 1524/5 when they downed-tools, demanding, among other things, payment for work done for nobles and the curtailment of the rights of those same nobles to ill-treat them on whim. Thinking it a boost to their cause to have Luther on-side, they approached him for public support of their grievances, he responding with a diatribe entitled *Against the murdering and Thieving Hordes of Peasants* which actually called for their slaughter. Acutely aware that he operated under the protection of the nobles, Luther called upon his benefactors: 'Let all who are able, cut them down, slaughter and stab them, openly or in secret, and remember that there is nothing more poisonous, noxious and utterly devilish than a rebel.' Taking him at his word, the nobles did exactly that and butchered over 100,000.

Nor was he any more beneficent when it came to dealing with those unlucky enough to find themselves in his personal service: 'We must govern them [all servants and slaves] Turkish-fashion; so much work; so much food, as did Pharaoh deal with the Israelites in Egypt.' As for the Jews, in his 65,000-word rant, *On the Jews and Their Lives* (1543) Luther described them as a 'base and whoring people, that is, no people of God, and their boast of lineage, circumcision and their law must be accounted as filth' for they 'are full of the devil's feces ... which they wallow in like swine'. The synagogue he deemed 'an incorrigible whore and an evil slut' and advocated that all good Christians should throw 'pig-shit' at every Jew they encountered. There is much more disgusting drivel in the same vein and, in keeping with his passion for lists, he presents his readers with an eight-point 'Final Solution' to what he saw as the Jewish Problem.

First to set fire to their synagogues or schools and to bury and cover with dirt whatever will not burn, so that no man will ever again see a stone or cinder of them...

Second, I advise that their houses also be razed and destroyed...

Third, I advise that all their prayer books and Talmudic writings, in which such idolatry, lies, cursing and blasphemy are taught, be taken from them...

Fourth, I advise that their rabbis be forbidden to teach henceforth on pain of loss of life and limb...

Fifth, I advise that safe-conduct on the highways be abolished completely for the Jews...

Sixth, I advise that usury be prohibited to them, and that all cash and treasure of silver and gold be taken from them... Such money should now be used in ... the following [way]... Whenever a Jew is sincerely converted, he should be handed [a certain amount]...

Seventh, I commend putting a flail, an ax, a hoe, a spade, a distaff, or a spindle into the hands of young, strong Jews and Jewesses and letting them earn their bread in the sweat of their brow... For it is not fitting that they should let us accursed Goyim toil in the sweat of our faces while they, the holy people, idle away their time behind the stove, feasting and farting, and on top of all, boasting blasphemously of their lordship over the Christians by means of our sweat. No, one should toss out these lazy rogues by the seat of their pants.

If we wish to wash our hands of the Jews' blasphemy and not share in
their guilt, we have to part company with them. They must be driven
from our country. We must drive them out like mad dogs."

Naturally, this and many of his other ramblings found great favour
with a later German anti-Semite of the 1930s who would make much
use of Lutheran texts to impart a quasi-divine spin to the horrors he
was about to unleash. In one of those eerie echoes that history can
sometimes produce, Martin Luther (1895–1945) was the name of the
German Foreign Office official delegated by Heydrich to sort out
the nuts-and-bolts of the Nazi Final Solution and set up the Wannsee
Conference so that all could be ratified and rubber-stamped. One
can only presume that the parents of one of the greatest Christians
of the twentieth century, Dr Martin Luther King (1929–1968), knew
nothing of the reality of the man for whom they baptized their son.

On the secular side, Luther's attitudes to women, sex and the
human body in general were strange to say the least and perhaps
best left unexplored. Beset by alternating bouts of constipation and
diarrhoea he developed what can only be described as an unhealthy
obsession with his bowels, recording in minute detail each successful
visit to the loo and the relief he found in his frequent enemas. Most of
his writings are riddled with anal references so we can safely assume
that this obsession permeated all other aspects of his life. Indeed,
Catholics take malicious glee in reminding any who will listen that
the Protestant movement, no pun intended, was born in a lavatory
as the enteric cleric did, by his own admission, pen his ninety-five
points while so enthroned at home. And, let joy reign unbounded,
Luther's loo was discovered in 2004 by Lutheran theologian/
historian, Dr Martin Treu, who made such discovery when
excavating a cloistered garden at the Luther home in Wittenberg.
The team unearthed a small annexe which was basically a loo of
considerable size and comfort. 'Treu's loo' measured 9 metres by 9
metres and incorporated under-floor heating and numerous fixtures
and fittings normally associated with a study. Presumably Luther
figured that if he had to spend half his life in there he might as well
make it as tolerable as possible. After musing what Luther might have
used when finished 'We still don't know what was used for wiping
in those days…paper would have been both too expensive and too
stiff', Treu, who seems to have got rather more excited about the
find than it warranted, enthused that future visitors to the Luther

Museum would be able to view and even sit on the great man's lavvy – be still, my beating heart.

THE ROUEN-ATION OF JOAN

The usual account of 'Joan of Arc' has her as a heroine of the early fifteenth century when she led the French armies to countless victories before being captured by the Burgundians who sold her to the English to be burnt as a witch in the marketplace of Rouen. But she wasn't French; her name wasn't Joan of anything; she never commanded any army nor even fought in battle; she was not tried by the Inquisition, which instead branded the trial an illegal mockery; she did not stick to her guns but recanted all at her trial; she was not executed for witchcraft but for her having gone back on her recantation and she was not the tomboy with a knife-and-fork hair-do as is her modern cinematic portrayal.

She was born at Domrémy in Lorraine in 1412, this an independent duchy not part of France until 1766. Her father, originally named Jaques Darce, which is close, had abandoned even that name by before marrying Isabeau and producing his daughter. He was inordinately proud of having made a pilgrimage to Rome in his youth, so much so that he changed his name to Jacques Rommee and his daughter was christened Jehannette, not Joan. The Rommees were not of simple peasant stock; Jacques was a highly successful farmer and leading citizen who threatened to 'strangle her with my own hands if she goes into France'. From that, if nothing else, we may safely assume that 'Domremyites' considered themselves anything but French. Having said that, Jacques allegedly had no objections to the family being ennobled by the French Crown after his daughter's equally alleged victories, which resulted in him being transformed into Jacques de Lys, so the family did get a *de* – perhaps.

Much that is known today of Ms Rommee comes from chronicles discovered in Notre Dame in the nineteenth century and not everyone is convinced that these documents are genuine. Even Roger Caratini, one of France's most prestigious historians, has both feet firmly planted in that camp:

> I'm very much afraid that precious little of what we French have been taught in school about Joan of Arc is true… She was, it seems, almost entirely the creation of France's desperate need for a patriotic mascot

in the nineteenth century. The country wanted a hero, the myths of the
revolution were altogether too bloody, and France more or less invented
the story of its patron saint. The reality is, sadly, a little different... Joan
of Arc played no role, or at best only a very minor one, in the Hundred
Years War. She was not the liberator of Orléans for the simple reason that
the city was never besieged. And the English had nothing to do with
her death. I'm afraid it was the Inquisition and the university of Paris
that tried and sentenced her... I'm afraid the fact of the matter is that
we were the ones who killed our national hero. We may have a problem
with the English, but as far as Joan's concerned, we really shouldn't.

Nor is Caratini by any means alone in thinking Joan a nineteenth-
century invention, this author can certainly recall having seen such
opinions expressed before, stating that if not an entire fabrication
then she was 'but one of many maids who followed the army as
a banner-carrier on the same daily pay as an archer'. If the entire
legend is to be accepted at face value, then we are expected to
believe that an uneducated sixteen-year-old farm girl who could
barely write her own name simply wandered into the French
Royal Court and, after telling of her 'voices' and quipping a few
prophesies, sauntered out as the Supreme Commander of the
French Armies despite the fact that she knew nothing of military
strategy, tactics, weaponry and artillery. Even if the Dauphin had
been daft enough to make such an appointment, is it realistic to
believe that the existing commanders and the rank-and-file would
meekly fall into line behind her?

If she was all the legend hails her to have been then one would
expect there to have been countless portraits and accounts of her
in her own time, yet there is nothing. The first 'biography' was not
written until the seventeenth century by Edmund Richer (1559–
1631), Head of the Faculty of Theology in Paris, his manuscript
lying unpublished in archives until 1911. The next person to tackle
the subject was Lenglet du Fresnoy in 1753. He was followed
yet another century or so later by Jules Quicherat who in 1841
discovered the suspect cache of documents mainly relating to
her trial, in Notre Dame. Quicherat beavered away until 1849 to
produce a five-volume work that most take to be the definitive
work on her life, trial and death. Impressive as far as it goes, but this
hardly constitutes an unbroken chain of observation and assessment
leading back to the early fifteenth century.

Accepting that there really was a Joan on trial for her life, there are more than a few misconceptions attached to those proceedings. According to the Notre Dame documents, the only member of the Inquisition present was Jean LeMaistre who, despite threats from the English, kept raising objections over the illegality and shambolic ineptitude of the proceedings. As stated she was not tried as a witch but over her claims that her voices were divine and, according to the records, for 'violating the norms' by wearing armour and prancing around at the head of an army. This sounds like the kind of perception someone in the nineteenth century might have about fifteenth-century mores; in fact, this was commonplace, and across the fourteenth and fifteenth centuries countless women led armies and wore armour. Jeanne de Monfort (d.1374) orchestrated the defence of Hennebont in armour and from horseback before breaking out at the head of a 300-strong column of cavalry and fighting her way through to Brest on the northern French coast. Phillippa of Hainault, wife of Edward III, led a 12,000-strong army against Scottish invaders; while Jeanne de Belleville was often to be found stamping round France at the head of her men and, in 1383, none other than Pope Boniface wrote in glowing terms of the deeds of Genoese ladies in their fine armour fighting in the Crusades. Margaret of Denmark, Jeanne de Penthièvre, Jaqueline of Bavaria, Isabella of Lorraine, Lady de Châtillon, even the treacherous Burgundians had female artillery squads who dressed decidedly butchly; no, France was teeming with martial maidens in armour and if this failed to upset the Pope why did the good clerics of Rouen get their cassocks in a twist over one more?

Most suspiciously, those trial records present a highly articulate and very well-read defendant engaging in such stunningly erudite banter and demonstrating such a knowledge of the finer points of theological philosophy that she drew grudging admiration even from those present who were determined that she would burn, come what may. At her trial she was still only nineteen and still illiterate, so whence all that knowledge? Nor did she stick to her guns; after contemplating the prospect of being burnt to death she wisely opted for a recantation, agreeing that her 'voices' were doubtless of Satanic inspiration. She also agreed to stop wearing the male attire which the Bishops deemed a blasphemy proscribed by biblical texts. Her u-turn was accepted on 23 May 1431 and reprieve granted, but, she was again caught in drag on the 29th of the same month and burnt as a relapsed heretic in Rouen the next day. Naturally, as alleged of countless other heroes sent to the stake or funeral pyre, her heart was so pure it refused to burn; this was even claimed of Shelly's pump to validate the purity of his verse. It makes a nice touch but Joan's heart would have swelled, popped, shrivelled and sizzled, just like anyone else's.

That said, not everyone accepts that she did burn. The extant archives of Rouen show that the city fathers authorized a payment of 210 livres to Joan 'for services rendered by her at the siege of the said city' on 1 August 1439, some eight years after Joan was supposedly converted to saintly oxide in the market-place of the same town. These archives were first unearthed by Daniel Polluche (1689–1768) and later re-evaluated by Joseph Octave Delepierre in the nineteenth century. In 1898 Dr E. Cobham Brewer, he of *Phrase and Fable* fame, wrote:

> M. Octave Delepierre has published a pamphlet, called *Doute Historique*, to deny the tradition that Joan of Arc was burnt at Rouen for sorcery. He cites a document discovered by Father Vignier in the seventeenth century, in the archives of Metz, to prove that she became the wife of Sieur des Armoise, with whom she resided at Metz, and became the mother of a family. Vignier subsequently found in the family muniment-chest the contract of marriage between "Robert des Armoise, knight, and Jeanne D'Arcy, surnamed the Maid of Orleans." In 1740 there were found in the archives of the Maison de Ville (Orléans) records of several payments to certain messengers from Joan to her brother John, bearing the dates 1435, 1436. There is also the entry of a presentation from the council of the city to the Maid, for her services at the siege (dated 1439). M. Delepierre has brought forward a host of other documents to corroborate the same fact, and show that the tale of her martyrdom was invented to throw odium on the English.

And there are other sources claiming Joan to have been alive after 1431; *The Ancient Registers at the Maison de Ville of Orléans* and *The Chronicle of the Dean of St Thibault-de-Metz* both make reference to a post-Rouen Joan. Either way, Polluche laid out his arguments in *Probleme Historique sur la Pucelle. (sur son Mariage)* (1749), this forming in part the foundation for Delepierre who first published his findings in *The Athenaeum* dated 15 September 1855.

The trouble is that all purported as fact is either shadow or contradiction as, apart from the occasional and sometimes unpublished academic work, little is heard of her until Napoleon decided to resurrect her as a cult figure, dipping his brush deep into the paint pot of tradition to depict the popular image. As stated, many consider her role and importance in the Hundred Years War to have been grossly exaggerated, if not entirely fictional and, to be fair, it is rather difficult to imagine a battle-hardened French Army being convinced that they would be led to victory by some slip of a foreign farmer's daughter who didn't know her arbalest from her hurlbat. And if she did lead her sub-commanders to such stunning victories, where are all the glowing testimonies from them, paying her tribute? At the end of the day we have a vague tale of a teenager who heard voices and 'saw things'; we have all sat next to one of those on a bus without going home to boast of having shared the journey with a saint. She claimed her two main 'voices' were those of St Margaret of Antioch and St Catherine of Alexandria – she of firework-fame since she was supposedly martyred on a burning wheel. Although in previous days the lives and times of these two were accepted as fact, it has since been established beyond the doubt of even the most fervent hagiophile that neither of these women existed which leaves us with a perhaps fictitious person guided by the spirits of two other fictions. None of this prevented Joan from being canonized in 1920.

WHAT DID YOU EXPECT?

The Spanish Inquisition? Often imagined to be the only one, this was a bit of a late-starter launched in 1478 by Ferdinand II of Aragon and his wife, Isabella I of Castile, those nice people who thrust Columbus on the New World. Although the Vatican had been running a series of Inquisitions since the late twelfth century, Ferdinand and Isabel decided to have their own show, so it is wrong to imagine the Spanish to have been the only inquisition and equally wrong to perceive it as an instrument of Vatican suppression. This is not to say that the Boys on the Hill didn't inflict atrocities of their own, just that the Spanish Inquisition was outside their remit and very much the idea of Ferdinand and Isabella. That said, all Catholic countries and dominions had, at one time or another, an Inquisition; even Peru got its own show, but the abiding image of the Spanish Inquisition comprising a bunch of sexually repressed clerics getting their jollies through torture and 'probing' innocent women who had been selected for their dedication through false accusations of witchcraft is pure nonsense. While the Inquisitors were hardly a bunch of woolly liberals, the abiding image we have of their carryings-on is a hand-me-down from the highly efficient Protestant propaganda circulated to divert attention from the atrocities *they* were committing throughout the rest of Europe on a scale that would have made Torquemada's eyes water.

Actually, the Spanish Inquisition was far and away the most even-handed and the least brutal of all such institutions as illustrated by its meticulous records and the known parameters within which it had to operate. Nor was it the 'playground' of frothy-mouthed clerics in pointy hats; there was the assiduously imposed counter-balance of secular lawyers, insisting on hard proof of transgression. As for the widespread myth that the Spanish Inquisition became an instrument of persecution aimed at Jews, Muslims and members of all other faiths, this too is wrong; it had jurisdiction over Catholics and Catholics alone. Apart from 'crimes of faith', the Inquisition was also active in the prosecution of adultery, bigamy, sodomy and other moral issues but its leniency made it a highly desirable option to those in the grip of the civil system, many of whom sat around spouting blasphemies until said authorities had no option but to hand them over to the Inquisition whose prisons were the best in Europe of their time. The much-maligned Torquemada insisted on a regime of cleanliness, decent food, a change of clothes for all inmates and a considerable degree of protection for women prisoners to save them from the unwelcome attentions of their jailors and other inmates. Basically, you had a far better chance of surviving the Spanish Inquisition than the civil system which was frequently little more than a veneer of legality for some baying mob set on a lynching. Contrary to popular opinion, it was the civil authorities who capriciously incinerated heretics, not the Church.

All that said and done, to attract the attentions of the Spanish Inquisition was no laughing matter; it most certainly had teeth and was not afraid to bite. It also became the preferred 'weapon' for some against *Conversos*, Jews who had embraced Catholicism so they could continue to live and prosper in Spain. Most had the suspicion, with justification, that some *Conversos* were simply paying lip-service to Catholicism while continuing their real faith in secret. And there was the usual anti-Semitic jealousy of their wealth which would fall forfeit if found guilty. This repugnant phase was very much a feature of the first fifteen years or so of the Spanish Inquisition's operations, largely under Torquemada (appointed 1483) but executions throughout this period only ran to about 130 per year; 2,000 in total. Abhorrent by modern standards, maybe, but this has to be seen in the context of the times; many of those tried were indeed guilty of heresy, then considered a grave crime by all, and throughout that same period the rest of Europe slaughtered perhaps 60,000 heretics and 'witches'. As these excesses gathered pace the questionable motives for prosecution were addressed by Pope Sixtus IV in a letter to the Bishops of Spain dated 18 April 1482.

> In Aragon, Valencia, Mallorca and Catalonia the Inquisition has for some time been moved not by zeal for the faith and the salvation of souls but by lust for wealth. Many true and faithful Christians, on the testimony of enemies, rivals, slaves and other lower and even less proper persons, have without any legitimate proof been thrust into your secular (note) prisons, tortured and condemned as relapsed heretics, deprived of their goods and property and handed over to the secular arm to be executed, to the peril of souls, setting a pernicious example and causing disgust to many.

Although Ferdinand wrote back telling the Pope such accusations were groundless and he should mind his own holy-business, the king did appoint Tomas de Torquemada to regulate the affair and make sure Spain could never again stand accused of such base motives. Big ships have enormous turning circles and the Spanish Inquisition was no exception; things did improve, but slowly. The vast majority of those brought before its courts were acquitted and, when the Inquisitors went on tour of the rural regions they always announced an Edict of Grace. This was a period of thirty days within which anyone with any real crime to confess or anyone who thought their enemies might try to frame them, could present themselves for confession and absolution. This well-intentioned gesture invariably backfired as all and sundry rushed to confess anything they could think of, as well as anything anyone else might think of, to place themselves in the clear. The travelling Inquisitions, finding themselves clogged with such a case load, frequently opted to issue a blanket absolution to every living soul in the area before beating a hasty retreat from the tsunami of would-be penitents. After the initial excesses had calmed down the Spanish Inquisition almost became a victim of its own leniency; designed to be funded by confiscation of monies and property from those they found

guilty, the Spanish Inquisition was always in dire-straits and having
to borrow money from the Crown to keep going.

By 1500 each office of the Inquisition comprised two Dominicans,
one legal adviser, a constable, a prosecutor and at least a dozen support
staff, all of these being lay persons – the wages bill must have been
a major headache. In all, throughout its 350 years of operation the
Spanish Inquisition brought about the execution of 5,000 persons – an
average of about a dozen a year. Yes, the Inquisition used torture but
so too did everyone – even present-day America has found it a handy
tool – so let us not for one minute consider that a crime exclusive to
the Spanish Inquisition, which only employed it in about 2 per cent of
the cases brought before it. If torture was to be used then it had to be
restricted to fifteen minutes with an option of a second dose, but never
a third. These were the days when English dungeons were full of racks
and thumb screws and a starving waif in London could be hanged for
stealing a loaf of bread. Across the sixteenth and seventeenth centuries,
'Merrie' England hanged 30,000 'witches' (they were never burned
at the stake in England or the New World) while the German witch-
hunts doubled that figure. By contrast, the Inquisition prevented such
atrocities with its announcement that it had investigated and found
there to be no substance to tales of witches and black magic, and that
those who brought forward spurious charges against harmless old
women would find themselves the focus of the Spanish Inquisitors.

At the end of the day, the Spanish Inquisition was far removed
from the popular portrayal in which the Catholics refer to it as 'The
Black Legend'. More assiduous in its record-keeping than most, the
files of the Spanish Inquisition reveal that between 1540 and 1700 it
heard just over 49,078 cases which resulted in 703 executions and,
in all, the total executions only just exceeded 5,000 throughout its
350 years of operation. Set that against the rest of Europe killing over
150,000 heretics and witches in one ten-year period alone, and the
Spanish Inquisition does not come out looking so black after all.

WE'LL TAKE MANHATTAN!

The motley crew of the *Mayflower* who pitched up on the shores of
America were not called the Pilgrim Fathers, they were not Puritans,
they did not put ashore because they had run out of beer, they were not
the first Europeans to go to America with the notion of establishing
settlement and they did not step ashore at Plymouth Rock.

Mayflower and her companion, *Speedwell*, set out from Southampton on 15 August 1620 but had to put into Plymouth after *Speedwell* sprung a leak. With repairs effected, the fleet-of-two put to sea but, yet again, *Speedwell* started to take on water, this forcing another embarrassing return to Plymouth. As it would later transpire, this tendency to leak was the result of sabotage inflicted by crew-members anxious to wriggle out of their one-year commitment to the venture and, within a month, they had their way. *Speedwell* was declared unfit for the voyage. All those keen to continue transferred to *Mayflower* which set out alone on 16 September 1620 with 102 passengers, plus crew, landing in America on 21 November of that same year. Although under commission to land in the Hudson River and establish a colony at the northern tip of Virginia, the ship got a bit lost and, according to legend, with the captain worried about the dwindling stocks of beer, they put ashore to forage, with the first to alight stepping out onto the enormous boulder that would become revered by Americans as Plymouth Rock.

To the modern mind the mention of such a motive to put ashore makes the venture sound like a trans-Atlantic booze-cruise but all ships then loaded up with as much small-beer (weak) as they could carry because its alcohol content, although minimal, was enough to keep it free of contamination and thus present a far more serviceable alternative to fresh water. Be that as it may, the only mention of any beer shortage occurs in *Mourt's Relation*, the chronicle of the voyage and the first months ashore which was written between November 1620 and November 1621 by Edward Winslow (1595–1655) and William Bradford (1590–1697). The relevant text reads:

> That night we returned again a-shipboard with the resolution the next morning to settle on some of these places; so in the morning, after we had called on God for direction, we came to this resolution: to go presently ashore again and to take a better view of two places which we thought most fitting for us for we could not now take the time for further search or consideration, out victuals being much spend, especially our beer, and it is now the 19th of December.

Thus they had no cause for concern about the beer-stocks until a month after arriving and even then it would only be concern for there being enough for the crew on the homeward journey.

So, why such a myth and when did it rear its silly head? It seems we can blame this on Budweiser. In the first part of the twentieth century, with Prohibition looming an ever larger prospect, the major brewers, most notably Anheuser-Bush who make Budweiser, began a battle for the hearts and minds of Americans by trying to make the drinking of beer seem patriotic. As early as 1908 the company was running full-page ads in the *Washington Post* proclaiming beer to be 'The drink of the great' and that 'Our Pilgrim Fathers drank it'. In fact, the barley crop of 1621 is known to have been insignificant and the so-called Pilgrim Fathers were more likely making wine from the local grapes. After the repeal of the Volstead Act in 1933, United States Brewers Association came out fighting with campaigns cantered on catch lines such as 'It was Beer not Turkey that lured the Pilgrims to Plymouth Rock'. (The Volstead Act did not make it illegal to drink, only to manufacture, sell or transport alcohol, this fine distinction saving the authorities the embarrassment of having to arrest almost everyone on Capitol Hill and most of the clergy whose requirements for 'communion wine' went up ten-fold overnight – Praise-be! Another miracle!) But, beer or no beer, it was not at Plymouth that the *Mayflower* first dropped anchor but at Provincetown where the so-called Saints signed their *Mayflower* Compact and set up the New World's first Communist Party. It is worth mentioning here that the religious minority were not Puritans but Separatists, the former resolved to stay in England to 'purify' the Church of any influence from Rome and the latter just wanted to get away. It would be a couple of hundred years before anyone started talking about Pilgrim Fathers – the *Mayflower*'s crew called them Psalm-singing-puke-stockings.

Much is made of the signing of that Compact but, contrary to the general promotion of the event, it was by no means an unanimous declaration of anything. To begin with, only twenty-eight adults out of the 102 passengers belonged to the self-styled 'Saints'; the overwhelming majority of the party constituted Strangers, as the Saints insisted on calling their less-religious companions. ('Stranger' would long outlive the *Mayflower* settlers as a form of greeting to an unknown person encountered, a bit like the Australian 'Blue'). Anyway, when it came to signing the Compact and agreeing its terms, this was only undertaken by forty-one members of the party and thus the minority. Be that as it may, private ownership gave way to communal ownership for the greater good of the group which was to function without regard for the individual but for the commune. Communism lasted for several years at Plymouth, when they eventually arrived there, and was only abandoned because it failed due to the inevitable squabbles over who did what and why-the-hell-should-they if there was no incentive. But if Provincetown was the first landing site, how come Plymouth muscled in on the act with its big rock?

Basically, they did it with a lie. To begin with the name; it would seem quite logical that the settlement was named Plymouth by the settlers because that was the name of their port of departure, but Accomack, as the Indians called the place, had been named Plymouth by the English long before anyone else got there. Captain John Smith of the earlier Jamestown settlement (of which more later) had returned to England in 1614 and, while at court, had submitted a map of the area along with a request that the then Prince Charles replace all the 'heathen' names with others throughout New England, as they chose to call it. Plymouth just happened to be the name of the place on the maps when the puke-stockings got there – without landing on any rock.

One of William Bradford's contributions to the aforementioned Mourt's Relation says of the Plymouth landing on 11 December (Old Style):

> On Munday they sounded ye harbor and found it fitt for shipping; and marched into ye land & found diverse cornfields, & little running brooks, a place (as they suppose) fitt for situation. At least it was ye best that they could find, and ye season and their presente necessitie, made them glad to accepte of it. So they returned to the shippe again with this news to the rest of their people, which did much comfort their harts.

No mention of anyone alighting on any rock. The record goes on to mention other explorations and landings on 18 December (Old Style), these most likely being somewhere up the Town Brook river, near Plymouth, but again no mention of any handy landing rock. These were people lucky to have landed at all and, with years of hardship and privation ahead, no-one gave a damn what they stepped on to get ashore, just so long as they made it in one piece. The pre-eminent Harvard Professor of History, Edward Perkins Channing (1856–1931), who also won the 1926 Pulitzer Prize for History, actually went to a great deal of trouble to get maps, charts and details of the prevailing currents to prove conclusively that a ship of *Mayflower*'s dimensions and draught could not possibly have got anywhere near close enough to that rock for it to serve as a stepping-stone for those on board.

For the next century and a half no-one so much as mentioned any boulder at Plymouth, apart from bemoaning its presence and wishing there was enough gunpowder to blast it out of the way. Then, in 1769, a group of young blades from the leading families of the town, became distressed: 'at the many disadvantages and inconveniences that arise from intermixing with the company at the taverns in this town' and so resolved to organize the Old Colony Club for gentlemen who would routinely mark and commemorate 'the landing of our worthy ancestors' on a date which would wander between 21 and 22 December (New Style) over the next century before being finally and officially pegged at the 21st. The first Forefathers' Day dinner was a rather grand affair marked by much cannon fire and worthy oration and the whole thing gathered pace, the rock not getting in on the act until the local cleric, Deacon Ephraim Spooner, 'remembered' that back in 1741 when he, Ephraim, was but six years old, a wharf was planned that would cover over a massive boulder at the base of Cole's Hill, a civic development which brought forth the 95-year-old Thomas Faunce who insisted on being carried down to the beach in his chair so he could kiss goodbye to the very stone that his parents had pointed out to him as their true landing point. After a touching scene of the 95-year-old man slobbering all over the rock, the builders, quite unmoved, demanded he be dragged out of the way so that they could start work. As things turned out, the rock was just too damned big to blast so the wharf was built over the rock with its cap sticking through in the hope that the wheels of countless wagons would eventually grind it down.

As the American War of Independence (1775–1783) crept closer, Loyalist and Patriot factions in the town vied for possession of the stone, the latter winning when their Militia Colonel Theophilus Cotton turned up with his brigade and thirty oxen to move the stone to a site of prominence in the town. Unfortunately they broke the thing in two but, undeterred, contented themselves with the five-ton top section which was carted inland and dumped in a secret location for safe-keeping, as if it were just any old boulder, which, to be fair, it was. After the war the top section was brought back to town and, with the abandoned lower section now long covered over and lost, the top was housed in a variety of civic buildings until its other half was re-discovered as the threshold of an old warehouse. Although a joyous and serendipitous uncovering, this now left the town with two Plymouth Rocks which confused the tourists no end. Thus in 1880, the top section was dragged back to the beach to be re-united with its other half. That is, presuming the boulder retrieved from its inland resting-place after the war was indeed the right one?

WITCHES' BREW

The modern perception of witches and the Great Witch Hunts is well established: the witches all wore black cloaks and pointy hats; they met in covens of thirteen to worship Satan with live sacrifices before stripping off for a spot of massed horizontal-jogging; they held Black Masses in parody of the Christian Church for which they all ended up going snap, cackle and pop when burned at the stake by the medieval authorities. All false.

Although perceived as a phenomenon of the medieval era, the persecution of witches was then quite sporadic and comparatively rare with the Church taking no part in such matters until 1320; the peak of European and New World witch-hunts came much later, starting in earnest in the early sixteenth century and reaching a peak in the seventeenth century. The trial of the Witches of Pendle Hill in 1612 was the most celebrated in England and the Salem Trials the most outstanding of such idiotic events in New England. Both these trials were significant in that they were formal proceedings mounted by the authorities whereas most 'trials' were thinly-veiled lynchings presided over by self-employed 'witchfinders' who earned a good living by putting on such shows to entertain the mob. Even the infamous Matthew Hopkins, most active in the 1640s, had invented the title of Witchfinder General for himself; at no time did the civil or Church authorities employ such people, nor condone the activities of Hopkins and his kind. Between 1645 and 1647 Hopkins, for example, earned over £1,500 from towns throughout Norfolk, Suffolk and Essex that he had 'saved' from witches, this being a time when general labour earned four pence a day. But for all that, no witches were ever burned at the stake in either England or in New England; all were hanged or, on occasions, pressed to death with heavy stones. Small comfort to those so dealt with, but the popular Hammer-House-of Horrors image of witches screaming curses from the ever-rising flames is but a modern invention. The only people at risk of burning were heretics and those guilty of treason, this including counterfeiting or any woman who attempted or succeeded in murdering her husband, this classed as petty-treason. The last heretic to taste the flames was Edward Wightman, burned at Burton-on-Trent in 1612 and the last public burning in Great Britain being that of Catherine Murphy, a counterfeiter, who was so dispatched outside Newgate Prison on 18 March 1789. It was this incident, which rightly caused so much revulsion, which led such form of execution to be proscribed by law the next year.

Much of what is now imagined to have been standard practice amongst so-called witches came from the twisted minds of the persecutors themselves. It was murderous charlatans like Hopkins who decided, without any evidence at all, that their quarry must meet in groups of thirteen in mockery of the Last Supper; as anti-Christians they must worship the Devil, and the orgy-bit, well, that was just thrown in for fun. Naturally, when they set-to with torture on 'witches' to admit that all of this was true, it was not long before all confessed that such was indeed the case. But most of the unfortunates convicted and strung-up to the approval of the mob were just harmless women who were widowed or lived alone for whatever reason – over 90 per cent of 'witches' fell into this category. Hopkins & co were loath to pick on women who had male protection and were damned careful to restrict their attention to the lower orders of society who could not fight back. Many were traditional healers who, having saved a few villagers with their knowledge of herbs and potions, were rewarded with accusations of witchcraft. Not only does this indicate a certain lack of gratitude but it also set back medical knowledge by centuries as such women decided it was far too dangerous to run round saving the dying.

Generalisations are rarely helpful or accurate but it is fair to say that the rich more often died because they could afford doctors in such times, while the poor survived because they couldn't. The healers would, for example, encourage those in pain to chew willow-bark and treated more serious illness with the mould from bread that had gone off after noting that the poor, confined to their hovels by sickness, with nothing to eat but rotten bread, frequently recovered while the rich, with fresh food at their fingertips frequently died. The Witch Hunts drove much of this knowledge underground so we had to wait until the twentieth century for aspirin to be produced from the salicylic acid found in willow-bark and for others to rediscover the curative powers of the mould they would call penicillin.

Interestingly enough, one of the last times anyone tried to expand the reach of the Witchcraft Act was in 1770 when a proposal was entertained by Parliament to bring the use of cosmetics and 'body enhancement' under that umbrella. Even perfume was then frowned upon for its pagan origins. The word is structured on the Latin 'per fuma', through smoke, and first applied to the fragrant oils and such that were added to burnt offerings to mask the stench of burning flesh. The first women to make bodily use of these unguents were the temple prostitutes who so anointed their bodies to make themselves more alluring in the activities which funded said temples. That proposal read:

> All women, of whatever age, rank, profession or degree, whether virgins, maids, or widows, that from and after this Act impose upon, seduce or betray into matrimony, any of His Majesty's subjects by the use of scents, paints, cosmetics, washes, artificial teeth, false hair, Spanish wool, iron stays, hoops, high heels, or bolstered hips shall incur the penalty of the law now in force against Witchcraft, and the like misdemeanours, and that the marriage, upon conviction, shall stand null and void.

Fortunately for those in the ever-extending Barbie-queue of today, this never found its way onto the books.

And a final word about Pendle Hill, a uniquely tautological toponym. At first, the promontory was simply call Pen by early Cumbric/Welsh speakers, that denoting a head or hill and still much seen in Welsh place-names and even 'penguin' as based on 'pen gwyn', or 'white head', an allusion to the white eye-flashes on the bird. Old English speakers, asking the name of the hill and, being told Pen, added their own Del, as denoting a hill or the valley below it, as in the Yorkshire Dales. Early English speakers, given the name Pendle, added their own 'hill' to end up with a name presenting Hill-Hill-Hill. Pendle Hill is also the name of a particularly fine ale but with 'brew', like the Scottish 'brae', being another word for hill this is perhaps just too confusing. Ain't language grand?

THE LAST 510 YEARS

ALL RHODES LEAD TO CLIVEDEN

At the time of writing, a chap called Tom Cholmondeley has just been found guilty of shooting and killing local stonemason, Robert Njoya, back in 2006, for having the nerve to wander across his estates in Kenya's Rift Valley. In 2005, Cholmondeley got away with the fatal shooting of Kenyan Wildlife Officer, Samson ole Sisina, under strikingly similar circumstances, by pleading self-defence on the grounds that he believed the man to have been on his property to commit armed robbery. With it being his word against that of a corpse, Cholmondeley walked, but the interesting thing about him is the fact that he is the great-grandson of Hugh Cholmondeley, aka 3rd Baron Delamere, who, from those same expansive estates, presided over the unbelievably debauched bunch of ex-pats who flocked to what he christened Happy Valley. (The locals of the 1930s and '40s more bluntly called it Shag-Happy Valley with the present black residents opting for Trigger-Happy Valley). The depths of the drug-fuelled promiscuity of Delamere and his cronies were revisited with the Charles Dance/Greta Scacchi film, *White Mischief* (1988), which focused on the celebrated murder of Josslyn Victor Hay, aka the Earl of Erroll, in 1941, by person or persons unknown and for reasons still hotly debated. But the interesting thing about *him* is that he left a trail all the way from Happy Valley to the dining rooms of Cliveden in the rural bliss of Buckinghamshire.

Before looking at Cliveden (pronounced Cliv-den), more recently infamous as the setting for the very real treason of the 1963 Profumo Affair, as driven by the corrupting charms of Christine Keeler, it is perhaps best to look at the 1930s British elite as a whole to see that the average weekend guest at Cliveden was nothing out of the ordinary in such circles. There was then little difference between the Nazi elite of Germany and the British upper crust; each was as anti-Semitic and jack-booting as the other with the latter seeing the former as a great ally in that it stood as a bulwark against the evil of the 'Jew-fuelled Communism' encroaching from Russia. You could have taken a blind selection of any thirty-or-so men and women from the British ruling classes, closed your eyes and thought yourself at Cliveden from their general conversation and attitudes.

Vast swathes of the British elite, both social and commercial, were seriously intent on avoiding conflict with Germany at any cost and campaigned for any accommodation ranging through appeasement to turning a blind eye with a non-aggression pact or even agreeing some kind of alliance. The prime objective was the preservation of the British Empire and their own privileged positions within it. Such feeling ran all the way to the top; the recently released papers of the departed Queen Mother reveal just how in favour of accommodation she was, and, with the infamous and potentially far more damaging 'Box 24' of her papers still embargoed, many suspect there is more to be revealed. The extent of her pro-German sympathies can be gauged by her having sent a copy of *Mein Kampf* to Lord Halifax, still Foreign Secretary at the beginning of the Second World War, with an accompanying note telling the recipient to note the 'obvious sincerity' of the author. Halifax, to some a traitor, to others a misguided appeaser, was a well-known favourite of the Queen Mother, she making no secret of the fact that she wanted him to replace the more belligerent Churchill and sort things out with Germany.

The Duke and Duchess of Windsor were pictured in Germany giving the Nazi salute to Hitler in 1937 before taking a tour of a couple of the newly-built concentration camps, and there is much to suggest that Hitler kept them in the wings as puppet-royals to be placed on the throne in the event of a Nazi victory; there is also much to suggest that this idea was by no means unacceptable to the couple. After returning to a frosty reception in the UK, Edward was packed off to France where he was attached to the British Military Mission with the rank of Major-General. Here, according to Julius Graf von Zech-Burkersroda, German Minister to The Hague, he told the Germans all about the British plans for the defence of Belgium. When the Germans did invade France, the Windsors, with their safe-passage guaranteed and Hitler's promise that their French properties would be guarded against their return, made a leisurely exit to Lisbon where Edward gave such a defeatist interview that many considered it treasonous. Churchill certainly agreed and threatened him with a court-marshal if he did not get back to Britain immediately. In the closing stages of the war, an MI5 officer, who divided his time between his intelligence work and assisting the Royal Librarian, was dispatched to Germany in March 1945 to retrieve papers and letters from the Schloss Friedrichshof. These were in part the so-called 'Vicky Letters', sensitive correspondence between Queen Victoria and her German relatives and, it is claimed, damaging correspondence between the Duke of Windsor and Hitler. That MI5 officer was Anthony Blunt and was likely hand-picked for the job by the Queen herself; Blunt, the Queen's cousin, would soon be rewarded for his venture by the Queen appointing him Surveyor of the Royal Paintings at Buckingham Palace – and what a traitor he turned out to be. It is perhaps unfair to focus on the pro-German royals, but they illustrate the pinnacle of the considerable opposition in certain quarters of the British establishment to any kind of conflict with Germany. And so to Cliveden.

An impressive pile by any standards, Cliveden was then the social power-base of Nancy Astor (1879–1964) whose family web spread from her niece, actress and monologist, Joyce Grenfell, back to her 'American Cousin', Mark Twain; her father was American tycoon Chiswell Dabney Langhorne and Mark Twain the adopted pen-name of the author born Samuel Langhorne Clemens.

But the notion of her sitting like a black widow at the centre of a web of conspirators simply did not stand up to the light of initial inspection; Nancy was nowhere near bright enough and the so-called Cliveden set a myth – sort of. The man who started all the fuss was Claud Cockburn, prominent left-wing journalist and cousin of Evelyn Waugh, who coined 'Cliveden Set' in a series of 1937 articles he wrote in his communist *This Week*. Cockburn was convinced that a specific clique of pro-German people of influence routinely held meetings round Nancy's dinner table to plot how best to influence the government's thinking and attitudes. He further alleged that those considered 'useful' would be invited down to be groomed and cajoled into certain courses of action. Then, as now, the image of a bunch of fat cats cloistered in a stately home, selling their own country down the river over Pimms and cucumber sandwiches was an easy schtik to sell to the public which is why the myth of the Cliveden Set has lived on. Trouble was, Cockburn's trumpeting got everyone looking so hard for what wasn't there that they missed what really was. Nancy was too busy playing hostess-with-the-mostest to spot what was going on under her own roof. But the blue-bloods who did indeed routinely coagulate about Nancy's dinner table were 'seeded' by members of a far more shadowy cabal which some chose to call the Milner Group and, although others claim that this is both unfair and inaccurate, we shall use that tag here as a device of convenience.

Although himself an interesting character – his second wife, Jean Ross, was the inspiration for Sally Bowles in *Cabaret* and his granddaughter is the present-day husky-vamp actress Olivia Wilde – Cockburn was so busy trying to nail Nancy that he failed to see the real cabal which routinely used Cliveden shindigs as a cover for their meetings and other activities. This 'Milner Group' had its roots in the rather unpleasant societies and closed groups set up by both Cecil Rhodes (1853–1902) and Viscount Alfred Milner (1854–1925), both men dedicated to the continued expansion of the British influence. Rhodes, the immensely wealthy founder of De Beers and an imperialist of the first water, held an unswerving belief in the notion that there wasn't a country on earth that would not have its lot improved by being brought under British rule. Rather more worrying, he saw that rolling expansion working in unison with Malthusian population control and 'human weeding' through the eugenics championed by Sir Francis Galton (1822–1911), the most famous member of a family of Quaker gun-makers (pardon?). To this end, Rhodes founded the Society of the Elect in 1881, then a rather 'closet' group not formalised until 1891, which sat at the hub of peripheral groups set up by white-supremacist Milner as 'The Round Table'. As explored in full by Professor Carroll Quigley PhD of Harvard and Princeton in his *The Anglo-American Establishment: From Rhodes to Cliveden* (1949), after Rhodes' death the group went from strength to strength under Milner and continued to do so after his passing. A full list of the more prominent members can be seen with a google of 'Quigley's Roster of the Milner Group' and, needless to say, many of these same names cropped up with monotonous regularity at Cliveden.

Cliveden may have looked serene to the casual observer on these country weekends but, as with the swans gliding across the lake, there was an awful lot of paddling going on below the surface. The ubiquitous Earl Halifax was never away from the place and George Geoffrey Dawson, original Milner-man from South Africa but then editor of *The Times*, was always on hand to keep the group's aims and objectives in the public forum. Knowing they had to keep America 'on side' with their plans, the group counted among its members Philip Kerr, 11th Marquis of Lothian, who, as British Ambassador to America did all he could on that side of the Atlantic. On a more subtle note, aviator Charles Lindbergh was invited to Cliveden to form a bridge between the Milner Group and arch-Hitlerite Henry Ford, the only non-German to be mentioned in glowing terms in *Mein Kampf*. Hitler and Ford kept signed photographs of the other on their desks and Ford and Lindbergh had both received high honours from Hitler, so they were obvious targets for the Milner Group. The only major glitch in the group's overtures to Germany seems to have been caused by Halifax himself when, against all Cabinet advice, he made a trip to Germany in November 1937, his cover-story being that he was only accepting an invitation from Göring to go on a hunting trip. Upon his arrival at the first meeting, Halifax mistook the soberly-dressed Hitler for a footman and casually tossed him his coat as he walked past with Göring who did not much improve the situation by collapsing with mirth. Big 'oops' there! Anyway, to bring us full-circle, another devoted attendee at Cliveden, whenever in England, was Josslyn Hay, Earl of Erroll, a staunch member of the British Union of Fascists, and keen to raise the point of view of those back in South Africa, where the Milner Group had its roots.

As war loomed inevitable, life in Happy Valley proceeded as normal – normal for them, that is. Erroll's wife died of a heroin overdose in 1939 and the next year there arrived from England Sir Jock Delves Broughton and his new and much younger wife, Diana (née Caldwell). Within weeks of the Broughton's arrival in Kenya, she and Erroll were conducting a very public affair ending after Erroll was found shot through the head in his car on a deserted crossroads on the night of 24 January 1941. Broughton stood trial and was acquitted; there was not a shred of evidence against him and most were of the opinion that if all the white residents of Happy Valley went around shooting their unfaithful partners and their respective lovers then there would have been bodies all over the place. Broughton returned to England a few months later to be found dead in a Liverpool hotel, apparently from a self-administered drug overdose, and Diana remained in Kenya, contenting herself with a string of lovers (of both sex, some maintain) before 'settling down' in 1955 to marry the 4th Lord Delamere, grandfather of Trigger-

Happy Tom. And that might have been the end of the matter had not a distant cousin of the Delamere's, respected Kenya-based author Errol Trzebinski re-investigated the murder in the light of what she claims to be new evidence in the form of previously unseen documents and death-bed-confession of someone involved in setting up the killing.

In *The Life and Death of Lord Errol: The Truth Behind the Happy Valley Murder* (2000) Trzebinski makes the extraordinary claim that Erroll was assassinated by British Intelligence, specifically the SOE, because of something he knew or because of something he knew to be on the cards. It should be stated before proceeding that Trzebinski is no sensationalist given to the churning out of pot-boilers; she has published several well-received books on the history of Kenya and famous Kenyans and began this particular book with full access to the Erroll family archives. From an advertisement she placed in the jauntily titled *The Overseas Pensioner* she received a reply to her invitation for any background information from a lady called Anthea Venning, sister of the acclaimed Kenyan choreographer, Elanor Fanzan. Venning offered to put Trzebinski in touch with a chap called Tony Trafford who had inside information on the killing which he claimed to have been a SOE 'hit'. Trafford, a Kenyan-born Intelligence Officer who had by this time retired to the Isle of Wight, told Trzebinski that here he had met up with a retired Naval Intelligence Officer he would only identify as 'Edmund' who had, upon learning that he had not long to live, decided to impart all he knew about the killing. Trafford supplied Trzebinski with a detailed 25,000-word typescript outlining how the Cairo SOE office sent a team south to take out Erroll and leave it looking like a 'domestic'.

According to 'Edmund' (via Trafford), the job had been formally handed over to SOE at 2300hrs on 12 September 1940 with the newly opened Cairo Office told to expect a senior officer from London with a top-priority mission. That man, referred to as Alistair McDonald, informed the meeting, which included 'Edmund', that it was vital that Josslyn Hay be killed as soon as possible but he would not go into reasons why this had to be. The Duke of Hamilton, of whom more later, had made arrangements, through his contacts in Kenya, for McDonald to be kept fully briefed on the target's movements and patterns of behaviour, and Hay's dalliance with Diana Broughton was readily identified as the ideal cover for the killing. Two agents, named as Susan Melanie Van Der Pleyden and

James Hewitt (surely no relation?) were packed off to Happy Valley to infiltrate the set and pick their moment. It was not long before Susan realized that the best way to get close to Hay was the most obvious and she was soon spending the odd night with him. On the night of the killing, they simply waited for Hay to drop Diana off back home and then wait for him on the road back to his own place. Susan, feigning a breakdown, flagged him down, got into the car and shot him in the head. When Hewitt arrived on the scene, they shifted the body to the passenger footwell and then fired onto the car again from the outside to make it look as if all the shots had been fired by someone standing outside the car.

From here we enter into the realms of speculation with reference to the fact that it was only a matter of weeks later that Rudolf Hess few from Germany to Scotland on 10 May 1941 to visit that same Duke of Hamilton. Hamilton, whose pro-German attitudes and contacts had long since attracted the attentions of British Intelligence, was, according to Hess, expecting him, as were other prominent figures, keen to thrash out an Anglo-German accommodation. But of course Hess was mad, wasn't he? Hamilton was a leading light of a group called the Nordic League which itself had links to the Milner Group and other like-minded coteries and in 1936 Hamilton had been to Berlin and met with Hess and other leading Nazis, but not with Hitler himself, as is sometimes asserted. After war had been declared, the Nordic League morphed into the Right Club under the leadership of Archibald Ramsay and, apart from Hamilton, members included the likes of the Duke of Westminster, Lord Redesdale, the Duke of Wellington and A.K. Chesterton, cousin of the author, he later being the co-founder of the British National Front. The members tended to meet in the Russian Tea Rooms run by Russian fascist Anna Wolkof, an intimate of Wallis Simpson. Unfortunately for this little group, they had been infiltrated by B5B, a sub-division of MI5 which monitored subversive groups. B5B was under the management of Maxwell Knight, himself a fascist-turned-gamekeeper, who 'fed in' his mistress, Joan Miller. In 1940, certain factions in Germany made overtures to the Right Club to see if they could not find a way to bring the Anglo-German conflict to a satisfactory conclusion but MI5 was intercepting the majority of such correspondence. In the September of 1941, Albrecht Haushofer, a close friend of Hess since their student days, wrote to Hamilton: 'You ... may find some significance in the fact that I am able to ask you whether you could find time to have a talk to me somewhere on the outskirts of Europe, perhaps in Portugal'. This same letter also giving very strong indications that they in Germany knew full well which other parties in Britain would be sympathetic to such accommodation.

This letter too was intercepted by MI5 who felt it was high time to get a grip on Hamilton and induce him to play along but under their control; so 'convinced', he agreed to meet Haushofer in Lisbon with Colonel Thomas Argyll 'Tar' Robertson of MI5's double-agent section noting: 'Hamilton was at the beginning of the war and still is a member of the community which sincerely believes that Great Britain will be willing to make peace with Germany provided the present regime in Germany were superseded by some reasonable form of government... He is a slow-witted man, but at the same time he gets there in the end; and I feel that if he is properly schooled before leaving for Lisbon he could do a very useful job of work.' Fortunately or unfortunately, depending on how you look at it, before Hamilton shipped out for Lisbon Hess pre-empted all by dropping out of the sky on 10 May 1941, demanding to see Hamilton whom he sincerely believed to be expecting him. Churchill's knee-jerk reaction was to demand that every man-jack of the Right Club be banged up for the duration but he was rightly convinced by others that to have a whole bunch of British nobles incarcerated as traitors would hardly be conducive to public morale. The upshot of this was that only Archibald Ramsay, Anna Wolkoff and a few minor figures saw jail while all the British fascist aristocrats walked free. But we should be thankful for small mercies; the arrest of Wolkoff was witnessed by the eleven-year-old son of a neighbour, Len Deighton, later stating that this is what started him writing spy-stories.

So, that is the overall picture; each piece taken in isolation does not add up to much but with the same names and like-minded players criss-crossing each others' paths throughout perhaps it adds substance to Trzebinski's version that Erroll was indeed silenced because of something he knew about the imminent arrival of Hess. Perhaps he knew that Hamilton had been 'turned' and intended to warn contacts in Germany that Hess shouldn't waste his time which would certainly have been enough for SOE to top him and stop him spoiling such a propaganda coup. Who knows; but the comfortable image of a doughty and united Britain against a nasty and uniformly hostile Germany is obviously well wide of the mark. At the time of writing, Cliveden is owned by the von Essen Hotel Group and proudly boasts of selling the world's most expensive sandwich at £100 a round, which seems a lot to pay for a ham, chicken and egg sarnie, albeit garnished with tomato and a smattering of truffle, but perhaps that sums up this story to a 'tea'.

BEN DOVA'S ROVER

Perhaps through some confusion with *Titanic*, people tend to remember the *Hindenburg* airship as crashing and burning on its maiden voyage despite the fact that the zeppelin had by that fateful day completed seventeen trans-Atlantic crossings (ten to New York and seven to Brazil) and countless other journeys. Perhaps not surprisingly given the intensity of the fire shown on those old newsreels, most also presume that all on board perished, when in fact fifty-six of the ninety-two passengers and crew survived, a statistic in itself remarkable. But what caused the fire in the first place? Even today most presume it was due to the German's incautious use of flammable hydrogen to achieve lift, but there was no hydrogen leak; others have focused on the explosive/ flammable coatings to the exterior cloth but this does not pan out either. Some have even speculated sabotage but, instead of any one singular cause, why not consider a concatenation of all three; it is the only possibility that fits all the known facts.

Prior to the *Hindenburg*'s departure from Frankfurt on 3 May 1937 the SS repeatedly searched the airship from stern to stern and rummaged the baggage and frisked all wishing to board because there had been a continual drip of intelligence that the airship might become the target of anti-Nazi bombers determined to bring down Hitler's flagship. With all safely aboard, the take-off was next delayed by the last-minute arrival of passenger Joseph Spah, a German-born music-hall contortionist and acrobat, by then resident in America. His search, much more hurried and less diligent than those experienced by others, forced him to unwrap one package, which turned out to be a rather large and expensive-looking doll, before this was grabbed back from the official as an anxious crew-member shooed Spah on board at the behest of the irritated captain. Spah, whose stage name was Ben Dova, secured his pet Alsatian, Ulla, in a cage in a storage room to the rear of the airship and settled down for the trip. The *Hindenburg* did not make good time; fighting thick fog and headwinds all the way it was eight hours late in passing over Boston on the morning of 6 May but the passengers were all confident of landing at the Naval Air Station at Lakehurst, New Jersey, at 4pm. Unfortunately, thunderstorms caused Captain Max Pruss to abort this attempt at the last minute and take his passengers on a sightseeing trip along the New Jersey coast. He received a radio message from Lakehurst that all was clear on the weather front so he started his turn at 6:22pm, dropping his mooring lines to Lakehurst at 7:21. Four minutes later the *Hindenburg* was destroyed in a fire that lasted a scant thirty seconds.

The crippled airship dropped as it burned and those who could, including Spah, waited as long as they dared before dropping the last 10 or 15 ft to the ground and making a run for it. These people, it must be remembered, were in the gondola slung beneath the fire raging through the massive balloon above. Joining the other survivors in a hangar, Spah struck up a conversation with badly burned crewman, Erich Spehl, and promised to send a telegram to his German girlfriend stating only 'I live', nothing more, nothing less, but Spehl died a few minutes later. There is absolutely nothing to suggest that these two knew each other or had any form of contact; it is only worth mentioning because these are the two main suspects for sabotage. The presence of the dog gave Spah the excuse to repeatedly visit the restricted areas at the rear of the craft where the fire broke out; not only did he ignore all instructions to cease doing so but his final trip to 'ensure the dog was well' was so close to the aborted 4 p.m. landing as to make no sense and on this final occasion he was allegedly carrying that doll. In the post-crash investigation Spah was also stated by several of the stewards and cabin-crew to have been more than understandably agitated by the final delay in landing which, if he had placed some device with a timer, would be quite understandable. The suspicion aimed at rigger Erich Spehl rests in the main on the fact that the girlfriend he was so anxious to telegram was a known anti-Nazi activist and the fact that he himself was a keen photographer. Just before the first explosion in the rear, near Gas Cell Number 4, rigger Hans Freund and helmsman Helmut Lau both claim to have seen a bright flash as if from a camera flashgun. Spehl, who should also have been on duty in that area, was nowhere to be found.

Witnesses on the ground are agreed that the fire broke out aft but there was some disagreement as to the exact point where flames were first seen. Just to stick with the sabotage theory for a while longer, it is not impossible that this conflicting evidence resulted from their being two initial points of eruption; although unlikely, it is not completely impossible that both Spah *and* Spehl were up to no good but working independently, quite unaware of the other's plans, with the first device to detonate setting off the other. Either way, Captain Pruss was convinced that it was sabotage, his second-in-command, Captain Ernst Lehmann, died the next day convinced there had been an incendiary device and, shortly before his death, communicated his suspicions to Charles Rosendahl, Commander of the Lakehurst Air Station who, also firmly of the same mind, laid out the case for sabotage in *What About the Airship* (1938). The FBI at the time was likewise suspicious and conducted a full inquiry during which it became clear that both Pruss and Lehmannn, and their Third Officer, Anton Wittemann, had been warned that there might be some attempt at sabotage. They also found among the wreckage the burnt remains of a dry-cell battery that could have been used to trigger some timed incendiary device but, with the intensity of the fire and the standard of forensics in 1937, all were shelved as inconclusive.

The main problem with all suggested external causes – static discharge, lightning strike, St Elmo's Fire or whatever – is that all the evidence, be it statements of the surviving crewmen, those of the eye-witnesses on the ground and even those old newsreels, all point to a fire that started inside the airship and then ruptured through the skin. That said, once through that skin, the speed with which the *Hindenburg* was consumed was quite alarming; it was over 800 ft long, as big as *Titanic*, yet gone in thirty seconds. The possibility of a hydrogen leak can be discounted as the gas used to fill the *Hindenburg* was infused with garlic to make any leak immediately detectable. More recently it has been suggested that the cellulose acetate butyrate, aluminium oxide and iron oxide used to coat the exterior were responsible for setting up a thermite burn but, while the oxides are indeed components in solid rocket fuel and CAB can remain reactive after setting, the characteristics of a thermite burn in no way match the fire seen on the newsreels. While those oxides were included in the coating they were not present in anything like the quantities needed to set up a thermite burn, had they been then the *Hindenburg* would have been too heavy for any hydrogen lift. Also, a thermite burn would have set up temperatures reaching 2,500°c and the aluminium skeleton would have melted at 630°c yet it was all there after the fire abated. Even if the external coatings were involved they cannot have been solely responsible as they would have needed an external instigator – and the fire broke through from within.

So, what are we left with? It is known that before the fire there was no hydrogen leak since no-one mentioned the smell of garlic. Certain members of the crew were adamant that they heard and saw some kind of 'incident' near Gas Cell 4 to the rear of the craft where Spehl should have been on duty and also the restricted area to which Spah made repeated visits despite his being told to desist from 'visiting his dog'. Hydrogen burns with an all-but-invisible blue flame yet the structure was consumed by orange-red flames. The fire started inside the balloon to the aft of the craft, right near Gas Cell 4 and then raced towards the prow. The only thing that matches all that is some sort of pyrotechnic incident in the vicinity of Gas Cell 4 causing a hydrogen fire to burst through the skin unseen where it immediately ignited constituents in the coatings, those two elements helping each other along the body of the balloon, bursting ever more gas cells in its self-exacerbating progress. We will never know for sure if the instigatory factor was sabotage as the only two likely suspects are dead. Both were decidedly anti-Nazi but neither comes across as a callous killer willing to die along with others just to achieve some political statement against Hitler. If either, or both, had placed some time-bomb it would have been done with the docking time of 4 p.m. in mind and the device set to go off after all had safely disembarked. This would tally with Spah's widely noted agitation and Spehl's mysterious absence from his station.

As stated, Spehl died on the airfield from his burns and Spah continued his career with his last appearance on film being possibly somewhat ironic. Readers who have seen the hunt for the Nazi war-criminal in *Marathon Man* (1976), with its chilling and still much-parodied catchphrase 'Is it safe?', may remember the opening scene in which two old men get into a road-rage incident in New York. One is German, the other Jewish and their rolling conflict ends with the death of the former in a ball of flame to set the whole plot in motion. The actor who played the aggressively anti-Semitic German, brother of the missing war-criminal, was Joseph Spah.

BLITZ-MYTHS

With the full connivance of the government of the day, we are left with the abiding image of chirpy Cockneys laughing at the Luftwaffe's best attempts to reduce their homes to rubble as they huddled in friendly masses in the London Underground singing 'Roll out the Barrel'. Needless to say, it was nothing like that; there was no 'Spirit of the Blitz', many were on the fiddle, one way or another, and instead of some imagined tightly knit community looking out for each other, Blitz-time London was often a time of dog-eat-dog.

If one can put precise dates to such a sprawling event, the Blitz is generally said to have run from 7 September 1940 to 19 May 1941 and during that time the crime rates went through the roof. Murder, rape, mugging and looting were rife and, certainly at the onset, the event was a class-war with the masses largely abandoned to their lot while those who could afford it fled the city each evening for their country retreats. The rich and privileged who opted to remain in London overnight spent their time in supposedly secure 'velvet bunkers' such as the underground quarters of the Savoy or the underground ballroom of the Café de Paris. On the night of 15 September, a panicked mob of over 100 burst into the Savoy demanding sanctuary only for the management to phone the Police who, fortunately for the interlopers, failed to turn up until after the all-clear had sounded. Those who boogied the night away at the Café de Paris were less fortunate.

British character-actor, Ballard Berkeley, whose swan-song would be the portrayal of the dotty Major in *Fawlty Towers*, who was then a Special Constable, was sent to the Café after it took a direct hit on the night of 8 March 1941. Two 50 kg mines found a lucky route through the Rialto roof to crash straight onto the underground dance floor where the blast-containment factor took its toll. Britain's first black band-leader, Ken 'Snakehips' Johnson, had been decapitated on his podium and, rather eerily, was still standing headless when Berkeley got there to see others, killed by the blast alone, sitting dead at their tables without a mark on them. Most shocking of all, however, was Berkeley's account, still held by the Imperial War Museum, of the looters working with impunity as the rescuers went about their job. Wallets, ration-books and personal papers that could be sold on the black market were quickly lifted while looters with stronger stomachs were busily cutting fingers and hands from the corpses to more quickly harvest the rings, watches and other items of jewellery. Nor were such attentions the province of the rich alone; looting during the Blitz was a pandemic. Any house hit was immediately stripped of anything worth taking by the neighbours and blackout gangs routinely prowled the streets. Nazi Germany endured a much lower rate of such behaviour because it ruthlessly imposed the death penalty – frequently on the spot without the inconvenience of trial – whereas Britain, initially reluctant to even acknowledge its population capable of such action, took a more liberal approach. The first looters did not even appear at the Old Bailey until 9 November 1940 and of that clutch of twenty defendants, ten were members of the Auxiliary Fire Service, a fine body of men and women whose ranks were infiltrated by those given to robbing the corpses they dragged out of the rubble. In fact, their ranks were greatly over-subscribed by spivs who saw it as an ideal cover for such activities.

Others found more subtle fiddles. The National Assistance Office, responsible for compensating those who had been bombed out, was, understandably, somewhat over-worked at the time and incapable of checking up an all claims presented. The first 'chirpy Cockney' to go to prison for taking advantage of this situation was a chap called Walter Handy who got three years for claiming to have been bombed-out nineteen times in five months. The blackout also gave cover to entrepreneurs who seized the chance to raid military establishments to steal guns and indulge in a little armed robbery. Meanwhile, out in the country, those safe from the Blitz fiddled their government's depleted assets with false claims for nonexistent evacuees and the moneyed escapees from London saw it as their right to run double and treble ration-book scams so they did not go short at their dinner-parties. Back in London, the working classes were dying in their droves through lack of adequate shelter and a government which, unbelievably, initially forbade the use of Underground stations as shelters – there was apparently a fear of people needed for the War Effort going subterranean and not coming out until it was all over. Eventually, this ridiculous thinking relaxed and Londoners did indeed go troglodyte, with the inevitable black-market in tickets to gain access and then more 'spiving' of access to the beds and rudimentary facilities. And, in the crammed conditions, other 'chirpy Cockneys' set about robbing the sleeping, pick-pocketing the unwary and raping women at knife point to keep them quiet.

One of the most high-profile of the 'toffs' prosecuted for selfish harvesting of others' assets was Ivor Novello (1893–1951), songster and darling of the elite who got a spell in Wormwood Scrubs for using black market petrol tokens so he could run his Rolls Royce in and out of the city from his bolt-hole in Maidenhead. Arrogant to the end, he tried to bribe the official serving him the summons and then entered a plea of not guilty when he clearly was. All this angered the court which might otherwise have let him off with a reprimand, so, to the cries of 'Jolly poor show' from his cronies in the public gallery, he was led off for an eight-week stretch during which he shared accommodation with a young Frankie Fraser who himself would later find fame as Mad Frankie Fraser, enforcer for the Kray twins who have their own claim to historical fame as the last prisoners of the Tower of London. Called up for their National Service in 1952 and stationed at a barrack within the Tower complex, they went AWOL after beating up their training sergeant and were caught and returned to cells in the Waterloo Block.

In a misguided attempt to bolster the rapidly flagging morale, the government put out propaganda films showing people partying and going about their daily routine, quite unperturbed by the bombing; George VI and his Queen Consort, the recently deceased Queen Mother, were cajoled into an ill-advised tour of London's bombed-out East End where they were booed, jeered and pelted with rubbish. Later, she would foolishly issue a statement saying that, after some stray bomb had glanced off the side of Buckingham Palace, she felt she could look East Enders in the eye – as all knew full well that she and her husband retreated to the rural safety of Windsor Castle every night, this hardly improved matters. But who started the bombing of civilians?

Needless to say, the British public were left in no doubt at the time that deliberate bombing of civilians was the unwarranted act of an unscrupulous enemy; this is still the prevailing perspective. But the British began the bombing of German civilians as early as the night of 15/16 May 1940 with strikes in the Ruhr. To quote the influential British historian, J.F.P. Veale (1897–1976) 'It is one of the greatest triumphs of modern emotional engineering that, in spite of the plain facts of the case which could never be disguised or even materially distorted, the British public, throughout the Blitz Period (1940–1941), remained convinced that the entire responsibility for their sufferings rested on the German leaders'. Scottish academic and historian, Angus Calder (1942–2008) made it even clearer in his *The Peoples' War* (1969):

> It may be inconvenient history but England rather than Germany initiated the murderous slaughter of bombing civilians thus bringing about retaliation. Chamberlain conceded that this was "absolutely contrary to international law". It began in 1940 and Churchill believed it held the secret of victory. He was convinced that raid of sufficient intensity could destroy Germany's morale, and so his War Cabinet planned a campaign that abandoned the accepted practice of attacking the enemy's armed forces and instead made civilians the primary target. Night after night RAF bombers in ever increasing numbers struck throughout Germany, usually at working class housing, because it was more densely packed.

And, J.M. Spaight CBE (1877–1968), by far the leading authority on airpower throughout the first half of the twentieth century and Principal Assistant Secretary of the Air Ministry at the time, puts it in a nutshell: 'We began to bomb [civilian] objectives on the German mainland before the Germans began to bomb [civilian] objectives on the British mainland… Because we were doubtful about the psychological effect of propagandist distortion of the truth that it was we who started the strategic bombing offensive, we have shrunk from giving our great decision of May 11th, 1940, the publicity it deserves.'

There is however one alleged act of brutality that can now be dismissed as pure invention – the supposed strafing of civilians fleeing the firestorm horrors of Dresden. Still considered a war crime by many, the necessity of the wholesale bombing of this city from 13–15 February 1945, a mere twelve weeks before the capitulation of Germany, continues to be argued, but tales of RAF Mosquitos and American Mustangs machine-gunning women and children in the streets are a persistent fiction. The former were only involved in the raids as guides and, having dropped their markers, peeled away and left the bombers to it. As for American Mustangs, there were none within fuel-range of Dresden and, after the firestorm had started, the kind of low-level flying required for strafing runs would have been totally out of the question. Little consolation to the perhaps 40,000 fried alive, but it simply did not happen.

COOK'S TOURS

When the history books debate the first and true discoverer of any landmass what they are really arguing is the case of the first white European claimant. The Chinese knew all about Australia in the thirteenth century and the Malays were constantly popping across to the north coast on protracted hunting trips. Even restricting the field to Europeans, James Cook (1728–1779) comes a long way down the list and it is hardly fair to use the term 'discovery' in connection with his antipodean ventures since he was given his charts and directions by an Admiralty long aware of the continent's existence.

Leaving aside outlandish theories holding the Phoenicians to have established a civilization there in the tenth century BC, the first believable claims of sightings come from the French and Portuguese on behalf of minor sixteenth-century explorers and rovers. Whilst it is true that a sixteenth-century Portuguese coin was allegedly unearthed in 1996 'somewhere on the Mornington Peninsula, near Melbourne, by a metal-detecting chap known only as "Bob"' this does not necessarily validate claims made on behalf of Cristovao de Mendonca (d.1532) who, some would maintain, sailed down the east coast in 1522 and into the Bass Strait where the coin was found. Just because a sixteenth-century coin is found, it does not necessarily mean that it was dropped there in the year it was minted; those with a theory to sell have been known to go out and dig up exactly what they have been looking for!

By all the rules of the white/European game, the little-known Willem Janszoon (1570–1630) is the man who discovered Australia. On 26 February 1606 he sailed into what is now called the Gulf of Carpentaria and dropped anchor in the Pennefather River on the western shore of Cape York in Western Australia. He began charting over 300 miles of coastline and in March tried to establish a settlement, a venture thwarted by friction with the locals which, according to Janszoon was down to their being mindless savages, although the oral tradition of the area blames the Dutch for kidnapping the women and trying to bully the men into hunting and labouring for them. Either way, after losing about a dozen men in the interminable round of tit-for-tat encounters, Janszoon upped-sticks and left Cape Keerweer, that being the Dutch for 'turnaround'. This first and true landing in Australia by Europeans is well recognized in

Australia itself – a replica of Janszoon's ship, *Duyfken* is on permanent moorings in Wollongong Harbour, New South Wales.

Throughout the next century, the Dutch were all over the place, charting, mapping, establishing settlements in the land they called New Holland. The first Englishman to take a serious interest in the place was pirate/navigator William Dampier (1652–1715) who landed early in 1688 on the north-western coast near Kings Sound and reported his findings upon his return to London in 1691. In January of 1699 he was given command of HMS *Roebuck* and a commission to further explore Australia, this beginning in the July when he started to chart over 900 miles of coast from Shark's Bay to Roebuck's Bay. He returned in 1701 to be court-marshalled for cruelty which, in the Royal Navy of the day, gives a strong indication as to the size of the man's mean-streak which would a few years later be responsible for the inspiration for *Robinson Crusoe* (1719). After being booted out of the Navy, Dampier returned to the life of a privateer/pirate at the helm of the *St George* which was accompanied by the smaller *Cinque Ports*. By October 1704 the ships were off the Chilean Coast when crewman Alexander Selkirk fell out with his own captain, Thomas Stradling, and Dampier over the seaworthiness of the *Cinque Ports*.

Refusing to continue further, he demanded to be put ashore at next landfall which just happened to be the deserted island of Juan Fernandez; as things turned out, Selkirk was right to be worried as the *Cinque* sank with few survivors shortly thereafter. For his part, Selkirk would have to languish on his island until rescued by Captain Woodes Rogers (1679–1732), first Governor of the Bahamas, who pitched up off Juan Fernandez on 1 February 1709 in a privateer called *Duke*. Naturally the poor chap was elated at his salvation but it speaks volumes for the character of Dampier that when the longboat neared the mothership and Selkirk saw his old enemy leaning over the side, he demanded to be put back on his island. Common sense prevailed and Selkirk returned to England to meet Daniel Foe who converted his tale to the classic. Actually, neither is famous by the right name: Selkirk was born Alexander Selcraig (1767–1721) in Lower Largo, Fife, but had to change his name and go on the run to avoid being dragged before the local Sessions on 27 August 1695 for 'indecent behaviour' in the local church, of all places, and the author was born plain old Daniel Foe (1659–1731). So often was he referred to as D-Foe, to differentiate him from his father, James Foe, or J-Foe, that he adopted the format and claimed association with French nobility. But back to Australia.

It was nearly a century after all such ventures that James Cook was hired by the Royal Society in 1768 and sent south with orders to observe the transit of Venus at Tahiti, which he did before sailing on to land on the eastern coast of Australia on 19 April 1770, so how he manages to grab all the glory is a mystery. By May, he was anchored in what he first called Stingray's Bay, then Botanists' Bay and finally Botany Bay but it is a myth that any convicts were subsequently landed here. The first of many transportees arrived on 18 January 1788 but the commander of the fleet deemed the sandy and infertile soil unsuitable for settlement and so sailed north until he found more suitable land at the site which would become, in time, the city of Sydney. Cook of course died on Hawaii on his third voyage but not quite in the way that it was trumpeted in the press of the day. We still have the image of the noble captain remonstrating with his men for firing on innocent natives armed only with sticks and stones and paying for it with his life as the ungrateful brutes hacked him down from behind. Not quite.

On 17 January 1779 Cook anchored up in Hawaii's Kealakekua Bay while those on shore were gearing up for their festival of Makahiki, a sort of harvest festival in honour of their god of fertility, Lono. Just as there were silly stories stating Cortés to have been perceived a god by those he went to rob, there were equally silly stories about the 'ignorant' Hawaiians thinking Cook to be Lono and thus showering him with immeasurable bounty. In truth, far from thinking him a god, the Hawaiians were seriously ticked off by the grasping nature of the interlopers, most of whom took full advantage of the festive hospitality and lack of aggression demanded throughout Makahiki, going seriously over the top when it came to the women and other temptations on offer. By the time Cook & co quit the island on 4 February, all were heartily glad to see the back of them. Unfortunately, a couple of days out, *Resolution* sprung her foremast and was forced to return, this time to a less than gracious reception: Makahiki was over and with it the religiously required tolerance. Each venture ashore ended in a clash and when one of the ship's boats went missing, Cook, rather foolishly, led a party ashore on 14 February with the intention of taking the chief hostage against its return. At the inevitable confrontation, Cook cut loose with a double-barrelled shotgun before he and his party were rushed and overwhelmed and Cook's body dragged away by his killers. One of the ship's junior officers led a reprisal raid of disputed brutality and this officer, William Bligh, would later meet his own South-Seas waterloo aboard the ill-fated *Bounty*. God knows what the Hawaiians did with the rest of James Cook but they later returned his scalp and some bones to his crew who gave the neatly-wrapped package, weighing a scant 9 lb, a Christian burial at sea.

At the end of the day, great sailor and navigator that he was, Cook neither discovered Australia nor advocated its settlement; indeed, he saw little merit in the place. He charted from Cape Everard to the Torres Straits but that was it; the major impetus behind the settlement and colonization of New Holland, as he called it, was the English botanist, Sir Joseph Banks (1743–1820) who had been with Cook on that first journey. Actually, he was also the driving force behind the *Bounty* voyage and instrumental in Bligh's later appointment as Governor of New South Wales where he presided over yet another mutiny. But that, as they say, is another story.

THE DEVIL'S TATTOO AND GHOSTS IN THE MACHINES

It must be said that one feels vaguely uncomfortable exonerating the Nazis of any Holocaust crime but, in matters of such enormity, the truth is all we have to honour the dead. No matter how popular the myths – and no matter how horrifyingly possible and believable – at no time did the Nazis render down their victims for soap, glue or fertilizer; they never hunted through the inmates for tattooed Jews to flay to make lampshades for SS headquarters and only Jews in Auschwitz inducted from the summer of 1943 onwards were tattooed with their IBM number and other identification marks. Most Jewish historians are of the mind that these myths should be exposed for what they are to prevent the Holocaust Denial mob seeking false comfort in them on the basis of a 'one thing false – everything false' premise.

The bars of 'Jewish' soap myth was actually a re-working of an earlier myth, spread by the British throughout the First World War, this claiming that the German Army was rendering down its own casualties to harvest the fats they were so short of due to the success of the British blockades. The originator of the myth was perhaps Brigadier General John Charteris (1877–1946), Head of

British Military Intelligence under Sir Douglas Haig; we have to say 'perhaps' as he both acknowledged and denied authorship of the lie. In his acceptance of the accolade of authorship, Charteris stated that the idea came to him when viewing two separate batches of photographs; one showing the Germans in retreat, loading the dead onto any available transport, and another showing convoys of lorries taking dead horses to a rendering plant. It was March in 1917 and, at such time, Charteris was desperately trying to convince China to have nothing to do with the Germans; knowing of the Chinese veneration of the dead and their deeply rooted cultural aversion to any desecration thereof, he said the idea came to him in a flash to jiggle about with the photographs and the captions to make it look like the Germans were rendering their own dead. Within hours, photographs apparently showing 'German cadavers on Their Way to The Soap Factory' were travelling under courier to Shanghai. Speaking after the war at the 1926 National Arts Club Dinner in New York, Charteris explained that he had concocted the lie for Chinese consumption and had no inkling at the time that the rest of the world would be so taken in.

But taken in it was. While the lie was a propaganda coup *extraordinaire* in China, where this alleged profanation of the dead is thought to have been a key instigatory factor in the subsequent Chinese declaration of war on Germany in August 1917, the story bounced back into the West, gaining increased acceptance and credence with every country it moved through. The British public got their first whiff of the tale on 17 April 1917 when *The Times* splashed it all over the front page, the imaginary human rendering plants now having picked up the title *of Kadaververwerkungsanstalts*, not the catchiest name to roll off the tongue but decidedly 'German'. Citing various sources throughout France and Belgium, the editorial proclaimed:

The factory is invisible from the railway. It is placed deep in forest country, with a specially thick growth of trees about it. Live wires surround it. A special double track leads to it. The works are about 700 ft long and 110 ft broad, and the railway runs completely around them. In the north-west corner of the works the discharge of the trains takes place.

The trains arrive full of bare bodies, which are unloaded by workers who live at the works. The men wear oilskin overalls and masks with mica eye-pieces. They are equipped with long hooked poles, and push bundles of bodies to an endless chain, which picks them with big hooks, attached at intervals of 2 ft.

The bodies are transported on this endless chain into a long, narrow compartment, where they pass through a bath which disinfects them. They then go through a drying chamber, and finally are automatically carried into a digester or great cauldron, in which they are dropped by an apparatus which detaches them from the chain. In the digester they remain for six to eight hours, and are treated by steam, which breaks them up while they are slowly stirring the machinery.

From this treatment result several procedures. The fats are broken up into stearin, a form of tallow, and oils, which require to be redistilled before they can be used. The process of distillation is carried out by boiling the oil with carbonate of soda, and some of the by-products resulting from this are used by German soap makers. The oil distillery and refinery lie in the south-eastern corner of the works. The refined oil is sent out in small casks like those used for petroleum, and is of yellowish brown colour.

In the weeks that followed, *The Times* carried a hail of letters from people claiming to have witnessed such horrors first-hand and other publications picked up on the story, including *Punch* magazine which promoted a famous cartoon showing the Kaiser addressing new recruits, saying he could make use of them dead or alive. On 30 April there were questions raised in the House of Commons with MPs seeking assurances that none of the British fallen were being so 'harvested' and, despite it being pointed out that '*kadaver*' was never used in German of anything other than an animal carcass, the myth rolled on, even repeated in print after it had been thoroughly debunked by Arthur Ponsonby, Baron of Shulbrede (1871–1946) in his *Falsehood in War Time* (1928). It was early in 1941 that the human-soap myth was resurrected with a twist; this time the Germans were supposedly processing the dead from the concentration camps for the production of soap. The bars in question, which were even presented at the Nuremberg trials (Exhibit USSR-393), were stamped with what people chose to perceive as 'RJF' and, during and after the war, it was widely believed that this stood for *Rein Judisches Fett*, or Pure Jewish Fat. In fact, with the I and the J interchangeable in German, the logo was in fact RIF and stood for *Reichsstelle fur Industrielle Fettversorgung*, or the Reich Centre for Industrial Fat Provisioning. As things turned out, this 'soap' was a poor substitute which, on post-war examination, was found to contain no fat whatsoever – human or otherwise.

But the myth was firmly rooted in the fertile ground of the only-too-real Nazi atrocities; people were understandably prepared to believe them capable of anything. Rabbi Stephen Wise, the influential head of both the American Jewish Congress and the World Jewish Congress, declared in the November of 1942: 'Jewish corpses are being processed into such war-vital commodities as soap, fats and fertilizer by the Germans. They are even exhuming dead Jews from their graves and paying Germans fifty marks for each body they dig up.' As the full horrors of the camps became open knowledge in 1945, countless survivors gave harrowing accounts of their trauma at having to wash with soap made of their executed comrades and even the world-famous Nazi-hunter, Simon Wiesenthal helped to perpetuate the myth, writing in *Der Neue Weg*, an Austrian-Jewish Community paper, that:

> During the last weeks of March the Romanian press reported an unusual piece of news: In the small Romanian city of Folticeni twenty boxes of soap were buried in the Jewish cemetery with full ceremony and complete funeral rites. This soap had been found recently in a former German army depot. On the boxes were the initials RIF, "Pure Jewish Fat". These boxes were destined for the Waffen-SS. The wrapping paper revealed with completely cynical objectivity that this soap was manufactured from Jewish bodies. Surprisingly, the thorough Germans forgot to describe whether the soap was produced from children, girls, men or elderly persons.

It is pointless and perhaps callous to cite other examples of such false claims, for there are many, enough to say that the myth was so widely believed that it was even referred to in the summing up at the Nuremberg Trials and so widely believed that the hunt began for the head of such nightmarish programme. Focus settled on Dr Rudolf Spanner of the Danzig Institute through some garbled testimony of laboratory assistant Sigmund Mazer who gave lurid accounts of great vats of human remains boiling away. On further investigation, Mazer's testimony fell apart and proceedings against Spanner were quietly dropped. Walter Z. Laqueur, one of the most reputable Jewish historians, caused a bit of a storm by addressing the myth in his *The Terrible Secret* (1980) and stating the human soap fears to be imaginary, and Gitta Sereny, respected Holocaust historian and child-abuse expert who has more than once crossed swords with Holocaust denier David Irving, stated in her *Into That Darkness* (1974, reissued 1995) that: 'The universally accepted story that the corpses were used to make soap and fertilizer is finally refuted by the generally very reliable Ludwigsburg Central Authority for Investigation into Nazi Crimes'. Deborah Lipstadt, the decidedly feisty Jewish historian who, together with Penguin Books, successfully stood against Irving who was suing both for libel, stated in 1981 'The fact is that the Nazis never used the bodies of Jews, or for that matter anyone else, for the production of soap'. This is also the opinion of Professor Yehuda Bauer of Israel's Hebrew University and Shmuel Krakowski, Archives Director of Israel's Yad Vashem Holocaust Centre.

But what of that other recurring horror-story concerning one Ilse Koch, (also known as the Bitch of Buchenwald) the deranged wife of said camp's Commandant, Karl Koch. That she was a prize bitch and treated the camp as if it were her own personal playground is beyond doubt, but she was pretty low down the ranks of depravity when compared to others; her enduring fame is due to the myth that she ordered tattooed prisoners to be killed carefully so that they could be flayed to make book bindings and lampshades. A rather dowdy and stumpy little sadist, were it not for this myth no-one would ever have heard of her, but the lampshade tale put forward at her trial captured the public imagination, with Woodie Guthrie sitting down to write songs about her nightmare-approach to interior design and her spectre being raised in several fictional books and films. At the time of writing Kate Winslet's Oscar-tipped *The Reader* (2009), is doing the rounds, inspired, if that be the right word, by the proclivities of Koch and in June 2009 the plot of an episode of *CSI–NY* pivoted on the suggestion that Ilse Koch had so behaved. She may have been a loathsome and sexually depraved sadist but neither she nor anyone else in the camps selected tattooed Jews for execution just so they could be flayed to make pretty lampshades for SS headquarters or, as is frequently asserted, Koch's own home. According to Diana Saltzman, Director of Collections at the Washington Holocaust Memorial Museum:

> None of the lampshades that have surfaced over the past fifty years
> have ever turned out to be real... There is no proof that this practice
> has ever occurred...Tales of such ghastly shades have circulated
> for decades. They stemmed, in part, from considerable newspaper
> coverage after WWII about human lampshades made at Buchenwald
> concentration camp.

The myth of human body-parts being used to produce 'artefacts'
appears to stem from a film made by Billy Wilder at the liberation
of Buchenwald in 1945. At one point in the documentary, the
camera focuses on a table holding shrunken heads, what appear
to be sections of tattooed skin and a rather mundane-looking
table-lamp which the voice-over chillingly pronounces to be: 'a
lampshade, made of human skin, at the request of an SS officer's
wife'. Not only is there no proof that any of the items shown were
anything other than imported 'props', but, rather suspiciously,
the lamp disappeared after filming. Were it truly such a terrible
indictment of the Nazi camps – as if one were needed – then one
would think it would have been carefully preserved for the trial
of Ilse Koch in August 1947 at Dachau and secured thereafter.
There was a lamp brought forward by the prosecution lawyers who
pronounced it to be one of many made of human skin and body-
parts, but this too turned out to be goatskin. She was also alleged
to have had light-switches made out of dehydrated thumbs, gloves
and handbags made from flayed prisoners and several books bound
with human skin, yet none were found. It should be said here that
books bound in human skin, tattooed or otherwise, abound in
the libraries of countless universities and other institutions across
Europe and America; theses ranging from Bibles to court records
and from atlases to books on anatomy. In the nineteenth century
it was common for the trial records of murderers to be bound in
the skin flayed from the condemned after hanging; most famously,
this was the fate of William Corder whose skin went to bind the
records from his trial for the infamous 'Red Barn' murder of Maria
Martin in 1828. And before anyone protested that this was 'back in
the nineteenth century', the last person to use human skin bindings
was Dale Carnegie (1888-1955) on special volumes of his *The
Unknown Lincoln* (1932). Dale, of course, was the chap who wrote
the sycophants' handbook, aka *How to Win Friends and Influence
People* (1936).

At the end of the day, it certainly appears that the prosecuting officers in the military courts were determined to go for the sensational and were not too fussy in their methods of obtaining it. Knowing that they had an extremely 'sticky' target, they opted for the 'sling as much mud as you can and see what sticks' principle with all sorts of unsubstantiated allegations being thrown at the repugnant Ilse, most of them clinging: she forced inmates to rape each other at gunpoint; she rolled around naked in her garden, visible from the camp, and shot at any man who so much as looked in her direction; she whipped and tortured countless prisoners and, most sensational of all, selected tattooed Jews to be killed by lethal injection so they could be skinned to provide her with gloves, handbags and, most famously, lampshades. But the frame-up was sloppy and unconvincing because the prosecution team was not initially aware of Koch's previous trial in German courts in 1943 which left them tripping over their own chronological mistakes.

Ilse Koch was quite depraved enough without such invention being introduced by the American prosecutors who were initially unaware that all these claims had been investigated by the German Judge Konrad 'The Bloodhound' Morgen (1909–1982) who, after eight months of relentless digging into the Kochs' time in Buchenwald, threw out all such allegation as ridiculous rumour. And before anyone suggests that this German judge was of the type predisposed to turn a blind eye to such horrors, Morgen had Karl Koch put up against a wall and shot for embezzlement of camp funds and the murder of two medical orderlies whom he killed to make sure they could never tell anyone about the treatment he needed for syphilis contracted through homosexual affairs. The main problem with the Ilse Koch/body parts myth as raised by the Americans and filmed 'in chilling reality' by Wilder is that is that Morgen's investigation of the gruesome-twosome was conducted in 1943 and covered alleged irregularities that had occurred at Buchenwald between 1937 and 1941, after which Koch was transferred as Commandant of Majdanek Concentration Camp. By the time the Americans liberated Buchenwald in 1945 neither of the Kochs had been there for years, so it is interesting that her collection of horrors was so readily found. The prosecution team made a serious error of judgement when they told the court that Morgen himself had seen Koch's collection of horrors because when he was finally found and brought forward he made it clear that he had seen no such thing nor would he perjure himself to back up their lies. Ilse Koch was, in his opinion a revolting specimen, guilty of many crimes, he had no doubt, but all the tales of bits and pieces of bodies being turned into everyday items was nothing but hysterical rumour that had circulated in the camp for years. The prosecution tried leaning on Morgen with physical intimidation and threats of his being turned over to the Russians if he did not play ball but he remained adamant. Quite how the Americans thought they were going to frighten a man who spent his Hitler years prosecuting high-ranking Nazis itself questions their judgement, but that is another story.

At risk of appearing in any way to be defending such a creature as the Bitch of Buchenwald or her husband, the decidedly camp Commandant, it can be stated with all considered certainty that neither they nor anyone else during their regrettable administration of Buchenwald engaged in such exploitation of human skin or other body parts. Not only was this the opinion of Morgen but also of countless others. General Lucius D. Clay, Commander in Chief of US Forces in Europe and Military Governor of the US Occupation Zone of Germany, from 1947 to 1949, who would later review Ilse Koch's case and reduce her sentence to howls of public protests, stated:

> There was absolutely no evidence in the trial transcript, other than she was a rather loathsome creature, that would support the death sentence. I suppose I received more abuse for that than for anything else I did in Germany. Some reporter had called her the "Bitch of Buchenwald," had written that she had lamp shades made of human skin in her house. And that was introduced in court, where it was absolutely proven that the lamp shades were made out of goat skin.

She was sentenced to life imprisonment on 14 August 1947 having been found guilty of participating in a 'common plan to violate the Laws and Usages of war' no mention whatsoever of any specifics of the popular imagination. When General Clay reviewed her case in the comparative calm of October 1948 and commuted her sentence to four years, he first addressed that public outrage in his *Decision in Germany* (1950):

Among the 1,672 trials was that of Ilse Koch, the branded "Bitch of Buchenwald", but as I examined the record I could not find her a major participant in the crimes of Buchenwald. A sordid, disreputable character, she had delighted in flaunting her sex, emphasized by tight sweaters and short skirts, before the long-confined male prisoners, and had developed their bitter hatred. Nevertheless these were not the offenses for which she was being tried and so I reduced her sentence, expecting the reaction which came. Perhaps I erred in judgment but no one can share the responsibility of a reviewing officer. Later the Senate committee which unanimously criticized this action heard witnesses who gave testimony not contained in the record before me. I could take action only on that record.

The point should perhaps not be laboured further, suffice to say that everyone who has looked into these gruesome allegations, be they the most blinkered denier or the most vehement Nazi-phobe determined to find something, everyone has come up with the same answers: the shrunken heads were tourist tat from South America and all lampshades, claimed to be Koch 'originals' turned out to be made of goatskin or some such. There are in existence some five or six patches of withered skin boasting crude tattoos but the exact nature of these, human or animal, and whence they came is likewise unclear.

Upon her release from Lansberg Prison, Koch was immediately re-arrested by the German authorities who re-imposed her life sentence in 1951 for crimes committed against German citizens, these being beyond the jurisdiction of any Allied court. Although she protested her sentence to the International Human Rights Commission it was upheld and she eventually hanged herself with her own bed sheets in 1967.

And so to that other Jew-tattoo myth; the notion that all inmates of the camps had their IBM number tattooed on their inner-left forearm. Although perhaps small consolation to Holocaust victims as a whole, both Jewish and non-Jewish, this was only ever the case in the notorious complex at Auschwitz.

The logistics of the Holocaust was run with chilling efficiency by IBM–Germany, aka Dehomag, (*Deutsche Hollerith-Maschinen Gesellschaft*) and their Hollerith punch-card system. Built into each person's reference number were elements indicating any relevant skills – carpentry, engineering, or whatever, as well as other indicators as to their religious, sexual and political inclinations. While some IBM offices ran the complicated railroad schedule for the shipment of Jews and other 'undesirables' from all over occupied Europe, either to the death-camps or to slave-labour factories, other bureaux tracked the movement of slave-workers, responding to requests such as 'we need 300 non-communist engravers and diamond-cutters; Jews acceptable, but no homosexuals'. IBM would run the database and collect the 'lucky' winners from the last tray in the line. More sinister was the fact that all the main death-camps had on site IBM offices keeping track of who was alive, who was dead and who was scheduled for extermination, in the IBM Hollerith coding numbers. At certain positions in the 'bar-code' '8' indicated a Jew while '11' denoted a Gypsy, while '5' indicated that the person had been executed and '6' indicated that they were scheduled for the gas chamber. Page fifty of the Auschwitz Camp telephone book, for example, shows the 'Hollerith-Buro' on extension 4495.

Each inmate or slave-worker had their IBM number sewn into the clothing and could be shot for not remembering it but the practice of tattooing did not really begin until the spring of 1943 and then only in Auschwitz. At first this tattoo was that person's number as issued by the camp IBM office but since this system was largely geared to the tracking and inmates and slaves up until their final '5' or '6', by 1943 the extermination programme had ratcheted up to such an alarming rate that the IBM offices could no longer keep pace with the murder-rate leaving the Nazis to go it alone with their own somewhat random system. At first, this was done with a large metal stamp with interchangeable numbers comprising several needles, the whole thing being slammed into the upper left chest before ink was sprayed on what was essentially a bloody wound. It would be 1944 before Auschwitz began inflicting tattoos on the inner left forearm and by then these insults had no relevance at all to the numbers issued by the still-functioning IBM Holocaust-support teams. Quite how many Jews and non-Jews were so callously number-crunched is anybody's guess but, given the time-scale of the tattooing programme and its restriction to the Auschwitz complex, the number of inmates so tagged must, against the entire Holocaust death-toll, represent a rather small proportion, although they numbered in their thousands.

It must be repeated that it is distasteful in the extreme to have to explain in such detail how the antics of the Bitch of Buchenwald were grossly over-rated; how the original soap-myth was a British invention and how 'only comparatively few' Jews were actually tattooed with a de-humanizing number and to further explain such horrors to be largely figments of the imagination amid a panoramic nightmare that was only too real and unbelievably true; distasteful but very necessary. All holocaust historians are adamant that, for the sake of those who died and for those who endured, no myths or exaggerations should be allowed to flourish in case they are put to use by the Holocaust deniers as props to their ridiculous argument that the Holocaust itself was a Jewish-Allied lie to discredit a noble cause.

FIRE FROM HEAVEN?

Firmly fixed in the general imagination is the notion that the Great Fire of Chicago was started on the night of 18 October 1871 by Mrs Catherine O'Leary's cow kicking over a lantern in her barn which stood to the rear of her family's home, just off Dekoven Street. But there were four fires that night and none started by any truculent bovine.

The Chicago conflagration broke out some time around 9 p.m. on the very windy night of 18 October and destroyed over 3 square miles of the city before burning itself out the next night leaving at least 250 dead and 100,000 homeless. The city was looking for a scapegoat and Michael Ahern, a reporter on the *Chicago Tribune*, decided to give the people what they wanted. All that was known for sure was that the fire had broken out somewhere on or near Dekoven Street so, with the Irish being at the bottom of the pecking order, Ahern picked on the O'Learys and plastered them all over the front page as the authors of everyone's ruin. Not until 1893 did he admit the fabrication but by that time it was all too late for the O'Learys who had to move and bury themselves among the stockyards on the city's notorious Southside. But while general history has focused on the Chicago fire, most missed the wider picture and the possibility that all had been caused by blistering hot fragments from Biela's Comet as it broke up over the American Midwest.

As stated, four fires broke out that night and all of them around Lake Michigan with the one at Peshtigo dwarfing that of Chicago and its study giving the British and American Air Forces the knowledge that they needed to create the incredible firestorms at Dresden and Tokyo during the Second World War. Frequently referred to as America's forgotten fire, this was the biggest and most devastating in the country's history and it is bordering on the incredible that the comparatively minor Chicago fire managed to put this event in the shade. With temperatures in excess of 2,000°c the real death toll is not known but could have been anything up to about 2,500 with 1.2 million acres laid waste and twelve towns consumed therein by a fire of truly epic proportions. At its peak there was a wall of flame over 1 mile high across a 5 mile front that was racing along at about 100 mph, jumping rivers like they weren't even there. Subsequent study of the fire and the flaming tornadoes it generated produced what is known as the Peshtigo Paradigm which, as stated, was employed by British and American bombers to replicate such conditions as best they could at Dresden and Tokyo where the death tolls exceed those of Hiroshima and Nagasaki.

The meteor theory was first mooted in 1883 and largely dismissed, despite countless witness reports of balls of fire falling from the sky and spontaneous ignitions of blue flame which would be consistent with the methane found in comets and meteorites; a similar blue-flame phenomenon was reported by members of the Fire Department in Chicago. More recently, American physicist Robert Wood PhD, presented his conclusions on the subject in a lecture to the Aerospace Corporation and the American Institute of Aeronautics and Astronautics in March 2004 when he asserted that there was much in the way of new evidence to support the notion that the fires had been caused by Biela's break-up showering the earth with white-hot debris. Wood proposed that the main bulk of the comet crashed into the Great Lakes and that residual and peripheral fragments of frozen methane, acetylene and other combustibles scattered the area producing the fires. Wood – and other proponents of this theory – says that only such a scenario could explain the sudden eruption of so many fires across such distribution. He also highlighted the facts that a 58 lb lump of meteorite had been found on the shores of Lake Huron and that in the early 1990s geologists had found a massive impact crater 200 ft below the surface of that same lake where drilling crews had reported meteorite finds. Also, an aerial view of the spread of the fires and their distribution matches what can best be described as cone-shaped shotgun splatter.

Obviously we will never know for sure what happened that night but it is high time to stop blaming Old Mother O'Leary and her much maligned cow. As fate would decree, the O'Leary house survived the fire only to be finally torn down in 1956 to make way for the Chicago Fire Academy.

FIRST AMONG SEQUELS

It is fixed in the general mind that Robert Walpole (1676–1745) was the first Prime Minister of Great Britain and George Washington the first President of the United States of America, however in reality both men come well down the list of tenures. Walpole, whose tenure began in 1721, was appointed First Lord of the Treasury, not Prime Minister; the letterbox at 10 Downing Street still announces to the world that the residence is that of the First Lord of the Treasury.

In Walpole's day and for quite some time after, 'Prime Minister' was a grave political insult – the Duke of Wellington would later issue a warning that anyone who called him a prime minister during his term of office could expect an invitation to pistols at dawn. The title was first carried by the sinister Cardinal Richelieu, appointed in 1625 to carry out Louis XIV's dirty work, and it was with this 'baggage' of pejorative overtones that the designation arrived in England. Throughout the seventeenth, eighteenth and for a large part of the nineteenth century, 'Prime Minister' was used as a sneer implying that the butt of the insult was nothing more than the King's 'poodle' or mouthpiece. The *OED* notes eighteenth-century use of the designation to be 'odious' and 'applied opprobriously to Walpole and disowned by him, as later by Lord North', he holding the office of First Lord of the Treasury from 1770–1782.

By 1905 the term had become 'respectable' enough for official recognition and the first man appointed Prime Minister of Great Britain was Henry Campbell Bannerman. On 5 December that year he was acknowledged First Lord of the Treasury and on 10 December, when the title had been granted formal recognition, he was also declared the first Prime Minister. As for Washington being the first President, this is sure to be the 'correct' answer in any quiz and an accolade afforded him in most reference books, but it is nevertheless wrong; he was the seventeenth.

The first 'President' elected by the Continental Congress was Peyton Randolph who held the office for a short term in 1774 after which Henry Middleton took over for a while before handing the reins back to Randolph who gave way in 1775. Next, John Hancock ran things until 1777, when he was followed by Henry Laurens (1777–1778), John Jay (1778–1779) and Samuel Huntington (1779–1781). The Continental Congress then gave way to the Articles of Confederation which appointed Presidents of the United States in Congress Assembled, these being Samuel Huntington (1781), Thomas McKean (1781), John Hanson (1781–1782), Elias Boudinot (1782–1783), Thomas Mifflin (1783–1784), Richard Henry Lee (1784–1785), John Hancock (1786–1786), Nathaniel Gorham (1786), Arthur St Clair (1787) and, finally, Cyrus Griffin (1788), who handed over to George Washington. The first of Washington's predecessors to serve after American Independence was Hanson who was addressed as President by Washington himself; when Hanson wrote to Washington to congratulate him after his victory over the British at Yorktown, Washington replied with a letter addressed to the President of the United States, so there was obviously no doubt who Washington deemed the president of his country.

The most remarkable American 'president', and one of whom few have heard, is David Rice Atchison (1807–1886) who slept through his entire term of office – supposedly one day on 4 March 1849; a feat not to be repeated until Ronald Reagan stepped up to the plate. Argument regarding the legality of his one-day tenure depends on how one interprets the law regarding the precise point at which a man becomes legally and constitutionally the President, but the facts are these. Outgoing President James K. Polk's term of office expired on 3 March 1849 which was a Saturday and, having religious objections to a Sunday inauguration, the incoming Zachary Taylor put off the ceremony until the Monday. Atchison at the time was the President pro-tempore of the Senate and, since the United States cannot be without a leader even for a day, or so the pro-Atchison lobby would have it, he was technically the leader of the country until Taylor was sworn in. Having tarried long at the Saturday night celebrations himself, Atchison slept the Sunday through and, according to his housekeeper, snored like a pig. In 2009, a similar argument arose after Barack Obama fluffed his lines and had to retake the oath. Both Obama and his vice-President, Joe Biden, were sworn in on 20 January 2009 with Obama having to retake his oath the next day, causing some to hail Biden as yet another President-for-a-day.

One final word on the subject of the inaugural oath, 'So help me God' is not a required suffix to the oath, although some incumbents have added it with a flourish, they falsely believing that Washington himself had done so.

HANGED, DRAWN AND QUARTERED

There are two myths attached to this once-popular form of public entertainment that survive today only in the realms of metaphor. The first is that such barbarity belongs to the dark and long-gone days of history, and the second lies in the generally presented wording, as in the heading.

Properly, the phrase is 'drawn, hanged and quartered', a typical reading of the sentence being:

> You are to be carried to the place from whence you came (back to prison, in other words) and from thence you shall be *drawn* on a hurdle to the place of execution where you shall be *hanged* by the neck but not till you are dead for, while still living, your body is to be taken down, your privy member cut off, your bowels torn out and burnt before your face; your head will then be severed from your body and your body divided into four *quarters* and they to be disposed of at the King's pleasure. And may God have mercy upon your soul.

The 'hurdle' was a crude cart, hence the expression 'being in the cart' as indicating dire trouble, and since the Tyburn killing-ground was to the west of the city of London, criminals also coined 'gone west' to explain the absence of a peer who had gone for a spin in the municipal tumbrel. Anyway, there is nothing to be gained by dwelling on the numerous victims of this decidedly 'cruel and unusual punishment' as history is littered with examples of the treasonous meeting such an end to the roars and guffaws of the mob; what is little known, however, is that the revolting sentence remained very much in use until well into the mid-nineteenth century, it being last passed in 1848 on Irish activist William Smith O'Brian (1803–1864) but, as his dates indicate, it was not carried out. Not so lucky were the five members of the Cato Street Conspiracy, a far-sighted group who sought to improve their fellows' lot by knocking off half of the Tory Cabinet of Lord Liverpool's government.

Although they did not get as far as enacting any of their half-baked plans, and only conspired to kill a few fat cats, all five ringleaders were handed down such a sentence to be carried out in public outside Newgate Prison on 1 May 1820. As a last minute thought, the boweling-and-bobbitting bit was cancelled in case it upset the more sensitive members of the considerable mob which turned up to see the fun. After being left dangling for about half an hour for a slow hanging, each was taken down and decapitated with a surgeon's saw before the head was held up to the crowd with the required admonition: 'Behold the head of a traitor'. As for O'Brian in 1848, he was lucky enough to have his sentence overturned before he was transported for life, eventually settling down in Tasmania. The sentence was next handed down to two other Fenians called Burke and O'Brian in 1867, this being 'commuted' to a standard hanging on pleas of clemency. The last public execution of any kind was the hanging of Fenian Michael Barratt, again at Newgate on 26 May 1868 with the sentence involving drawing, hanging and quartering being removed from judges' arsenal in 1870.

The other gallows-myth is that those who survived a bungled execution were automatically entitled under law to walk free – while this was on occasion allowed on compassionate grounds, it never had legal backing; several prisoners have 'come back to life' after the gallows and most were strung up again although, as stated, some were released on the whim of the local magistrates. The most celebrated such case is that of John Lee who came to be known as the man they could not hang. Condemned to swing at Exeter prison in 1885, the trap-door repeatedly refused to open each time they placed him on the spot. Three times he was returned to his cell while tests were carried out and each test went like clockwork, but every time Lee was brought back the drop-trap refused to open – even after Lee himself, perhaps by that time keen to be done with the matter – obligingly jumped up and down on the offending trap as the executioner cranked away on the release lever for all he was worth. This gruesome spectacle proved too much for the governor of the prison who, making awed pronouncements of divine intervention, ushered Lee back to his cell. The sentence was commuted to life-imprisonment, but public pressure, sharing the governor's belief in divine intervention, eventually secured Lee's release after which he shipped out to America where he died of natural causes in 1933. As things turned out the prison governor was actually right in part;

God had played a part if only by proxy. It seems there was a warped board on the platform and every time they tried to nudge Lee from this mortal coil the prison chaplain was standing on the one spot guaranteed to cause this board to jam the trap. Every time Lee was removed for tests, the only other missing factor was the chaplain.

The first authenticated case of someone erroneously presumed dead on the gallows is that of Anne Green, hanged at Oxford in 1650 for infanticide. Having been left turning slowly in the wind for over an hour to entertain the crowd, she was cut down and taken to the offices of Dr William Petty for dissection. To the chagrin of Petty and his companions, Anne came round and sat up to be granted a full reprieve – but it seems our trans-Atlantic cousins are made of sterner stuff. In 1932 an American murderer named Jack Bullen actually survived the electric chair and surprised all and sundry by leaping out of his coffin. He was strapped back into 'Old Sparky' and left until well done. In Louisiana there was the more celebrated case of Willie Francis (1929–1947) who, found guilty of murder, was strapped into the chair on 3 May 1946 but no matter how long they left him there he showed a marked reluctance to die. Returned to his cell he would wait another year while all the legal arguments for clemency came to nought; he was returned to the chair for a more successful outcome on 9 May 1947. This entire misconception of automatic reprieve rests on a fine legal point; the law demands that the *sentence* be executed, in the sense of carried out – not the condemned man and if the prisoner survives the attempt then the sentence has not been executed.

HARRY'S CLAIM

One of the best-known and oft-quoted lines from *The Third Man* (1949) comes from the exchange between the two main characters, Holly Martins and Harry Lime, the latter extolling conflict as the crucible of all that is worthy: 'In Switzerland they had brotherly love – they had over 500 years of democracy and peace – and what did that produce … the cuckoo-clock!' Orson Wells may have delivered the line with panache but with little or no accuracy; there was no democracy; the cantons were constantly at each other's throats and embroiled in external wars and the cuckoo-clock was a German invention first seen in 1629 in the Black Forest. So, one of the most famous lines in cinema manages to embrace four historical errors within twenty-four words; not bad going.

That said, the myth of Swiss neutrality and aversion to war had been doing the rounds for decades before Wells delivered his lines; in fact, the Swiss liked a ruck as much as anyone else and when they did not have a war of their own to keep them amused they operated as one of the most prolific providers of mercenaries in Europe, with the Swiss Guard at the Vatican still going strong. Just sticking to Harry Lime's scale of 'five hundred years of peace' from the date of the film we have the Swiss-Thurgau War of 1460 by which the latter was overcome and absorbed into the 'cantonese' structure; the Swiss-Habsburg War of 1468, the Swiss-Burgundian War of 1474–1477; the Swabian War of 1499; the Swiss-Milanese and Neopolitan War 1499–1504; the Swiss War with the League of Cambrai in 1508; the War of the Holy League 1510–1515; the First and Second Kappel Wars of 1529 and 1531 … and so on and so on until the Sonderbund War of 1847. This was the last of countless civil wars, Switzerland having had more of these than any other three European nations put together. Switzerland did declare neutrality in 1815 and has done very nicely out of that stance ever since it tired of being an extended battleground between the French and the Russians. And it all depends on what one means by 'neutral' – throughout the First and Second World Wars neither Britain nor Germany respected any notion of Swiss neutrality and Switzerland itself walked a damned thin line which was hardly in keeping with the spirits of their national myth.

During the First World War, the Swiss were extremely embarrassed when Robert Grimm (1881–1958) of their National Council was caught red-handed in Russia in 1917 by British Intelligence, trying to broker a deal for peace between Russia and Germany only; needless to say, Britain was less than impressed. The standing joke about the Swiss in the Second World War was that they worked six days a week for the German war effort and spent the seventh day praying for an Allied victory so they could keep all the Nazi gold they had squirrelled away. Throughout the war 84 per cent of Switzerland's considerable munitions and weapons production went to Germany, along with bomb-sights, various other forms of instrumentation and optical aids. On the importation side of things, the Swiss bankers had no qualms about accepting trainloads of gold and riches, stolen from the murdered millions, and exchanging them for the hard cash Germany needed to keep the panzers rolling; there are many who put forward a persuasive argument that this brand of Swiss 'neutrality' prolonged the war and increased the death toll.

Nor should the Swiss be perceived as pacifists; they have always had a very firm military policy and are only too willing and able to back up their neutral status with more than a Swiss army knife. At the beginning of the war Hitler had plans to invade Switzerland but Operation Pine Tree was shelved when it dawned on the little Corporal that, although numerically inferior, the Swiss were armed to the teeth and had in place a policy of aggressive retreat to the Alpine passes that they knew like the backs of their hands, where they could tie up an invasion force for years. On top of that, every household owned a gun, with the average Swiss being more than capable of shooting assorted appendages off a flea at considerable distances. This is still the case; everyone in the country has to go through basic military training and keep ready a gun at home. Perversely, Switzerland has the lowest national rate of gun-related crime; so low in fact that no-one bothers to note down the figures anymore). Allied and German planes routinely invaded Swiss airspace so the Swiss took to shooting them down with their German-built BF-109 fighters (mistakenly referred to as the Me-109); they downed a dozen German planes in the four weeks from mid-May to mid-June alone. They shot at British and American planes as well; America in particular taking exception to such antics and 'accidentally' bombing a few Swiss towns while Britain too started to 'mistake' Swiss towns for German targets. The Swiss were rightly sceptical as to how genuine were these claims of instrument-error, this scepticism fuelled by certain Allied commanders, British and American, muttering that the Swiss could do with a good bombing as they were nothing but a bunch of German sympathizers. The average 'gnome in the street' was convinced that the bombings were 'hints' that they should re-think their economic co-operation with Germany. Things went a bit far with the bombing of Zurich itself on 4 March 1945 by six American planes claiming they thought themselves to be over Freiburg which is about 300 miles away. In what has to be the first criminal prosecution for 'friendly-fire', the lead pilot and navigator, Lts William R. Sincock and Theodore Q. Balides were put under courts martial in England with American Air Force Lt. Col James Stewart (he of Hollywood fame) presiding. Their acquittal did nothing to appease the Swiss who by now were complaining that their streets were being strafed with monotonous regularity by 'lost' Allied fighters.

As for Harry's final error, the cuckoo-clock was not a Swiss invention but a German one, first inflicted on the world by occupants of the Black Forest in the late 1620s. The Swiss stole the idea in the late nineteenth century and built it into twee chalet-style housings to sell it in the thousands to tourists coming to take up the new craze invented by the English – recreational downhill skiing. Until the English got the idea that it might be a jolly wheeze to hurl oneself off a mountain with planks of wood strapped to the feet, denizens of snow-bound countries only really used skis as a means of getting about on the flat; only the English thought of skiing as fun. Switzerland boasts numerous statues and monuments to the memory of Sir Arnold Lunn (1888-1974) to express their gratitude for his having instituted the ski-resort business and, with it, the cuckoo-clock trade. The travel-firm he started to run Alpine tours grew into the Lunn-Poly giant.

One final Swiss-myth concerns the Renaissance-style uniform of the aforementioned Papal Swiss Guard which was not designed by Leonardo da Vinci who was long-dead by the time the outfit was adopted in 1914. It was designed and championed by Jules Repond, the Guard Commander from 1910–1921.

HITLER'S SUPERIOR RACE MEETING

The 1936 Berlin Olympics has virtually taken on a life of its own with the main myth, still touted, maintaining that black American athlete, Jessie Owens (1913–1980), punctured the Nazi image of superiority and was publicly rebuffed by Hitler for his 'crime'. In fact, he was treated a whole lot better by the Nazis than he was by the American public and his own government. Although Owens is the only black American who is popularly remembered, there were in fact eighteen others who, between them, picked up four gold medals, four silver medals and two bronze. There were also thirteen Jewish medallists – winning eight gold, four silver and two bronze. These competitors in the main came from Hungary and Poland but there was one German Jewish medallist, champion fencer Helene Mayer (1910–1953), who picked up a silver in the individual foil. Rather controversially, she wore a swastika-armband and gave the Nazi salute when she mounted the podium to receive her medal. And as for Hitler's dreams of grandstanding German superiority, the host country was far and away the winner with eighty-nine medals in all.

Used to segregation in America, Owens would later recall his astonishment upon arriving in Germany where he was allowed to ride the same buses and eat in the same restaurants and stay in the same hotels as white people. Before the commencement of the Games Owens was approached by another Adolf, one of the brother-partners of the Dassler Shoe Company, who, despite being a enthusiastic party member, knew a good thing when he saw it and was prepared to incur the ire of the other Adolf to get it. Dassler persuaded Owens to compete in his track-shoes which not only made Owens the first black sportsman to find a sponsor but also did wonders for the profile of Dassler's in Germany where Owens was soon to become a hero. The rest, as they say, is history; Owens left Germany's 'children of the corn' panting in the dust, taking four gold medals in the process, but Hitler never snubbed him and the crowd roared with approval at every appearance of the black athlete and pestered him for autographs wherever he went.

It is true that on the first day Hitler only shook hands with and congratulated German victors, which prompted the Olympic Committee to tell him on the second day that the accepted form was to congratulate all or none. Hitler opted for the latter. Owens had not competed that day so the issue never arose but as he himself recorded: 'When I passed the Chancellor he arose, waved his hand at me, and I waved back at him. I think the writers showed bad taste in criticizing the man of the hour in Germany.' He also went on to point out: 'Hitler didn't snub me – it was FDR who snubbed me. The President didn't even send me a telegram.' While the white medalists were invited to the White House for a celebration, Owens and the other black medalists were left out in the cold. He did get a party at the Waldorf-Astoria Hotel but while the white guests trooped in through the front doors he had to go in through the service entrance at the back of the hotel and ride the freight elevator up to his own reception. Just how irked, if at all, Hitler was by Owens' performance is a matter of debate, maybe not at all, as two years later his long-jump victory was included in *Olympia* (1938), the propaganda film of the Games made by Leni Riefenstahl (1902–2003), Hitler's flick-chick who would later rely on concentration camp inmates for slave labour on her film sets with those en route to the camps working as extras before being sent to their fate.

Far from being welcomed home a hero, Owens was reduced to working as a janitor, petrol-pump attendant and other such jobs befitting an Olympic champion. Other times he would barnstorm the country putting on tin-pot shows which always included his party-piece, running against racehorses: 'People say that it was degrading for an Olympic champion to run against a horse but what was I supposed to do? I had four gold medals, but you can't eat four gold medals. There was no television, no big advertising, no endorsements then – not for no black man, anyway.' Actually, his famous horse-trick was a con; his assistant always made sure the starting pistol went off in the horse's ear, causing it to rear up in an almighty wobbler to give Owens the time to get halfway down the 100 yard track before the rider had got his mount into stride. After that, the horse was covering 3 yards for every one of his and, as Owens himself acknowledged, had the track been 10 yards longer he would have lost every time.

As for his German sponsor, Adolf, he and his brother had a profitable war making jackboots for their chums but, after a bitter and very public post-war argument as to which of them had been the more enthusiastic Nazi and SS officer, brother Rudolf stormed off to set up on his own as Puma. Adolf, who was acutely aware that his Christian name was the kiss of death on any international market, decided to take the pet-form of Adi, and bolt it on to the first four letters of his surname to found Adidas. Understandably, Riefenstahl's film career stalled after the war but, feisty to the end, she married her sixty-year-old boyfriend, Horst Kettner, in 2003 when she was still a sprightly 100 years old, before popping her clogs a few months later. Kettner was her main cameraman and they had been together since she was sixty and he twenty.

HOUGHMA-GANDHI

Westerners have long specialised in the form of self-delusion whereby anything or anyone exotic and remote simply has to be wonderful, wise and hold the secrets of the universe. On a mundane level, this means that ingredients in cosmetics will only work wonders if extracted from obscure plants found up the Orinoco; mediums' spirit-guides have to be ancient Egyptian princesses, never a bus-driver from Cleethorpes, and on the spiritual level, disaffected youths can only 'find themselves' in India where they learn inner-truths at the feet of gurus who invariably have a Roller parked round the corner. But when it came to Gandhi, still widely perceived as some sort of saint-in-a-bed-sheet, Europe and America fell wholecloth for the myth he so cleverly wove for himself. The broad picture is of Gandhi the great humanitarian; Gandhi the vigorous opponent of race and class divides; Gandhi the pacifist who abhorred all violence; Gandhi the fount of boundless love for his fellows who liked nothing better than sitting cross-legged in his loin-cloth at his spinning wheel, running up clothes for the poor and needy. Sarojini Naidu (1879–1949), Indian political activist and poet, once wryly observed: 'It costs the nation millions to keep Gandhi in the style of poverty to which he is now accustomed.'

The longevity of the Gandhi-myth is likely now assured, helped along greatly by the highly sanitized and biased *Gandhi* (1982), Sir Richard Attenborough's Academy Award-winning blockbuster. It has been suggested that this film was little more than a Gandhi PR exercise because the Indian Government put up one third of the production costs and kept a lunging rein on the production to ensure they had a say in the direction and 'slant' of their investment; if true, this would explain why the film marched determinedly down the Gandhi-was-a-sainted-martyr route with nary a mention of the fact that Gandhi's devotion to the repellent caste-system was such that he went on one of his tedious fasts when there was talk of removing some of the restriction on the Untouchables to alleviate their misery and oppression. When the film covered Gandhi's time in South Africa (1893–1914), this was presented as his struggle to improve the lot of the oppressed black majority which is far wide of the truth. Gandhi hated the 'Kaffirs' as he insisted on calling them; his objection was to high-caste Indians being lumped together with the 'black savages'. There was no mention of his considering Hitler to be not such a bad chap and suggesting that the Jews would be better off offering themselves up to the slaughter than resisting their eradication and doubtless it was thought too tricky to show how Gandhi liked to sleep naked with pre-teen girls, in pairs and also naked, selected for their 'pertness' to 'stiffen his resolve' for celibacy. Yeah; right. Very much a case of 'damn, failed again, must try harder tomorrow night'.

Mohandas Karamchand Gandhi (1869–1948), his surname meaning 'green-grocer', was raised in Gujarat and, at the age of thirteen, was married off to an older woman; the fourteen-year-old Kasturba Makhanji (1869–1944). He was a father by the age of fifteen and, throughout his entire life, seems to have been highly active in the 'houghmagany' department, as the Scots call it, while relegating his wife to a life of humiliation and, some say, routine domestic violence. (There were countless rumours and allegations but, since Kasturba herself never uttered a word, there can be no proof). Naturally, like all good hypocrites, while he was worshipping anything in a sari, he was at the same time commanding everyone else, married couples especially, to shun carnal pleasures for anything other than procreation; married couples should only have sex, he said, for as many times as it took to ensure pregnancy and to then abstain until they wanted another child. Before he started taking young girls to his 'test-bed', Gandhi had several affairs with women, Indian, European, married and single; in South Africa he enjoyed a dalliance with Millie Polak, wife of Henry Polak. They were both activists, but he failed to control her to his exacting standards, she openly ridiculing the risible dietary strictures he tried to impose on her and his insistence on his co-workers observance of chastity. Tiring of the challenge, he broke off their affair, or she did, with him next turning to Maud Polak, Henry's more compliant sister. Next was Esther Faering, a young and impressionable Danish missionary, and finally Saral Devi who Gandhi called his 'spiritual wife', much to the chagrin of Kasturba. There was also an affair with Madeleine Slade, daughter of a British Navy Officer stationed in Bombay, who he called Mirabehn.

It seems it was some time in 1938 that Gandhi decided to start nightly tests of his ability to resist the sexual allure of pre-teen girls and assorted young women; all had to sleep naked and, just to make doubly sure of his resolve, Gandhi would often take them to bed in pairs. Some as young as twelve, several girls later acknowledged that they did often 'render service' to Gandhi but refused to elaborate further. There was Sushila Nayar who always bathed with Gandhi before settling down in his bed, Gandhi later claiming that he 'kept his eyes tight shut' in the bath. There was Lilavati Asar, Sharada Parnerkar, Amtul Salaam, Prabhavati Narayan and a host of others but his favourite was his brother's granddaughter, Manu, this causing a real scandal. Equally eyebrow-arching was his other incestuous bedding of another young and married niece, Abha, who was perhaps fourteen. When her husband, Kanu, found out that she had been roped into goosey-Gandhi's sexual charades he was less than pleased and, despite his youth, confronted the great man to give him a piece of his mind. Gandhi 'explained' that, apart from trying to test his inner demons, he liked the warmth of another bod or two in the sack to fend off the night chills. Kanu said that he quite understood and, to save his wife any further such duty, he and a friend would be her stand-ins; it seems Gandhi was not sufficiently appreciative of the offer as to ever call for Kanu at bedtime. And the young girls' reward for having 'rendered service' was to have Gandhi give them an enema in the morning; Gandhi's defenders can waffle on all they like about great men having great eccentricities that defy the understanding of hoi polloi but, not to put too fine a point on it, Gandhi was a dirty old man who today would run the risk of being convicted as a paedophile.

As for Gandhi the pacifist, why was he never awarded the Nobel Peace Prize? Perhaps because he was not a pacifist but so fond of war that he volunteered for three of them and constantly made statements supporting bloodshed and violence. Sergeant-Major Gandhi of the British Army served in both the Boer War (1899–1902) and the Zulu War of 1906 and was only prevented from signing up for the First World War by a bout of pleurisy. After his self-reinvention as the simian-like aesthete – some called him Bandy-Gandhi behind his back, while Sarojini Naidu called him Mickey Mouse to his face – Gandhi tried to gloss over his war career with the British, claiming for example that in the Zulu War he only ran stretcher-bearer teams to care for wounded Zulu – What? British Army stretcher-bearers strictly for the enemy? Well, according to his own dairy recording events of July 1906: 'At about 12 o'clock we finished the day's journey, with no Kaffirs to fight'. (That is the term Gandhi always used of the black South Africans, despite it being the Afrikaners' equivalent of 'niggers', but we shall get to the reality of his 'crusade' in that neck of the woods later). Having been rejected as unfit for military service in 1914, Gandhi returned to India to begin a massive recruiting drive to raise men to fight in the British Army under the slogan 'Twenty recruits from every village'; as one can see from the man's history, Gandhi wasn't against violence per se, only against its use when it was not the best route to the objective: 'I do believe that where there is a choice only between cowardice and violence I would advise violence'. And, when the Nawab of Maler Kotla announced that local violence would be quelled by the shooting of ten Muslims for every Hindu killed in the prevailing riots, Gandhi gave this draconian response his public blessing. He frequently acknowledged that 'war may have to be resorted to as a necessary evil' and publicly sang the praises of Subbas Chandra Bose who raised over a million Indian men to fight first for Hitler and then throw their lot in with the Japanese. In fact, it was during the Second World War that Gandhi's pronouncements began to get increasingly 'eccentric':

> I do not consider Hitler to be as bad as he is depicted. He is showing an ability that is amazing and seems to be gaining his victories without much bloodshed'.

– So, limited bloodshed is OK?

> I appeal for cessation of hostilities ... because war is bad in essence. You want to kill Nazism. Your soldiers are doing the same work of destruction as the Germans. The only difference is that perhaps yours are not as thorough as the Germans ... I venture to present you with a nobler and a braver way, worthy of the bravest soldiers. I want you to fight Nazism without arms or ... with non-violent arms. I would like you to lay down the arms you have as being useless for saving you or humanity. You will invite Herr Hitler and Signor Mussolini to take what they want of the countries you call your possessions. Let them take possession of your beautiful island, with your many beautiful buildings. You will give all these but neither your souls, nor your minds. If these gentlemen choose to occupy your homes, you will vacate them. If they do not give you free passage out, you will allow yourself, man, woman and child, to be slaughtered, but you will refuse to owe allegiance to them ... I am telling His Excellency the Viceroy that my services are at the disposal of His Majesty's Government, should they consider them of any practical use in advancing the object of my appeal.

Nor does Israel have much time for Gandhi after his pre-war announcement that: 'The cry for a national home for the Jews does not make much appeal to me... It is wrong and in-human to impose the Jews on the Arabs.' Also, while writing to Hitler, addressing him as 'friend', he later opined: 'But the Jews should have offered themselves to the butcher's knife; they should have thrown themselves into the sea from cliffs.' Equally, there is considerable groundswell opposition to any statues being erected to Gandhi in South Africa where his struggle with the rules of apartheid was not what most imagine it to have been. Gandhi was there to extend and redefine apartheid, not to crush it.

Gandhi, it must be remembered, was a firm believer in the caste system with all its draconian rules and strictures that made apartheid look positively benign; it was not the separation of white and non-white that offended him but the fact that high-caste Hindus were lumped together with 'savage Kaffirs' and had to suffer the indignity of queuing up and travelling with them instead of having their own doors, buses and what-have-you; Gandhi did not want the removal of apartheid; he wanted it refined and extended. Best leave it to the words of the Mahatma himself to illustrate his regard for the South African black population. The following are all taken from *The Collected Works of Mahatma Gandhi*.

A general belief seems to prevail in the Colony that the Indians are little better, if at all, than the savages or the natives of Africa. Even the children are taught to believe in that manner, with the result that the Indian is being dragged down to the position of the raw Kaffir.

– December 1894.

Ours is one continual struggle against a degradation sought to be inflicted upon us by the Europeans, who desire to degrade us to the level of the raw Kaffir whose occupation is hunting and whose sole ambition is to collect a certain number of cattle to buy a wife with and, then, pass his life in indolence and nakedness.

–Vol. 1: pp.409–410.

Of course, under my suggestion, the Town Council must withdraw the Kaffirs from the location. About this mixing of the Kaffirs with the Indians, I must confess I feel most strongly, I think it is very unfair to the Indian population and it is an unfair tax on the proverbial patience of my countrymen.

–Vol. III: p.429.

It is a gross injustice to seek to place the Indian in the same class as the Kaffirs.

–Vol. V: p.226.

Are we supposed to be thieves or free-booters that even a Kaffir policeman can accost and detain us wherever we happen to be going?

–Vol. VII, p. 395.

The British rulers take us so low and ignorant that they assume that, like the Kaffir who can be pleased with toys and pins, we can also be fobbed off with trinkets.

−Vol.VIII: p.167.

Kaffirs as a rule are uncivilised − their convicts even more so. They are troublesome, very dirty and live like animals. Each ward contains nearly 50 to 60 of them. They often start rows and fight amongst themselves, The reader can easily imagine the plight of the poor Indian thrown into such company.

−Vol.VIII: p.199.

Some Indians sink to contact with Kaffir women; I think such contacts are fraught with grave danger. Indians would do well to avoid them altogether.

−Vol. X: p.414.

There are endless examples of Gandhi's racist attitude towards black South Africans which fitted perfectly with his unwavering support of the caste system under which your status at birth dictated your entire life with the vast majority of Indians relegated to a life of isolation from certain temples, restaurants − indeed any public place where their 'unclean' presences would require all high-caste Indians to run screaming for protracted ritual cleansing after stoning the interloper to death for his transgression. If you were born into the level of the lowest of the low, the Untouchables, then that is where you must stay − only slightly higher were the Pariahs and we all know what their name fell to. While Gandhites love to remember their mentor as the champion of the Untouchables, no Eliot Ness he. The true champion of the Untouchables, and the man annually revered in India for having been such, was Dr B.R. Ambedkar (1891–1956). Ambedkar was also one of the first to see through the Gandhi-act, cautioning others not to fall for it as Gandhi was not a saint but a very clever politician. When Ambedkar started a move to secure the rights of the Untouchables to have the right to vote for their own representatives Gandhi went on hunger-strike to the death until Ambedkar pulled the plug on the idea. When recovered, Gandhi claimed his objections to the scheme were: 'Give the Untouchables separate electorates and you only perpetuate their status for all time.' All but his most ardent supporters saw this as a phoney veneer to the real reason which was

Gandhi's fear that the 60 million Untouchables would, with their own electorate, throw in their lot with the 100 million or so Muslims and, together, challenge the virtual dictatorship of 180 million strong Hindu lobby.

Gandhi's love of the oppressive caste system can be seen in his own words in a series of articles, written throughout 1921 by him for a journal called *Nava-Jivan*, which show his ease with the notion of most being hog-tied to drudgery for life, with no escape; like any structured elitism, it doubtless can be seen as noble and righteous when, as Gandhi did, one views it from near the top.

Why should my son not be happy to be a scavenger if I am one?

I believe that if Hindu Society has been able to stand it is because it is founded on the Caste system.

I do not believe that inter-dining and inter-marriage are necessary to national unity.

Among the Vaishnavas many women are so orthodox that they will not eat with (certain) members of the family nor will they drinks from a common water pot. Yet, have they no love? The Caste system can not be said to be bad because it does not allow inter-dining or inter-marriage between different Castes.

To destroy the Caste system and adopt a Western European social system means that Hindus must give up the principle of hereditary occupation which is the soul of the Caste system. I have no use for a Brahmin [top-Caste] if I can not call him a Brahmin for life. It will be chaos if every day a Brahmin is to be changed into a Shudra [a class of labourer] and a Shudra is to be changed into a Brahmin.

Gandhi's long-suffering wife died in 1944 because, according to many, he refused to allow doctors to give her the 'alien' treatment of a course of penicillin injections, such invasion of the body being against his Hindu tenants: 'If God will it, He will pull her through.' Not long after, he himself was struck by malaria but saw his way to taking a life-saving course of quinine and, even later, saw no problem with British doctors operating on him when struck with appendicitis. On 30 January 1948 Gandhi was taking his customary stroll when gunned down by Hindu Nationalist, Nathuram Godse (1910–1949) who was executed the next year. The popular perception of this shooting is that it was one lunatic act that came out of the blue to eliminate a universally loved character, whereas there had been a series of attempts on Gandhi's life stretching back to 1934, with Godse being involved in five of these abortive attempts.

HOW THE WEST WAS SPUN

Most nations have a careful hand in the crafting of their own history and the USA is no exception. When it came time to build the enduring image of the cowboy and settler of the Wild and Woolly West, both were painted as men who could determine their own destiny and the course of history with a gun and a willingness to use it. Unfortunately there are still many Americans who, believing this to be true, seek infamy in the shadows of that myth with countless students and, for some strange reason, postal-workers (hence 'going postal', for violent and irrational behaviour) routinely paying the ultimate price in college and work-place slaughters. The cowboy was the embodiment of taciturn, yet fundamental goodness; the gunslinger a rough-diamond samurai, the doughty settlers, pushing ever Westward, did so in constant peril of slaughter by hostile Indians who screamed 'Whiteman speak with forked tongue' as they rode round encircled wagon-trains until they got dizzy or shot. Obviously it was little like that; first the cowboy.

For a start, no-one went around calling anyone 'cowboy' as the term was a serious insult, first coined in the War of Independence (1755–1783), when it denoted Loyalist assassins who used cowbells to entice Patriot farmers into the shrubbery to look for what they presumed was lost stock. After the war it only applied to rustlers who mounted raids across the Mexican border so, those content with the standard number of holes in their bodies opted for 'wrangler' or 'drover'. The average 'cowboy' was aged about sixteen and likely dead by his mid-twenties, not from any dramatic shoot-out but from a riding accident or pneumonia. They did not parade around bristling with side-arms as few could afford them; a 'modern' Colt revolver would be something like nine month's wages to such men who lived and died on a dollar a day. The heyday of the cowboy lasted a mere twenty years and at least a quarter of them were African American and another quarter of their number made up of Hispanics, yet it is exclusively the white man riding tall in the saddle that modern America chooses to remember.

As the railways reached new towns, such as Abilene and Dodge City, the cattle drives increased to fill those stockyards but progress, like old age, cometh not upon its own and the advent of these rail-heads also caused a social upheaval in such towns, as the property up-wind of the stockyards rocketed in price leaving the poorer members of the community living 'on the wrong side of the tracks'. But these towns were not the wide-open, shoot-'em-up places of modern imagination; you had more chance of being gunned down in Victorian London than in Dodge or Tombstone and there were many more guns per capita in the American East than in the West. Towns subjected to the double-edged bounty of the burgeoning beef-trade made sure they hired highly competent thugs and killers, such as Wyatt Earp and his motley crew, to enforce restrictions on the carrying of firearms within the city limits; between 1870 and 1885, which was about the end of the day of the cowboy, there were a scant forty-five killings in total racked up by Abilene, Ellsworth, Wichita, Dodge and Caldwell put together. Abilene, widely acknowledged as the wildest of all those cow-towns, recorded that from 1868 to 1870 nothing happened at all. And what of the gunslinger; that lone-wolf, prowling the West, racking up an increasing number of notches on his shooting-iron? Hardly.

If you google 'a complete list of old West gunfights' you will be led to a grand total of … twenty-four, including the over-vaunted gunfight at the OK Corral, which did not take place at said location. That spat between two groups of criminals, one led by Wyatt Earp and the other by Ike Clanton, actually took place on vacant land beside Fly's Boarding House in Tombstone on 26 October 1881; only thirty shots were fired in as many seconds and only three died; a modern turf-war resulting in three deaths would not even make it to the front page. The truth is that no-one ever faced off in a dusty street at noon because most gunfights were impromptu and more often as not drunken arguments that had got out of hand. The vast majority of deaths in such circumstances resulted, not from some lightening-fast draw but from concealed weapons; derringers held up the sleeve or in the boot. The revolvers of the day weighed between 4 and 5 lb; just see how long you can hold two bags of sugar out at arm's length without shaking. It must also be remembered that it was not until the turn of the twentieth century that smokeless ammunition was available so in the raddled huts that passed for saloons in the West no-one would have been able to see a thing after the first couple of shots. With the weapons and ammunition of the day, none of the so-called gunslingers or sharp-shooters could hit a barn door beyond 20 yards; Frank James, reckoned to be a far better shot than his deranged brother, Jesse, was lauded for being able to place twenty shots in a 10 inch circle at 20 yards; that of course was with him taking his own sweet time about it; shooting at moving targets or someone who was shooting back would have been another matter altogether. Those determined to see old age tended to carry a shotgun when there was business to attend to.

Few of the famous names lived up to their modern image; Billy the Kid was a grubby little back-shooting psycho who perhaps killed three or four people rather than the twenty-odd he claimed; Earp was far more criminal than anyone he ever arrested and the over-feted Wild Bill Hickok was not only a rather nasty piece of work but a lousy shot due to early-onset glaucoma. While Marshall of Abilene in 1871 he got drunk and started beating up a saloon girl called Jessie Hazel and likely would have killed her had not a chap called Phil Coe, owner of another saloon, intervened to give Hickok a dose of his own medicine. A few days later, Hickok strolled casually up to Coe in the street, whipped out two derringers and shot him in the chest; his eyesight by now already failing fast, he did not recognize his own deputy, Mike Williams, approaching to see what all the fuss was about, and, just to round the day off, shot him in the head – twice. The next year, Hickok was out buffalo-hunting with his sidekick, Newt Moreland, and gunned down three unarmed Sioux, just for approaching his camp and asking for some coffee.

All the guff about notches in the butts of frontier Colts stems from a joke played by Bat Masterson on a gun collector in New York. Masterson was one of the longest-lived and more successful of the Western characters, dying in 1921 at his desk in the offices of the *New York Daily Telegraph* where, bizarrely, he ended up as Sports Editor. Constantly pestered by a gun collector for one of his old frontier pieces, Masterson bought an old Colt from a pawn-shop, cut twenty-odd notches into the butt and sold it on for an indecent profit. The whole snake-eyed gunfighter myth was dreamed up by Ned Buntline who promoted people like Hickok and that other old fraud, Buffalo Bill Cody, in cheap novels that sold so well that they made him one of the wealthiest writers in nineteenth-century

America. It was Buntline who invented everything from the myth of the fast-draw, shooting from the hip and the fanning of revolvers for rapid firing which, although physically possible reduced the limited accuracy of such weapons to zero.

And what of the intrepid settler, huddled in their circled wagons, fighting off the Plains Indians so intent on their destruction? Sure, there was conflict between the tribes and those crossing their lands but the Indians killed were pitifully few compared to the predations on such convoys meted out by other whites. Most wagon trains crossed the plains without incident as the Indians quickly realized it was best to steer clear of these mobile disease-traps. The major cause of death on the wagon trains was not being visited by hostile Indians but by typhus, cholera, drowning and accidental shootings/arguments among the travellers themselves. The most infamous attack by Indians on any wagon train remains the Salt Creek Canyon 'Massacre' in which four white travellers died and the Warren Train 'Massacre' of 1871 in which seven of the twelve wagon drivers were killed while hauling supplies to US Army forts. Satanta, the Kiowa warrior who led that attack, obviously considered it a legitimate military target and those who scream 'massacre' neglect to mention that, just hours before, he had allowed an army ambulance train to pass unmolested. Michael L. Tate PhD, Professor of History and Native American Studies at the University of Nebraska, made quite a study of the interaction between the Indians and the wagon trains and his *Indians and Emigrants* (2006) is most revealing; between 1840 and 1860 over half a million people passed through the Indian territories in wagon trains with a scant 362 white deaths attributed to hostile action by Indians who either shunned the travellers or interacted in the main on a friendly basis, operating as guides or trade-intermediaries. No, the biggest and most vicious slaughter inflicted on any wagon train was the Mountain Meadows Massacre of 1857 in which Mormons murdered, raped and robbed about 128 men women and children from Arkansas as their Francher-Baker wagon train passed through Utah in the September of 1857.

It seems that the Mormons of Utah were not as tolerant as the 'savages' when it came to permitting the peaceful passage of strangers through 'their' land and when news of the imminent arrival of the Fancher-Baker train was received at the Mormon stronghold of Cedar City, the decision was taken by local Church leaders not to allow any reprovisioning, despite this being the last place en route to California for the purchase of food and other supplies. Due to their rather arrogant stance of virtual independence from the rest of the United States, the Mormons of Utah were expecting a visit from the US Army, and Church Leader Brigham Young, had ordered the conservation of all supplies in case of siege. Furthermore, the inbound wagon train was accompanied by a herd of over 800 head of cattle on which the local Mormons had their collective beady eye!

When wagon master Alexander Fancher realised that no-one in Cedar City was going to sell him anything, he ordered all in his charge to make ready to move out and do so peacefully. Still salivating over that herd, the pious Mormons decided to organise a raiding party to take off after the train and kill anyone who opposed them. Unwilling to carry their own can, they planned to make it look like the work of the local and largely peaceful Paiute Indians by dressing up like a Paiute war-party. This was most likely the idea of John D. Lee who, although vehemently opposed to any Federal interference in Mormon affairs, happily accepted wages from that same Federal government which paid him to operate as a constable and the local Indian agent. The plan to raid the wagon train was first mooted amongst the Cedar City Elders on 6 September and the few who objected to the raid had their consciences assuaged by the suggestion that a messenger be sent to Brigham Young, who was 250 miles away in Salt Lake City, asking for permission to proceed.

Not bothering to wait for any reply, the raiding party set out the next day to embark on what would turn into a five-day siege so any later claims that this was a moment of madness can be discounted. It is argued whether there were any real Indians in the party or just some of the Mormons in fancy-dress so the whole sorry affair could be blamed on the Paiutes; it was most likely the latter. Either way, by the time they caught up with the wagon train any thought of letting anyone live to tell the tale had long since evaporated; they intended to murder the lot. The initial attack brought down a few of the travellers but the rest soon circled the wagons and took up positions against what they thought to be an Indian attack. At this point the Mormons could have driven off the herd if that is all they wanted but this was obviously not enough for them. Across the next few days the Mormons kept their quarry pinned down in the heat, knowing they must be getting short of water, and then came the end-game of the plan. On 11 September, Lee himself approached the besieged train under cover of a white flag and managed to convince the travellers that a deal had been struck with the 'Indians', on the travellers' behalf, and that their lives would be spared if they put down their guns, abandoned all their possessions and livestock and walked out under Mormon protection. Seeing little alternative, the travellers agreed and, in accordance with Mormon instruction, the wounded left first in one wagon with the rest leaving on foot, first the women and children and last the men and boys. On the prearranged signal, each Mormon escorting the males shot the man or boy nearest to him, this gunfire being the signal for the other good Mormons to get stuck into the wounded and the women and children. The only ones not killed were eighteen children so small that Lee and his raiders deemed them too young to hold any recollection of the events. About that they were wrong.

Stripping all the bodies of anything worthwhile before leaving the dead to the tender mercies of the local wildlife, the Mormons rounded up the herd and wagons and took the whole kit and caboodle back to Cedar City for an auction. By this time, it is said by some, a letter had arrived from Young telling the loonies to leave the travellers alone but many suspect this to have been a forgery trying to ring-fence his reputation from the whole sordid affair. Either way, the surviving children were renamed and farmed out to Mormon families who could be trusted to keep their mouths shut while the conspiracy to blame the Indians began in earnest. Even after the full horror of the events became known up in Salt Lake City, Young dithered and hoped that it would all blow over with the Paiutes taking the rap; only when the truth leaked out did Young turn on his own; in 1859 he quietly 'retired' President Isaac Haight and other Cedar City Leaders with blood on their hands, but he did not excommunicate Haight and Dee until the whole sorry affair became a national scandal in 1870.

By this time several Paiutes had been murdered, most by 'avenging' Mormons trying to hide their guilt behind feigned righteous indignation, but in 1874 a Grand Jury put out warrants for the nine main instigators of the massacre. All but one of the re-housed survivors were returned to family back in Arkansas and, contrary to what Dee and his fellow murderers thought, they could still vividly recall members of that Mormon city strutting about in their parents' clothes and wearing their jewellery. Some of the nine went on the run with only Lee being executed by firing squad on 23 March 1877 on the site of the massacre in Mountain

Meadows. Always maintaining that he was 'only obeying orders' from the top of the chain, his last words recorded were: 'I do not believe everything that is now being taught and practised by Brigham Young. I do not care who hears it. It is my last word... I have been sacrificed in a cowardly, dastardly manner.' He left behind nineteen wives and sixty-seven children and, in the April of 1961, the Mormon Church, for reasons best known to itself, overturned his excommunication and posthumously reinstated Lee's membership.

Finally, we come to those 'pesky' Redskins. Much of what we 'know' about the culture and lifestyle of the Amerindian comes from the sliver screen but even the tribal 'names' we recognise from Westerns are nothing but inter-tribal insults and not the proper names of the peoples concerned. 'Apache' and 'Comanche' both mean the enemy; 'Eskimo' was the Cree nickname for the Inuit and means raw-meat eaters and the Huron were properly the Wendat. This last tribe got their nickname from their French allies who built on 'hure', the French for bristle-head, as it was this tribe and not the imaginary Mohican who wore their hair in the central plume so mimicked by punks today. Mohicans only existed in the Hawkeye novels of James Fennimore Cooper who seems to have confused the name of the Mohiingans. All films of Hawkeye and *Last of the Mohicans* (1992) feature, by definition, only a couple of Mohicans with long hair but whole brigades of Hurons with their plumes, hence the punk fashionistas gripping the wrong end of the stick. So successful were the Cooper novels that the Mohiingans got lumbered with 'Mohican' and are still referred to as such.

Indians only rode around and encircled wagons in Wild West Show arenas, the shape of which gave them no other option. Early cinema adopted the same device, and forgetting the famous cartoon of an Indian gazing at the mushroom-cloud from a nuclear test with the caption 'I wish I'd said that', no tribe communicated with smoke-signals. Fire was used to confirm or countermand some previously made verbal agreement – black smoke for 'Yes'; white smoke for 'No', or whatever – but no-one could use a blanket over a fire to send up coded messages for others to read. Scalping was a pleasantry introduced to the New World by the white settler; 'powwow' was actually the title of the man officiating at inter-tribal talks, not the negotiations themselves and tomahawks were never thrown in battle like some sort of war-axe. Totem poles were not items of idolatry, but commemorative affairs – the usual order of importance ran from the bottom up so that people standing in front of the thing could easily see what or who the pole was commemorating, thus making a nonsense of expressions such as 'low man on the totem pole'. 'Paleface', 'Happy Hunting Ground, 'Great White Father', 'I have spoken' and 'Whiteman speak with forked tongue' all came from the pen of Cooper and his kind. In addition, no Indian language ever included the greeting of 'How!'

Much as the wolf has dual and juxtaposed reputations – on one hand the slavering killer of men (there has in fact never been a single authenticated account of wolf-attack on man) – and on the other the nurturing image of wolves rearing abandoned children, so it is with the Amerindian. On the one hand we have the alcohol-intolerant, blood-crazed scalping rapist and, on the other, the gentle ecologist with simple but dignified philosophy that shames the fork-tongued whiteman who, cocooned in his technology, is blind to the damage he inflicts on Mother Earth.

The Indians were neither more nor less brutal than their white invaders; they just had different killing tools. The Indian most certainly did chop up his enemies with an axe, not because that turned him on but because cutting and stabbing weapons were all he had; the white men had guns which allowed cleaner kills but in much greater numbers and from much greater distance than could be achieved with any tomahawk or spear. The white settlers inflicted more slaughter on the Indians than was visited in return, not because they were evil but just because they could. Had the technological boot been on the other foot there would have been reservations all over England, filled with displaced lords and ladies giving dignified speeches lamenting the passing of the times as they rode free across the land, hunting the fox and baiting the badger, or whatever. The Amerindian and the white were the same beast; they just had different toys. As for the Indian being some spiritual and caring custodian of the land, taking only what was needed, this is just a load of twentieth-century romanticism.

Many is the canvas showing the intrepid Indian hunting buffalo from horseback with a bow and arrow, picking off one or two animals of which he would respectfully use every last part. In reality, the Indian was every bit as profligate and wasteful as modern society. A typical buffalo hunt more usually involved the setting of a prairie fire to stampede an entire herd over a cliff, known as a buffalo-jump, so the hunters could clamber down and cut out the tongues only for a feast; the rest, sometimes hundreds of carcasses, would be left to rot. Along many of their rivers the tribes hunted the beaver to extinction as they paid no heed to the animal's breeding times, simply taking as many as they could whenever they felt like it. The Indian had not the slightest notion of conservation, when they depleted an area they moved on to another and started all over again. True, the beaver's lot was not much improved by the advent of European trappers but, like the aforementioned imbalance in killing-capability, these men had far more sophisticated traps and a far larger market-demand to satisfy back home. Anyone interested in reading further into just how well the Indians treated their own lands should grab a copy of *The Ecological Indian: Myth and History* (2000) by Shepard Krech III PhD, this being but one of several books he has written about the lifestyles and realities of the Amerindians.

Most of the rubbish enjoyed today concerning the noble and philosophical Amerindian is based on two frauds, that of Grey Owl and the famous speech *not* made by Chief Seattle in 1854. The former, a celebrity conservationalist of the 1920s and '30s who made a fortune touring Europe in buckskins and feather headdresses, turned out to be a bigamous conman called Archie Belaney (1888–1938), who actually came from Hastings; his exposure set back the conservationist movement by decades. As for Chief Seattle's speech, so dear to the hearts of the knit-your-own-muesli brigade, he never said anything about conservation. In fact, as one of the last speakers of Lushootseed, a veritable nightmare of a language, no-one knows what on earth he said in 1854 as none present understood a word. All that is known for sure is that Seattle gave a speech in the city bearing his name in 1854 after a meeting had been called by its governor, Isaac Ingalls Stevens, to discuss the selling of Indian lands to white people. At some point, Seattle did rise to speak, causing some offence to the white contingent and no little amusement to the Indian, when he rested his arm atop the head of the seated and diminutive governor as if he were some kind of leaning-post. But he spoke in his native tongue which was simultaneously translated into Chinook, this being of no use whatsoever to those assembled; even members of other tribes present sat there shrugging and raising their eyebrows. Also present was Dr Henry A. Smith who in 1887 – thirty-three years later – presented to the *Seattle Sunday Star* what he claimed to be an English translation he had jotted down at the time. Smith's purported record of the speech bears no resemblance to the version touted today as there was not one jot of eco-babble, merely an expansive thank you to the government for the generosity of the price offered for the land. Far from being some sort of proto-eco-warrior opposed to the influx of the white population and their evil ways, Seattle was far and away the most pro-white of all the chiefs; he had long recognized the inevitability of the white influx and was very much a go-with-the-flow sort of chap.

'Additions' to the speech began in 1929 when Clarence B. Bagley reproduced Smith's version, with embellishments, prompting one John M. Rich to publish an even more flowery version in 1931 as *Chief Seattle's Unanswered Challenge*. In the 1960s, William Arrowsmith, an American classicist involved in the burgeoning environmentalist movement, added sufficient flourish to preceding forgeries as to inspire screenwriter Ted Perry to pen his own version as the voiceover to the film *Home* (1972), a mawkish tree-hugger produced by The Southern Baptist Radio and Television Commission. Although the film sank without a trace, Perry's invention seized the moment and before you could say 'Save the Whale!' it had swept America, reproduced in booklet form, wall-hangings and god-awful 'criminal' records of cigar-store-type Indian voices intoning the mantra of the Perry version over a background of drumbeat and howling Indian dirges. Although sections have been edited out to prevent readers slipping into a coma, most will doubtless recognise this:

How can you buy or sell the sky, the warmth of the land? The idea is strange to us. If we do not own the freshness of the air and the sparkle of the water, how can you buy them? Every part of the Earth is sacred to my people. Every shining pine needle, every sandy shore, every mist in the dark woods, every clear and humming insect is holy in the memory and experience of my people.

So, when the Great Chief in Washington sends word that he wishes to buy our land, he asks much of us. The Great White Chief sends word he will reserve us a place so that we can live comfortably to ourselves. He will be our father and we will be his children. So we will consider your offer to buy land. But it will not be easy. For this land is sacred to us.

This shining water that moves in streams and rivers is not just water but the blood of our ancestors. If we sell you land, you must remember that it is sacred blood of our ancestors. If we sell you land, you must remember that it is sacred, and you must teach your children that it is sacred and that each ghostly reflection in the clear water of the lakes tells of events in the life of my people. The water's murmur is the voice of my father's father.

I am a savage and do not understand any other way. I have seen a thousand rotting buffaloes on the prairie, [actually, Seattle never saw a buffalo in his entire life] left by the white man who shot them from a passing train. I am a savage and do not understand how the smoking iron horse can be made more important than the buffalo that we kill only to stay alive.

What is man without the beasts? If all the beasts were gone, man would die from a great loneliness of the spirit. For whatever happens to the beasts, soon happens to man. All things are connected.

You must teach your children that the ground beneath their feet is the ashes of our grandfathers. So that they will respect the land, tell your children that the Earth is rich with the lives of our kin. Teach your children what we have taught our children that the Earth is our mother. Whatever befalls the Earth befalls the sons of the Earth. If men spit upon the ground, they spit upon themselves.

This we know – the Earth does not belong to man - man belongs to the Earth.

All things are connected. Whatever befalls the Earth - befalls the sons of the Earth. Man did not weave the web of life - he is merely a strand in it. Whatever he does to the web, he does to himself.

Still today, few realize that this Perry version is a pack of lies underpinning a veritable industry; in 1991 a children's book, *Brother Eagle, Sister Sky: A Message from Chief Seattle* sold 280,000 copies in the first six months of its release and born-again conservationist, Al Gore, never tires of quoting great chunks of the Perry version. The Italians have a saying: '*se non e vero, e molto ben trovato*', if it is not true, it is very well invented, and you have to admit that the Perry version is bloody *ben torvato*; it just sounds spot on for the sort of thing a noble savage *ought* to have said.

JAMMIN' WITH THE BAND ABOARD THE UNTHINKABLE

Given the size and importance of RMS *Titanic* it was perhaps inevitable that so many myths would weave around her sinking: the owners had never boasted of her being 'unsinkable'; the iceberg ripped her open like an old tin can and she was racing through the ice-field at ridiculous speed in an attempt to claim the coveted Blue Ribbon for the fastest Atlantic crossing. In addition, the third class passengers were locked behind barred gates below to give the first- and second-class passengers first dibs on the lifeboats and, of course, the band played on, breaking into a sombre rendition of 'Nearer My God to Thee' as the ship slipped beneath the waves with the captain standing stoically on the bridge. Not only is all of this false but the iceberg was only the last of many nails in the ship's coffin, most of which were in place long before she sailed on her disastrous maiden voyage.

It was only after the sinking that the White Star Line became so successively active in their campaign to burke the fact that they had, on numerous occasions, pronounced both *Titanic* and her older sister, *Olympic*, to be unsinkable. In reality their campaign of false security had begun in September 1910 with the pre-launch publicity for both ships which read 'in as far as it is possible to do so, these two wonderful vessels are designed to be unsinkable'. By the time *Olympic* was afloat, this campaign had abandoned any qualifiers such as 'designed to be' or 'practically' and progressed to clear and promote unequivocal statements that both ships were 'unsinkable'. Captain Edward Smith, who managed to crash *Olympic* into a British warship and be on hand for the sinking of *Titanic*, never shut up about how it was physically impossible for either ship to sink. Even after it was common knowledge that *Titanic* had hit an iceberg, Phillip Franklin, Vice-President of International Mercantile Marine, a conglomerate that owned White Star and thus *Titanic*, was interviewed in the early hours of 15 April 1912 and, still unaware that by this time *Titanic* had actually sunk, told reporters:

We are absolutely satisfied that even if she was in collision with an iceberg, she is in no danger. With her numerous water-tight compartments she is absolutely unsinkable, and it makes no difference what she hits. The report should not cause any serious anxiety. In any event, the ship is unsinkable, and there is absolutely no danger to passengers. We cannot state too strongly our belief that the ship is unsinkable and the passengers perfectly safe. The ship is reported to have gone down several feet by the head. This may be due from water filling forward compartments; the ship may go down many feet and still keep afloat for an indefinite period.

There are countless other examples of presumably sane men pronouncing that under no circumstances could 70,000 tons of steel sink in water and those interested in reading further should google 'How the Titanic became unsinkable' and then take the first option.

The whole 'unsinkable' thing rested on the advanced technology built into the two ships and the watertight compartments which could be sealed off by the flick of a switch on the bridge. Unfortunately for all who died on *Titanic* the vaunt of 'latest technology' was a base lie and the so-called watertight compartments did not close all the way up – a bit like making blackout curtains that do not close to meet in the middle. To be truly watertight the compartment, when closed, would have to form a six-sided box but those of the *Titanic* were only five-sided; when one filled up, as was proved on the night in question, the intruding water simply overflowed from one compartment to the next, and so on. To scrimp on the construction costs, the makers had baulked at using the best possible steel for the plating and the rivets and opted for old and extremely 'conservative' technology throughout; far from being ahead of their time, *Olympic* and *Titanic* were years out of date by the time they were launched. *Titanic*, most crucially as things turned out, only had a single and inadequately small rudder; out of the water, her stern presented the profile and configuration of an eighteenth-century sea-going yacht; bigger perhaps but no different. There were numerous other liners in commission which had one large rudder for each of their three or four propellers and thus were capable of vastly superior manoeuvrability than that endured by *Titanic*.

Actually, there was one bit of up-to-date technology built into *Titanic*, the new-fangled helical gearing system on her steering. This had been developed by a bright young engineer called André Citroën (1878–1935) who realised that chevron-shaped gear-teeth would mesh more efficiently from various angles than the old-fashioned straight-cut teeth. Originally from Holland, the family had descended from a grandfather who sold lemons but decided that Citroën sounded a bit more up-market than Citron when they moved to France. Anyway, the Citroën dynasty moved on from components to car-manufacture but kept the symbol of their engineering origins, two interlocking helical gears, as the bonnet-badge still seen today. Naturally, that French giant today does not beseech the modern motorist to drive a lemon nor trumpet the fact that their origins lie in the steering-gear of *Titanic*; shame; a marketing opportunity missed; en-gin; ice; lemon; it's all there for the taking. Perhaps not! Anyway, the point is that *Titanic* was a floating leviathan which had all the helm-response of an arthritic sloth.

The next nail in this floating coffin was its captain, Edward Smith (1850–1912), who, despite being trumpeted by White Star as the most experienced man on the high seas, seems to have been anything but. Prior to taking command of *Titanic* he had captained *Olympic* with more than his fair share of scrapes and collisions. On completing her maiden voyage from Liverpool to New York he nearly sank one of the twelve tugs helping him into Pier 59 and in the September of that same year he managed to crash into HMS *Hawke* in open seas and tear the prow off said British warship. In February 1912 Smith managed to rip off one of his own propellers by passing over a charted wreck and it was the diversion of components from the building of *Titanic* to *Olympic* to get her seaworthy again which delayed the former's maiden voyage in time to meet the ice-packs. For reasons unfathomed, none of this dissuaded the White Star Executive from putting *Titanic* in Smith's hands for the maiden voyage, they describing him as a middle-aged man of vast experience which would only hold true had Smith planned on living until he was about 130 years old as he was sixty-two at the time. When he took *Titanic* out of Southampton he passed so close to the American liner, the *City of New York*, that his wash tore that ship from its moorings to come within 3 or 4 ft of collision. Well, as the Americans are fond of opining, there's no such thing as a free launch. Seriously though, someone should have taken the old chap aside for a quiet chat, and perhaps that did happen; just prior to his sailing Smith had announced that this maiden voyage of *Titanic* would be his swan-song; well, at least he got that right.

Once in open waters, *Titanic* made a steady 23 knots (26 mph) but it is unfair to say that Smith fancied himself in some Blue Ribbon race or that any of the White Star 'suits' aboard, specifically J. Bruce Ismay (1862–1937), Managing Director, put pressure on Smith to get his foot down and show the world what *Titanic* could do. This was certainly the impression given in the mawkish 1997 Leonardo DiCaprio/Kate Winslet film of the disaster. But Ismay was a numbers man; had *Titanic* arrived a day early he would have had hundreds of passengers on his hands demanding accommodation and subsidence, at his expense, while they waited for scheduled connections; he was not that stupid. This was the man who had ordered the reduction to the planned forty-eight lifeboats to the minimum sixteen as then required by law – Ismay was nothing if not cost-driven. It is also unfair to blame Smith for his holding steady speed while heading for the iceberg fields; true *Titanic* had been kept up to date with the latest information of the existence of icebergs in its path. However, it was then standard practice not to break speed in a ship like *Titanic* as all thought that anything large enough to cause serious damage would be seen in plenty of time for evasive action to be taken, as doubtless would have been the case had the watch been equipped with binoculars, which takes us to what appears to have been, quite literally, the key to the disaster.

With the unexpected lay-up of *Olympic*, thanks to Smith ripping off its propeller, one of the silver-linings, as far as White Star was concerned, was the unexpected availability of that ship's First Officer, Henry Tingle Wilde, who they deemed more experienced in dealing with the petulant demands of first class passengers than the already-appointed Chief Officer on *Titanic*, William Murdoch. The dry docking of *Olympic* allowed for a last-minute re-shuffle involving Wilde replacing Murdoch as Chief Officer on *Titanic*, he, Murdoch being relegated to position of First Officer, with the original First Officer, Charles Lightoller, being re-slated as Second Officer. This left Second Officer David Blair with nowhere to go but off the ship and, in a bit of a mood, he packed up his gear and quit *Titanic* just days before the departure, taking with him the key to the crow's nest locker. It is variously argued that this was a petulant gesture or simply an act of forgetfulness, it also being argued that the binoculars stored therein were his own personal set which he had also removed from the ship so even had he not flounced off with the locker-key there would have been no binoculars for the crow's nest watch to find in any event. Others maintain that there was indeed a set of company binoculars in that locker but no-one could find the key. Whatever; the crow's nest watch found itself without binoculars as *Titanic* approached the ice-fields; had they been so equipped they would almost certainly have been able to spot the iceberg and report its presence ahead in plenty of time for the bridge to take evasive action. Blair, it seems, hung onto that key, willing it to his daughter who in turn donated it to the International Sailors' Society. It was sold at auction by Christies on 22 September 2007, along with a postcard from Blair to his sister-in-law saying how miffed he was at getting bumped at the eleventh hour, these two items being bought for £90,000 by Shen Dougjun, a Chinese jewellery tycoon.

By the time Frederick Fleet and Reginald Lee, up in the crow's nest *did* spot the damned thing, there was little time to take evasive action; a better-built ship with multiple rudders might have responded in time to avert collision; who knows, but on the night of 14 April 1912 *Titanic* hit the 'berg a glancing blow with her right side, sustaining surprisingly little damage. Popular opinion still has the ship ripped open with a 100 ft gash but the hole was actually about 8 or 10 ft square; it was the massive 'holes' in the design of the ship which would set up the domino-effect through the 'watertight' bulkheads and take her to the bottom. As is well known, at first there was no particular concern, certainly not among the first class passengers who, still buoyed up by the arrogant lies of the ship's unsinkability; came out on deck to gawp at the 'berg and make fatuous comments. As the gravity of the situation dawned on the crew and then the passengers, the radio operator, Jack Philips, who himself would not survive the night, started sending out the standard CQD signals of distress. He did eventually try the newly instituted SOS as a last resort but it is a myth that this was the first time that that signal was ever transmitted.

The 1906 Radiotelegraphic Conference held in Berlin decided that a new international distress signal was called for and one that was immediately recognisable and transmittable even by an unskilled person. They picked on the pattern of three dots, three dashes, three dots which was intended to be transmitted as a composite block, no gaps, as it did not in fact stand for anything, not even the letters S, O and S, so all the stories that it stands for 'save our souls', or whatever, are just stories. The first ship to transmit SOS in danger was not *Titanic* but the American steamer *Araphoe* which, en route to Jacksonville from New York, broke her propeller-shaft on 11 August 1908. In fact, the radio operators of most nations fell in line quite quickly, it was only stuffy old Britain which clung to the tradition of CQD which, incidentally, did not stand for Come Quick – Distress. CQ was the standard call to 'All Stations' and D for 'distress'; it was the fact that so many mundane messages, such as time-signals, were preceded by CQ that it was rightly time for a change to avoid any confusion. The only distress call that does stand for something is 'Mayday', the standard vocalisation of the French '*m'aider*', 'help me'. Anyway, Philips did resort to SOS as events darkened and although this was not the first time the signal had been used it was certainly the event which convinced even the British that it was time to get in step with the rest of the world and instruct all shipping to abandon CQD in favour of SOS.

As *Titanic* began to settle in the water, the order was given for the lifeboats to be launched and here things did begin to unravel a bit. Despite the fact that there was lifeboat accommodation for less than half of those on board, the first boats were put to sea greatly under capacity; the first to be launched, Number Seven, with capacity for over sixty, put away from *Titanic* with only twelve people aboard. And there was soon panic deep below decks in the third class accommodation. Many films of the events have either plainly stated or tried to imply that the third class passengers were gated below to their doom like cattle to give the first class passengers full access to the lifeboat seating but this simply is not so. There were indeed gates between the third class accommodation and the most direct route to the lifeboat decks, this being through the first class accommodation. The gates were in place and routinely locked to prevent third class passengers wandering through first class and possibly helping themselves to the odd trophy or three but as the disaster unfolded these were unlocked. That said, the demographic of the death-toll does reveal the advantage of class and to a lesser extent, nationality.

Category	Number aboard	Number of survivors	Percentage survived	Number lost	Percentage lost
First class	329	199	60.5%	130	39.5%
Second class	285	119	41.7%	166	58.3%
Third class	710	174	24.5%	536	75.5%
Crew	899	214	23.8%	685	76.2%
Total	2,223	706	31.8%	1,517	68.2%

Out of the 2,223 passengers and crew there were only 706 survivors with the majority of death caused by hypothermia in those who, unable to get any place in a lifeboat, simply jumped for it with a lifebelt but did not long survive in the sub-zero waters. As readers can see from the above chart, the higher up the pecking order the better one's chances with first class enjoying an overall survival rate four times higher than third class.

Breakdown of Passengers by Gender

Women	Children	Men	Total
TOTAL ADULT FEMALE PASSENGERS Died: 112 Survived: 304 Survived: 72%	**TOTAL CHILDREN PASSENGERS** Died: 56 Survived: 56 Survived: 50%	**TOTAL ADULT MALE PASSENGERS** Died: 638 Survived: 130 Survived: 18%	**TOTAL PASSENGERS** Died: 806 Survived: 490 Survived: 37%
TOTAL FEMALE STAFF Died: 2 Survived: 20 Survived: 91%	**TOTAL CHILDREN ON CREW** None. (Although some were in their teens)	**TOTAL MALE STAFF AND CREW** Died: 701 Survived: 195 Survived: 21%	**TOTAL CREW AND STAFF** Died: 703 Survived: 215 Survived: 23%
TOTAL WOMEN Died: 114 Survived: 324 Survived: 72%	**TOTAL CHILDREN** Died: 56 Survived: 56 Survived: 50%	**TOTAL MEN** Died: 1339 Survived: 325 Survived: 19%	**TOTAL ON BOARD** Died: 1509 Survived: 705 Survived: 31%

Breakdown of Passengers by Class

Women	Children	Men	Total
FIRST CLASS WOMEN (SERVANTS TOTALLED SEPARATELY) Died: 4 (0) Survived: 6 Survived: 97% (100%)	**FIRST CLASS CHILDREN** Died: 1 Survived: 55 (2) Survived: 86%	**FIRST CLASS MEN (SERVANTS TOTALLED SEPARATELY)** Died: 104 (10) Survived: 113 (24) Survived: 34% (17%)	**FIRST CLASS TOTAL** Died: 119 Survived: 200 Survived: 63%
SECOND CLASS WOMEN (SERVANTS TOTALLED SEPARATELY) Died: 13 (0) Survived: 78 (1) Survived: 86%	**SECOND CLASS CHILDREN** Died: 0 Survived: 25 Survived: 100%	**SECOND CLASS MEN (SERVANTS TOTALLED SEPARATELY)** Died: 135 (4) Survived: 13 Survived: 8% (0%)	**SECOND CLASS TOTAL** Died: 152 Survived: 117 Survived: 43%
THIRD CLASS (STEERAGE) WOMEN Died: 91 Survived: 88 Survived: 49%	**THIRD CLASS (STEERAGE) CHILDREN** Died: 55 Survived: 25 Survived: 31%	**THIRD CLASS (STEERAGE) MEN** Died: 381 Survived: 59 Survived: 13%	**THIRD CLASS (STEERAGE) TOTAL** Died: 527 Survived: 172 Survived: 25%

Further Steerage Breakdown

Women	Children	Men	Total
THIRD CLASS BRITISH WOMEN BOARDING IN SOUTHAMPTON Died: 16 Survived: 14 Survived: 47%	**THIRD CLASS BRITISH CHILDREN BOARDING IN SOUTHAMPTON** Died: 17 Survived: 8 Survived: 32%	**THIRD CLASS BRITISH MEN BOARDING IN SOUTHAMPTON** Died: 110 Survived: 15 Survived: 12%	**THIRD CLASS TOTAL BRITISH BOARDING IN SOUTHAMPTON** Died: 143 Survived: 37 Survived: 21%
THIRD CLASS NON-BRITISH WOMEN BOARDING IN SOUTHAMPTON Died: 41 Survived: 27 Survived: 35%	**THIRD CLASS NON-BRITISH CHILDREN BOARDING IN SOUTHAMPTON** Died: 29 Survived: 9 Survived: 24%	**THIRD CLASS NON-BRITISH MEN BOARDING IN SOUTHAMPTON** Died: 174 Survived: 30 Survived: 15%	**THIRD CLASS TOTAL NON-BRITISH BOARDING IN SOUTHAMPTON** Died: 244 Survived: 66 Survived: 21%
THIRD CLASS WOMEN BOARDING IN CHERBOURG Died: 11 Survived: 17 Survived: 61%	**THIRD CLASS CHILDREN BOARDING IN CHERBOURG** Died: 4 Survived: 7 Survived: 63%	**THIRD CLASS MEN BOARDING IN CHERBOURG** Died: 51 Survived: 9 Survived: 15%	**THIRD CLASS TOTAL BOARDING IN CHERBOURG** Died: 66 Survived: 33 Survived: 33%
THIRD CLASS WOMEN BOARDING IN QUEENSTOWN, IRELAND Died: 23 Survived: 30 Survived: 57%	**THIRD CLASS CHILDREN BOARDING IN QUEENSTOWN, IRELAND** Died: 5 Survived: 1 Survived: 17%	**THIRD CLASS MEN BOARDING IN QUEENSTOWN, IRELAND** Died: 46 Survived: 5 Survived: 9%	**THIRD CLASS TOTAL BOARDING IN QUEENSTOWN, IRELAND** Died: 74 Survived: 36 Survived: 33%

Apart from the class factor in the survival odds there also seems to have been a cultural factor at work with Americans enjoying a far higher survival rate than anyone else, right across the board. Of the American passsengers in first class 67 per cent of them survived as against only 44 per cent of the British; in second class it was 47 per cent against 41 per cent and in third class 28 per cent against 15 per cent. Although British passengers, across the board, made up 53 per cent of the total lists they were not represented in the survivors in anything like that quantity. The Americans only constituted a mere 20 per cent of the passenger total but were nearly 20 per cent more likely to survive than their British counterparts. The only reason behind such a glaring discrepancy that has so far been put forward is manners; the British are internationally known for their ability to form an orderly queue whereas the Americans tend to be a trifle 'pushy' by comparison, this making them psychologically more suited to surviving in such circumstances while the band played on – or did it?

The *Titanic* band has become something of a metaphor but those playing on the last night were not a regular group because *Titanic* in fact had two separate musical groups; there was the five-piece led by Wallace Hartley, quite a famous musician in his day and a member of the equally famous family of jam-manufacturers, and a French/ Belgian trio which was more usually to be found in the ship's Café Parisien. The night of the sinking was the first time they had ever merged into an eight-piece and they had done so for that night only. That these men calmly played on for a while is beyond dispute, trying to keep the passengers – first class only, of course – calm and entertained while they waited to be allocated a place in a lifeboat. But just how long they kept this up and what they played last is greatly contended. The standard version of events is that they played right up until the end, breaking into *Nearer My God To Thee* as the ship went down, but this cannot be. As the end crept nearer the angle of tilt to the decks increased to the point that no-one could stay in any one place without hanging on to something, and definitely not stand there calmly playing a viola, or whatever. The originator of the 'Nearer My God To Thee' myth seems to have been first-class Canadian survivor, Vera Dick, who told all the newspapers that this had been the band's swan-song. The trouble with that is that Ms Dick was one of the first embarkees to the lifeboats and had quit the scene nearly an hour-and-a-half before the boat went down so she cannot have had any first-hand knowledge of anything that happened. She was perhaps compensating for the trauma by weaving a comfort-blanket of romanticised myth to shield her from viewing the ugly reality – if she was third class we could of course just say that she was a liar. Other more reliable witnesses say the band kept playing ragtime and lively waltzes as long as they could with the last number possibly being 'Autumn'.

For some reason, the most famous survivor was American Margaret Brown (1867–1932), thereafter celebrated in America as 'The Unsinkable Molly Brown', but her coffin-dodging prowess pales beside that of *Titanic*-survivor Violet Jessop (1887–1971). Perhaps something of a jinx, Violet had been a stewardess on the *Olympic* when Smith decided to play 'chicken' with HMS *Hawke*, and while *Olympic* was being refitted she transferred with him to *Titanic* and survived that sinking as well. Recovering from her ordeal, she joined the third sister-ship, *Britannic*, which was converted to a hospital ship during the First World War. This too sank, after striking a mine in the Aegean in 1916 and, despite being sucked under and battered against the keel, she survived that sinking too. The last *Titanic* survivor of all, Millvina Dean (1912–2009), died in her nursing home in Ashurst, Hampshire, just outside *Titanic*'s departure port of Southampton, where her nursing costs had been met in part by both DiCaprio and Winslet. At a mere nine-weeks-old, she was the youngest of all the passengers and died on 31 May, the 98th anniversary of the launching of the great ship, almost to the hour.

JOHN WHO?

The personification of the British bulldog breed is internationally accepted as the stout character of John Bull who was first drawn in 1712 by Dr John Arbuthnot (1667–1735). The caricature most certainly sprang from Arbuthnot's pen but it is more than likely that he had already heard such a name applied to the English by the French and asserted a masterly grip on the wrong end of the stick by presuming the name complimentary through comparisons to the creature's reputation for strength and stout heart.

The people of most European nations had blanket nicknames which were without exception coined by their enemies. To the English the generic Dutchman was 'Jan Kaas' or 'Johnny Cheese', this later corrupting to 'Yankees' when first hurled at Dutch settlers of early America by their English neighbours. The catch-all name for the French was 'Jean Crapaud' or 'Johnny Toad', in reference to the heraldic device of the old Frankish/French kingdom which incorporated golden toads; not only did this evolve into the ever-popular 'Frogs' but it also explains the otherwise rather worrying name of the crap dice so beloved by the Americans since its introduction to New Orleans by the French. Anyway, the point is that nicknames of Johnny this-or-that were always international insults and it seems that when Arbuthnot heard use of what he thought to be 'John Bull' he thought of the animal, with its aforementioned anthropomorphised attributes, presumed the name to be complimentary and drew accordingly. But in the French, from whence it seems the name originated, the closest one gets is Jean Boule translating to Johnny Liar, which is close in keeping with that nation's oft justified concept of 'Perfidious Albion'. If this is correct, as it likely is, the early eighteenth-century French must have been laughing their socks off when they saw how the English had adopted the insult.

KATE THE GREAT AND HER MATE

The most remarkable thing about Catherine the Great (1729–1796) is how she managed to bootstrap herself up from being an obscure German princess to holding absolute rule over one of the largest realms on the planet. She was intelligent, shrewd, witty, a veritable tiger in the political arena and if there is one thing that men hate, it is a smart woman – and one as smart as she was just had to be put in her place. The safest form of attack for misogynistic cowards has always been sexual ridicule and while it stretched credulity not one iota that there would be one idiot to dream up the myth that Catherine died attempting sex with a stallion it is depressing and disappointing that so many were ready to believe such rubbish – and still do. Lurid accounts of her imagined death can still be seen in print in the worst of 'Amazing Facts' books.

Born Sophie Friederike Auguste von Anhali-Zerbst-Domburg, ('Figchen' to her friends), she had to convert to the Russian Orthodox Church before marrying the Grand Duke who would, for all his sins and shortcomings, become Peter III of Russia. This she did on 28 June 1744, being baptized Ekaterina with the invented patronym Alexseyevna (daughter of Alexsey) thrown in for good measure. Barely sixteen she would, within as many more years again, dispose of her husband within months of his ascending the throne in January 1762 and take over the family business. Far from being resentful, the work-shy Peter was over the moon; in July 1762, already fatigued by six months of responsibility; he had decamped with his mistress to the Palace at Oranienbaum, leaving Ekaterina minding the store. This apparently politically stupid move, (his wife's ambitions by then were common knowledge), combined with his attitude of 'Oh *quelle domage*; you win, dear; well played; I'll just have to settle for a life of self-indulgence in the palace at Ropsha' gives sufficient grounds to the notion that Catherine did not so much stage a bloodless coup, as do exactly what Peter prayed for. Others were not so convinced of Peter's capacity for indolence and on 17 July, three days after the coup, a group of nobles, led by Count Alexei Orlov, went to Ropsha and cut short Peter's party. Although Ekaterina did not order this done, to her shame, she rewarded the killers instead of punishing them.

So much happened throughout her tenure – the mechanisation of agriculture and industry; inoculation programmes; the opening up of relationships with Japan, the invitation of foreign investment to kindle depressed regions of Russia – it is a sad reflection on human nature that all anyone now wants to know is how many lovers she had and whether or not 'un-bridled' lust was her final downfall. She did have affairs, a dozen in total; but why shouldn't she? All her lovers did very well out of the relationships, she remaining extremely generous long after the relationships had run their course, which places her in sharp contrast to male despots who could be vindictive and even homicidal when it came to cast-offs in the carnal department. She did indeed have a protracted affair with Grigori Potemkin (1739–1791), he of village-fame, but as for the suggestion that he used to 'pimp' for her, sending prospective candidates to some lady of the court for a dummy-run to make sure they would measure up for the ruler, so to speak, this is just more of the same puerile nonsense. Sometimes this 'stud-muffin' is said to have been Countess Bruce but the only boudoir cross-over between those two went the other way; Bruce actually took over one of Catherine's lovers, Ivan Rimsky-Korsakov, their grandson doing quite well in the music business. As for the ridiculous notion that Catherine was crushed to death when, hot-to-trot for her equine lover, there was a failure in the harness designed to prevent her four-legged friend from going too far; this is a silly myth which was perhaps started by the fragrance behind the still-popular Cussons Imperial Leather soap: Catherine the Great died of natural causes in her bed-chamber.

Another of the great Catherine myths, also concerning Potemkin, gave rise to the use of 'Potemkin village' for anything false or lacking substance. Catherine annexed the Crimea in 1783, first visiting her new acquisition on a tour of inspection, along the Dnieper River, in 1778 when, it is said, that Potemkin tried to 'big-up' her acquisition by building false villages all along the ordained route and importing so many animals from the region to the river banks that he instituted a famine. This piece of nonsense was started by Georg von Helbig, the Saxon Envoy to the Russian Imperial Court, who, as it turns out, did not make the trip and was miffed at not being invited. Not only did he hate Potemkin but also the myth had the bonus effect of making Catherine out to be a silly woman, unable to see past such a simple ruse. But back to the soap-connection.

In 1768 Count Grigory Orlov, one of Catherine's favourite lovers and older brother of the man who murdered Peter III, visited London and took the opportunity to call in at Bayley's of Bond Street where his request caused a few studious nods. He told the perfumers that he and a 'lady of his close acquaintance' had a 'thing' about the smell of leather in a stable's tack-room and that both desired a cologne redolent of the smell of hot and horsey leather. Perhaps this was all that was needed to start tales of 'forni-Kate' and her stable mate? Either way, Eau de Cologne *Imperiale Russe* was the result of Orlov's visit and regular shipments were sent out to the Russian Court, right up to the Revolution of 1917 and the death of the last of Catherine's kind, they being murdered, rather ironically, in Ekaerinburg, founded and named in her honour in 1723. Bayley's was acquired by Cussons in 1921, along with the recipe and its history, this inspiring the owners to produce a soap called Imperial Leather.

LIBERTÉ, EGALITÉ AND DECAPITÉ

If there is one thing that everybody knows about the French Revolution it is that it all kicked off with a rousing rendition of *La Marseillaise* and the guillotine going nineteen-to-the-dozen as the nobility got their comeuppance to the nodded approval of the Parisian knitting-club. It was, of course, nothing like that, if only for the fact that neither the guillotine nor *La Marseillaise* was around at the time. On the subject of the former, despite it being widely accepted that the guillotine was invented by Doctor Guillotin (1738–1814) and that he was the first to taste the whispering kiss of his own brain-child, the good physician from Saintes had nothing to do with the machine's inception. (It seems that the 'e' was added by British writers who, lampooning the French Revolution in verse, found that version easier to rhyme with than the proper name).

One of the earliest such machines on record is the Halifax Gibbet with the second being the Edinburgh Maiden, introduced by James Douglas, 4th Earl of Morton, for the execution of the Laird of Pennycuik. The exact date of this cannot be fixed but it is known that in 1566, on the evening of 9 March, Thomas Scott was executed by it for his part in the murder of David Rizzio, the secretary of Mary,

Queen of Scots. Ironically, the armed party that entered Holyrood House to kill Rizzio was led by none other than Morton himself who succumbed to the dubious charms of his own maiden on 2 June 1581 for his part in the murder of James Darnley, Mary's husband. It is more than possible that Morton dying on the instrument of his own introduction gave rise to the later Dr Guillotin myth. All of this took place a long time before the French Revolution which began in May 1789 with the so-called guillotine not adopted in France until 25 March 1792 after a long campaign by Dr Joseph-Ignace Guillotin who proposed its adoption on humanitarian grounds. Although this today might sound a trifle odd, in Guillotin's day decapitation was a luxury reserved for those of noble birth, commoners having to endure more protracted and inefficient methods of dispatch.

With the machine's official adoption imminent, Dr Guillotin and Antoine Louis, Secretary of the French College of Surgeons, commissioned a chap called Laquiante from the Strasbourg Criminal Court to run up a design, which he did, incorporating a *lunette*, or crescent-shaped blade. A German harpsichord maker named Tobias Schmidt was roped in to transform the design into reality and it was he who suggested the blade raked to 45 degrees as a far more efficient cutting tool. Everyone agreed; Schmidt's prototype was tried out on a few dead bodies from Hôpital de Bicêtre, pronounced a roaring success and set up for all to see in the Place de Grève. The first man to die on it was not Dr Guillotin but a common highwayman called Claude Pelletier who lost his head on 25 April 1792 – believe it or not, the last public guillotining in France took place at Versailles in 1939. Initially, the contraption was known as the Louisette but due to the Doctor's long advocacy of the machine his name soon took over. This did not please Guillotin or his family who, after the good Doctor's death from natural causes at the ripe old age of seventy-six, changed their name to disassociate themselves from the wholesale butchery of the Reign of Terror which, contrary to popular perception, killed off far more commoners than aristos.

Throughout the Revolution, some 17,000 were executed, before during and after the inception of the guillotine, but to put this into perspective, if that is the right word, between 1933 and 1945 16,500 people met a similar fate on the Nazi guillotines set up in Germany and Austria. But of the French Revolutionary death total, 85 per cent were commoners with only some 1,200 members of the nobility treading the boards to the entertainment of the crowds which were not, it must be said, led by the infamous but imaginary Tricoteuses, these ghouls being yet another invention of a largely hostile British press. All clouds, they say, have silver linings and 1,200 closed-down homes of the nobility were enough to give the world the restaurant. Until then, although there were private functions rooms one could hire for specific and catered events, there were no walk-in eateries and, with Paris teeming with unemployed chefs, butlers and other catering staff from the aforementioned stately homes, these people banded together to do the only thing they knew how. The dictionary definition of 'revolution' talks of something going through a complete cycle before returning to the point at which it began, and this is the reality of all political revolutions: the down-trodden stay exactly where they were in the first place – they just have a different set of oppressors. The first people through the doors of these new establishments to taste the food and enjoy the pampering that was once the province of those they had removed were the leading lights of the Revolution itself. *Plus ça change.*

As for the birth of *La Marseillaise*, that too came from Strasbourg but far too late to have been sung by the drunken mob that stormed the Bastille (1789) or any other of the opening events because, like the guillotine, it did not even exist until 1792 when it was written, not to stir up the mob, but to cheer up the French Army on the Rhine. Rightly worried about the morale of the troops providing his protection, Philippe-Frederic de Dietrich, mayor and businessman of Strasbourg, thought that it might be a good idea if someone came up with a rousing marching song for them and up to the plate stepped Rouget de Lisle, a Captain of Engineers with an ear for a catchy number. De Dietrich gave the nod for the tune to be issued with the uninspiring title of *War Song for the Army on the Rhine* and, not long after, a young doctor, Francois Mireur (1770–1798), who would later die as one of Napoleon Bonaparte's youngest generals in Egypt, took the song with him when he went down to Marseilles to join a newly raised brigade. By the time the column reached Paris he had them all singing it, and when they marched into the city on 30 July 1792 it sent the mob crazy, they setting fire to buildings and generally having a very 'French' time of it. The sway the song held over the mob was instrumental in rousing them to march on the Tuileries ten days later when, unable to find the royal family, they butchered 600 of the Swiss Guard and every man, woman and child in service therein. The French have always been up for a good riot but even the Revolutionary Council became worried about the strange effect *La Marseillaise* could have on the mob and fought in vain to restrict its singing in the streets. Finally, and reluctantly bowing to public pressure, the Convention sanctioned the song adoption as the official new national anthem in July 1795 but it was soon banned by Napoleon who feared its peculiar ability to raise the rabble. This ban was reiterated by Louis XVIII and again by Napoleon III; it was not until 1879 that the song was reinstated as the national anthem and again allowed to be sung in public without attracting dire penalty. As for the man who called for the song in the first place, he went to the guillotine in 1793 on the orders of Robespierre himself and likely to the chant of his own brainchild. His family had pushed long and hard for ennoblement and had been granted their wish just before the Revolution got underway – talk about not asking the gods for what you want. But the rest of his family survived to set up the industrial dynasty of de Dietrich & Cie, one of France's largest companies. The year 1793 was not a good one for the song's writer either; he was languishing in prison awaiting his turn to dance with Madam Guillotine when he was set free to die in poverty by the counter-Revolution.

LONG DAY'S JOURNEY INTO TRITE

The repugnant little peasant who would become Chairman Mao has to be the world's most successful killer – trebling the combined score of Hitler and Stalin – which must take some doing. He was also a liar. The Long March, of which he made so much, is a legend born of gross misrepresentations of which he himself seems to have been the author. Even his maths is poor: if he is correct in his assertion that the 370-day trek covered 8,000 miles then the army of 80,000 must have averaged 20 miles every day in some of the roughest terrain in China. It is doubtful that an athlete with a full support team could accomplish such a feat, so laden soldiers, women and children and a supply column would have no chance. The official account of the March is quite simple; under the guidance of Mao, the Central Red Army quit its southern bases in Yudu, in the province of Jiangxi and, from October 1934 to October 1935, fought its way north to Yanan in the province of Shaanxi. Here the flower of Communism blossomed – the town is still something of a 'pilgrimage' site for misty-eyed idealists – and Mao led his army back to victory and the foundation of New China.

For a start, there were three marches. Apart from the Central Army, the Second and the Fourth Red Armies were also in full retreat, all heading north. They were running from what they though would be their annihilation at the hands of Nationalist forces under Chiang Kai-shek but he had no intention of fighting them, he let them go, indeed, he dictated their path by surrounding them while leaving one 'door' open. But Chiang was no closet-Communist sympathizer; he had plans for the Red Army; if he drove it north through the provinces run by some extremely powerful warlords, he thought the presence of such a force on the doorsteps of such men might induce them to thrown in their lot with the Nationalists. Far from running some clever strategy of their own, the Communists were simply lab-rats. And as for Mao being in charge of the fiasco, this simply is not so: he had nothing to do with the planning of the so-called Long March as he was unpopular, rightly considered untrustworthy and thus kept outside the power-circle. He was not even told of the departure from Yudu until all but a couple of days before and after all had been settled.

Six weeks into the journey there was a clash with Nationalist forces along the Xiang River or the Hsiang River, depending on your choice of transliteration. Mao (who was still a long way from taking control of the army) always hailed this a dramatic conflict responsible for upwards of 50,000 casualties that 'his' forces sustained. It is true that the Central Army column was reduced from 86,000 to something less than 30,000 around this time, but the vast majority of these losses – as high as 90 per cent by some estimates, were due to desertion by peasant-soldiers who had been pressed into service at gunpoint and had not an inkling why they were trekking through the wilderness carrying the elite on litters. According to Mao's version of events, the next 'crucial' conflict happened at the Dadu River Bridge which ran over a deep gorge. With a Nationalist Army hot on their heels, Mao claimed that 'his' Reds came to this bridge to find it on fire and under the sights of several machine-gun nests on the far side. Twenty-two volunteers stripped off to fight their way through the flames and bullets to wipe out all opposition and clear the way for their comrades' escape. It simply did not happen. The reason that the Red Army crossed the bridge without a single casualty is that Chiang Kai-shek had ordered it to be left open and unguarded so making sure that the Reds made it to the other side; it was all part of his plan.

By the time the Reds made it to Yanan, Mao was well and truly in control, he having back-stabbed his way to power, literally and metaphorically. Once established in that city, Mao's concept of communistic equality soon became apparent to all – he beat Orwell to *Animal Farm* by ten years. Although hailed for years afterwards as the birthplace of Chinese Communism and a Mecca for political pilgrims, those who took the trouble to turn up while Mao was still there were sickened by the elitism and louche lifestyle of the self-appointed leadership; the sexually incontinent Mao dividing his time between sleeping with as many impressionable young girls as he could while muscling in on the lucrative opium trade which would amass him a personal fortune of over £400 million at today's values.

The first cracks in the official version of events appear in 2003 when two British researchers, Ed Jocelyn and Andrew McEwan, decided to retrace the route, which they accomplished in 384 days by averaging a more realistic 10 miles a day over the real distance of about 3,700 miles. Their subsequent book of their venture, *The Long March* (2006) made the observation that: 'Mao and his followers twisted the tale of the Long March for their own ends. Mao's role was mythologized to the point where it seemed he had single-handedly saved the Red Army and defeated Chiang Kai-shek.' In truth, Chiang was not defeated by anyone. In the December of 1936 he was planning an all-out assault against Mao in Yanan when several of his commanders, previous warlords brought on-side by Chiang's original plan, turned coat again and kidnapped him on 12 December, holding him hostage until he agreed to recognize the Communists and join forces with them to fight their common enemy, the Japanese.

Not surprisingly, their findings found little favour in Beijing which countered with a tight-lipped statement maintaining: 'The 25,000 *li* (a measure of about 500 meters) of the Red Army's Long March are a historical fact and not open to doubt.'

LUBBE'S BOOB

With the prevailing fashion – nay, passion – for a never-ending round of apologies for this or that long-past transgression, the exoneration of Marinus van der Lubbe (1911–1934) in January 2008 passed unnoticed, save the inevitable flurry of claims for compensation from charlatans that always emerge to confirm one's lack of faith in human nature. Opinion has veered between the arson being the work of the Nazis to its having been the work of loony-Lubbe alone, but it wasn't either of them; it was both.

Van der Lubbe, falsely presented by the Nazis to the world press as a half-wit, had been in Berlin for a few weeks only before the night of the Reichstag Fire on 27 February 1933. He had attended meetings of various Communist factions and been stunned at there being no resistance offered each time the police moved in to break up said meetings. Lambasting Berlin Communists for their lack of moral fibre, he repeatedly said that something big had to be done to attract world attention to the darkness of the Nazi regime. Strutting round known Communist haunts, demanding that they all rise up and set fire to public buildings, van der Lubbe cannot possibly have failed to attract the attention of Hitler's network of spies and informants who will have identified him as a potential asset they could use to stitch up the Communists good and proper. The Nazis must have played van der Lubbe like a fiddle.

The most likely scenario is that he was befriended by Nazis masquerading as passionate Communists who then played up to his obvious hunger for fame; obviously this can never be proved but in light of the fact that the Nazis clearly knew the night and time that the job would be done makes it more than probable. After a couple of abortive dummy-runs on the night of the 25th, when he tried to burn down an unemployment office and a section of the Imperial Palace, he was ready for the biggie; the Reichstag was gutted on the night of the 27th and van der Lubbe arrested at the scene, in a state of some undress and, far from protesting any innocence, proudly claiming sole responsibility. Hitler and the rest of his gang were quickly on the scene, ready with statements that Germany was in peril of a carefully orchestrated Communist plot and that the fire was the signal for the uprising, thwarted by patriotic Nazis who, as he spoke, stood guard round other buildings that were likely targets. Far from there being any such plot, the fire was the excuse for Hitler's assumption of sole control of Germany, for its own good and protection, of course. Germany saw many changes as a direct result of that fire, among them Göring's Department 1A, set up to interrogate van der Lubbe and anyone else that the Nazis thought might prove politically advantageous to have in the frame; given 'special powers' to cope with this freshly uncovered national emergency, this was the unit destined to 'blossom' into the Gestapo.

By the time the trial opened on 21 September, rumour of Nazi involvement was rife; by this time there was hardly a fire official or an arson investigator in the world who thought that the job could have been done by a single, half-blind man; even a first-rate 'torch' could not have ensured such devastation of a building that size on his own. Sefton Delmer, the German-born British foreign correspondent of the *Daily Express* who had been on site that night recalled that he had there met with Dr Alfred Rosenberg, Hitler's prime adviser on foreign affairs, who, in an unguarded moment had remarked: 'I only hope that this is not the works of our chaps. It's just the sort of damn silly thing some of them might do.' He also recalled Hitler being quite beside himself with excitement at the scene, running hither and thither before tripping over a hosepipe and being cautioned by Göring to calm down. And it was Göring's nearby residence that was connected to the Reichstag by an underground service tunnel through which it is most likely that a gang of trusted cohorts would have made their way to the other end to augment van der Lubbe's amateur efforts – while the Nazis could be sure of their patsy, the required result had to be guaranteed.

It is conjectured that a gang of about ten Brownshirt thugs from the SA, most likely under the leadership of Hans Gewehr, used the tunnel to get into the Reichstag at about 8 p.m. that night and, knowing they had an hour before their cronies brought van der Lubbe along to break in through a side window, spread their accelerants and gave them plenty of time to soak in. Van der Lubbe turned up around 9 p.m., broke in as planned and as soon as he started his own amateurish pyrotechnics, the place erupted in a fireball; no wonder the poor lad was found in a dishevelled and somewhat dazed state. Arch-opponent of the Nazi regime and one of the few conspirators in the bomb-plot against Hitler to survive, Hans Gisevius (1904–1974) was a the prime witness against Göring and testified at Nuremberg that: 'It was Goebbels who first thought of setting the Reichstag on fire' and Rudolf Diels (1900–1957), the first head of the Gestapo, would also testify that 'Göring knew exactly how and when the fire was to be started' and went on to explain that, prior to the fire, Göring had given him the list of people to be arrested after it started.

In addition, General Franz Halder (1884–1972), Head of the Army General Staff and a dour man not given to flights of fancy, stated in an affidavit that he had personally heard Göring boast about orchestrating the fire himself. He was attending a lunch to celebrate Hitler's birthday in 1942 when the subject came up, prompting Göring to slap his thigh and say: 'The only one who really knows about the Reichstag building is I, for I set fire to it.' Even if such men were lying there is a very solid corroboration of Nazi involvement that comes from a rather odd source; Hitler's Jewish speech-trainer.

Erik Jan Hannussen (1889–1933), the son of a synagogue caretaker, made for an odd Hitlerite but he was a devoted Party member and, as Germany's leading entertainer of the time, the largest single contributor to Party funds. He was the top Berlin stage-act, specializing in illusion, clairvoyance and, upon meeting Hitler for the first time, told him that: 'If you are serious about entering politics, Herr Hitler, why don't you learn to speak?' This was the year before the fire and, instead of stringing Hannussen up with piano-wire for his cheek, Hitler took this opportunist into his inner circle, allowing him to morph him from a beer-hall ranter into the orator he became. Hannussen taught Hitler the art of speech-delivery; the art of pause and how to pick the moment to crank it up; he taught him the art of crowd control and manipulation, and how to make whoever he was talking to on a one-to-one basis feel like they were the most important person in the world. But he got careless and greedy; the night before the fire, Hannussen held a private and high-priced séance for Berlin's elite in his luxury home, wowing the select guests with a vision of the impending fire. Now then, unless any reader actually believes that there are those who can see the future, this was a blatant misuse of insider knowledge which would soon cost Hannussen his life. But not yet; he still had his uses. The suspicion – and it is only a suspicion – is that Hannussen, also an accomplished hypnotist, had been working on van der Lubbe throughout the seven months between his arrest and his trial. Most present at the charade noted the main defendant's marked stupor throughout the proceedings in which he did not stand trial alone; a few leading lights of Germany's Communist Party were propped up in the dock alongside him for extra colour. This proved a double-edged sword for the Nazis; one co-defendant, Gregori Dimitrov, wise enough to conduct his own defence, took the opportunity of demanding that Göring himself took the stand so that he could cross-examine him, something that no court-appointed brief would have had the nerve to insist on, no matter how much his client demanded it be done. Needless to say, the sparks flew as Dimitrov asked Göring some rather probing questions about the night in question. But all was a foregone conclusion as far as van der Lubbe was concerned, beheaded after the inevitable verdict. To the collective ire of Hitler & co, the token Communists were acquitted, with one of them taken into 'protective custody' by the Gestapo-to-be immediately after the trial. Hannussen, his possible job of post-hypnotic suggestion done, had already been spirited away in the night, shot in the head and dumped in a shallow grave on the outskirts of the city, a couple of months after his gaffe.

MAKING THE MALTESE CROSS

The Maltese get very bristly when anyone questions their tradition that the island held out against Axis airpower with nothing more than a trio of Gloucester Gladiator biplanes, one of which is still on proud display in the Malta War Museum, purported to be that known as 'Faith'. The myth of Faith, Hope and Charity lives on but, since the names were invented after the event and there were at least eighteen Gladiators on the island, the wrecks of some being cannibalized into new ones, it is fair to say that the plucky little trio never existed at all. It should also be pointed out that there were also numerous Spitfires and Hurricanes on the island, plus a strong contingent of Blenheims and Beaufighters.

From 1940 until 1943, Malta's strategic importance again thrust it into the firing line to become the most bombed place on the planet throughout the war. London, Coventry, Hamburg, Berlin and Dresden have hogged all the limelight in the most-bombed tables but it is a simply matter of fact that Malta, measuring a scant 17 miles by 9 miles, found itself on the receiving end of a staggering 3,340 air-raids between June 1940 and July 1943. In one raid alone, that of 20 March 1940, 300 tons fell on the small airfield at Tarkali and across the following month of April, Malta took 6,728 tons. To put that into perspective, the infamous Coventry raid of 14 November 1940 was conducted with about 500 tons and throughout the Blitz years London took something in the region of 18,000 tons. The total tonnage dropped on Malta can only be guessed at but the details of the aerial defence are well recorded.

Allied surface vessels and submarine operations out of Malta were taking a heavy toll on the German convoys trying to keep Rommel supplied in North Africa, which explains the colossal aerial offensive on the island. In the opening phase of the assault on Malta, there were in fact 18 Gloucester Gladiators, serial numbers N5518 through to N5535 inclusive, which had been delivered in crates by HMS *Glorious* early in 1940. With the island not yet under attack, it was decided that six of these should be assembled and made combat-ready, with another five made ready and held in reserve. Throughout the defence of Malta, all of the original eighteen were at some time assembled or stood down for spares so it is impossible to know which, if any, formed the mythical trio. At the end of the day, the Faith, Hope and Charity tags were the later invention of the island press, trying to create some sort of embodiment of the incredible resistance the islanders had indeed presented. But the Gladiators were far from alone.

By July 1940 the Gladiators had been joined by seventeen Hurricanes, the first of many batches of such planes brought in by the carrier HMS *Argos*; in all some 300 Hurricanes, many with the new cannon fire-power, were delivered to Malta. The American carrier *Wasp* and the British HMS *Eagle* delivered over 100 Spitfires and a goodly number of Blenheims and Beaufighters. Given the immense strategic importance of Malta it is ridiculous to even contemplate its aerial defence being left to a trio of biplanes to hold back the combined might of the German and Italian air forces, so it is perhaps time to put the myth of Faith, Hope and Charity out to grass.

MAKING UP FOR LOST TIME

Had the early Vatican not decided to blend in with pagan traditions and peg Easter to the vernal equinox, we would never have had the myth of the time-riots of the mid-eighteenth century, April Fools' Day and a financial and tax year running April to April.

As it was building its power base, the main movers and shakers of the early Church figured they would have more success by pitching in with existing pagan festivals and gradually taking over from within than they would by confronting established traditions head-on and trying to drag people away from such rites. No-one has a clue what date Jesus was born on – the alleged fact that the shepherds were out tending flocks by night would indicate some time in June or July for that neck of the woods – but it is no coincidence that the Church plumped for 25 December, the same time as the Northern

Yule, celebrating the mid-winter solstice and the return of the next solar cycle, and a clutch of other solar celebrations. As for the other 'biggie' in the Christian calendar, Easter, it was decided to pitch that on the first Sunday after the full moon of the vernal equinox of the 21 March, another time of great pagan celebration. But the problem was the old Julian calendar and its accumulating inaccuracies which, over the centuries, had let everything slide a bit too far; by 1582 and the proposed adoption of the new calendar, the vernal equinox had slipped back from 21 March to 10 March so something had to be done to stop the Church getting out of step with itself.

Although named after Pope Gregory XIII (1502–1585) he had nothing to do with the conception and calculations of the Gregorian calendar, this instead being mainly the labours of the Jesuit astronomer Christopher Clavius (1538–1612), foremost in his field in the Europe of his day. Gregory did however champion the calendar's adoption but there was at first little interest in what was initially named the Clavian calendar as the civil authorities of most nations could see the upheaval of such implementation. In a shrewd move, the system was re-marketed as the Gregorian calendar to make it more user-friendly to Catholic countries. Protestant nations tended to drag their feet a bit, Britain and her colonies holding out until 1752 with the Eastern Orthodoxy being even more recalcitrant – Russia not falling into line until 1917, Greece and Turkey holding out until 1923 and 1926 respectively. But it was the implementation in Britain which gave rise to the myth that there were riots in the streets as the 'ignorant masses' rebelled to the chant of 'Give us back our eleven days!' While the abiding memory of such foolishness is down to the success of Catholic propaganda designed to ridicule the opposition, there was a kernel of truth to the tale.

There were indeed pockets of civil unrest and rebellion, not because people thought that they were going to die eleven days before their time, or whatever, but because landlords and business interests tried to con the public under cover of the changeover. This always happens; the changeover from L.S.D. to the present decimal currency was no different as that gave more modern sharks the chance to 'bury' a quite unwarranted increase in the translation of prices in 1971. When the calendar changed in 1752, 2 September was followed by 14 September, and it was this span of eleven evaporated dates that the ungodly sought to exploit in contracts, rental agreements and assorted other ways; criminals already incarcerated hoped to be released eleven days early, but this did not happen either. But, all in all, the reform as instituted and overseen by Philip Stanhope, Earl of Chesterfield (1694–1773), leading light of the Whig Party, went quite smoothly. Stanhope had been backed by George Parker, 2nd Earl of Macclesfield (1695–1764), a keen astronomer whose son, George Jnr, would stand as Whig candidate in Oxfordshire in the 1754 elections, where the poor chap was constantly heckled by jocular taunts about his father having stolen eleven days from the common man. Realizing they had a bit of a struggle on their hands, the Whigs abandoned any pretence of political integrity and embarked on a campaign of vote-buying through the hiring of taverns so they could put on freebie days for the locals. William Hogarth (1697–1764) pilloried such corruption in 'An Election Entertainment', a print showing all sorts of bloated drunks fawning over the candidates and, on the floor, front and centre, an abandoned banner demanding 'GIVE US BACK OUR ELEVEN DAYS'. All the artist was trying to stress was the fact that the mob soon stopped taunting the Whigs upon the offer of a free drink but the enormous success and wide circulation of the print ensured that later generations would be left with the notion that the electorate had taken to the streets in their thousands demanding the return of a small portion of their lives which had been stolen.

Other shifts of festivals and calendar reforms through history have likewise left their mark; our September, October, November and December, although now the ninth, tenth, eleventh and twelfth months of the year were, as indicated by the first element of their very names, once the seventh, eighth, ninth and tenth of the Roman calendar brought to England by the Invasion. That Roman year began in March, hence the numerical disparity of the aforementioned months, with the new year marked by a festival commencing on 25 March with its octave on 1 April, a perfectly sensible day to celebrate the re-birth of the land and so forth. With the adoption of the Gregorian calendar, New Year was shifted to its present position which not only made a mockery of the names of September, etc, but also gave rise to the tradition of marking the old new year with small gifts and practical jokes, hence April Fools' Day. One can swap calendars and play around with the dates till the cows come home but said cows will stubbornly continue to breed at their own natural cycle and the crops will continue to flourish at the same time each year, no matter what you call the harvest month. With the bulk of the nation's wealth directly or indirectly dictated by the agricultural sector, all the major rent days had to stay put, leaving the financial year forever locked in April. When income tax was first imposed in 1798 and presented to the nation as a temporary measure to fund the Napoleonic Wars, this new breed of parasite had to quickly acknowledge that even they could not get blood out of stone and likewise fell into line with an April to April collection schedule. Most reference books are unanimous that such conflict came to an end with Waterloo in 1815, so we should perhaps lobby our MPs to ask why we still pay this 'temporary measure', and demand the return of a lot more than a lousy eleven days.

MONKEY TRIAL OF JOHN T. SCOPES

In 1925 the small town of Dayton, Tennessee, found itself the focus of international attention when J.T. Scopes, a teacher at the local High School, was to be tried under the Butler Act which forbade the teaching of the principles of evolution. The famous Monkey Trial, as it became known, was immortalized in the classic play and film, *Inherit the Wind* (1960), a portrayal of the event which greatly distorts the facts of the case. Scopes is depicted as the pioneering young idealist battling against the forces of banal legislation and fundamentalist religious mania, but no victim of circumstances he; the whole affair was cooked up by local business interests with Scopes' connivance. The motives for the charade were financial rather than ethical.

The dubious bounty of the Roaring Twenties had been but a distant rumble to Dayton and local trade was not in good shape. What the town needed, reasoned the local tradesmen, was to be put on the map in a big way. George Rappleyea, who ran the local coal and iron works, got together with a chap called Robinson, who ran the town drugstore, to see what they could cook up. Robinson also happened to be the chairman of the local school-board and so it was most likely he who concocted the idea of going up against the much-debated Butler Act. Naturally, a teacher would have to be prosecuted so they sent for Scopes, who was actually the football coach, but who also stood in for lessons on algebra, chemistry and physics – not biology as is usually maintained. Already known to be opposed to the Butler Act, Scopes was more than willing to serve as the catalyst.

The date was set for Scopes to teach the heresy of evolution and the next day he was arrested by Robinson who quickly leaked the story to the press. According to Scopes' own book, *The Centre of the Storm* (1932) not one of them had an inkling of the size of the kraken they were about to awake. As the limelight hotted up, the main protagonists stepped into the arena; William Bryan, politician and a renowned fundamentalist, offered his services to the prosecution and the equally renowned atheist, Clarence Darrow, offered his services free of charge to the defence.

So well-known is the complete and utter destruction of Bryan by Darrow's cross-examination that many 'remember' Scopes to have won his case, but he was in fact found guilty as charged. Having scored an overwhelming moral victory for sanity, Darrow pleaded his client guilty and accepted the fine of $100 – a peculiar move for a lawyer who knew his client to be wholly and provably innocent of the charges before the court. The final irony of the whole farce was that on the preordained day Scopes never made it to school to teach the lesson; he was home sick all day. His fellow conspirators considered this a minor inconsequentiality and proceeded as planned. Aware of this, Darrow refused to put his client on the stand in case the truth came out and ruined his day in court with Bryan.

During the brief eleven days of the trial it seemed Rappleyea and Robinson had hit pay-dirt, local trade boomed with the massive influx of those who came to see the clash of the Titans, but as is the norm in such events, only the lawyers and the press made anything out of the circus. The world forgot Dayton as quickly as it had found it and, having been 'taken apart like a dollar watch' Bryan died a few days after the trial which soured Darrow's victory a mite. As to the victory for sanity, this too was short-lived; Scopes' much publicized failure to secure an acquittal encouraged Mississippi and Arkansas to pass similar laws; as late as 1966 an Arkansas teacher successfully enforced its implementation but this decision was later quashed by the US Supreme Court which over-turned the verdict in *Epperson v. Arkansas*. Scopes himself slipped back into anonymity dying ironically enough in 1967, the year the Butler Act was finally repealed in Tennessee.

NOT ALL IT'S CRACKED UP TO BE

The so-called Liberty Bell was not made in America and did not get such a name for its having been the bell that tolled in Philadelphia to announce the Declaration of Independence. In fact, it was not given that name until 1839 and, prior to that, was held in such high esteem that the local administration of Philadelphia had tried to sell it off as scrap and, when there were no takers had offered it free to anyone who would cart it away. Again there were no takers since the tower it hung in was in such a state of disrepair that none thought it worth the risk or effort to get the damn thing down. Finally, it did not crack when first rung to herald Independence; it first cracked on its testing bed before it was hung anywhere.

The Philadelphia State House Bell was actually cast in the London workshops of Thomas Lester's foundary in Whitechapel in 1752 and shipped to America where it cracked on its first testing. It was re-cast locally by John Pass and Charles Stow only to crack again; they had another go, this time adding more copper, and while it held sound on trials everyone agreed that the tone was dull and uninteresting. Pass and Stow conducted a third re-casting before, with all and sundry now thoroughly disenchanted with the whole venture, the result of their labours was positioned in its tower in the June of 1753 and forgotten. The Assembly commissioned a replacement from Whitechapel but when this arrived it was deemed no better than the Pass-Stow bell and thus relegated to the cupola above the State House. The Pass-Stow bell was rung on certain State occasions over the next twenty years but lay silent on the Declaration of Independence in 1776 because the tower was by now in such a dilapidated state that all thought it too dangerous to start swinging a two-ton bell about therein. Along with all the other major bells in Philadelphia, the Pass-Stow bell was removed to safe storage during the ensuing war, after which it was returned to the city to languish in a stable until 1785 when a new State House steeple was built to house it. The bell was tolled quite a few times without incident – the death of Benjamin Franklin in 1790, the death of Washington in 1799, and other such occasions – but in 1828 the city tired of its flat and uninteresting tone and commissioned local foundryman John Wiltbank to provide a new 4,000 lb bell and to cart away the Pass-Stow bell and the one in the Clock Tower.

Wiltbank ended up being sued by the City Assembly who held him in breach of contract as he only carted away the Clock Tower bell, leaving the Pass-Stow duffer in situ. Wiltbank argued that the $400 allowed for the scrap value of that bell against the cost of the new bell would be eaten up in the removal costs and leave him out of pocket. The court ruled a compromise in which Wiltbank paid the court costs and the city kept the Pass-Stow bell, which now legally belonged to Wiltbank, as a long-term loan. Now regarded as a white elephant, the bell was sidelined on future occasions of import until someone remembered its inscription from *Leviticus* 25–10: 'Proclaim Liberty Throughout All The Land To All The Inhabitants Thereof'. This prompted the anti-slavery magazine, *Liberty*, to show the bell on its front covers throughout 1837 and, with other like-minded publications following suit, the Pass-Stow bell became 'The Liberty Bell'. Now raised from disgrace to national status, the bell was chosen to ring the lead for the marking of the anniversary of Washington's birthday in 1846 – and it promptly cracked again, this time so seriously that it was rendered unusable.

Ringable or not, the bell was now an icon with its status raised even higher by the 'imaginative' writings of Philadelphia-based writer George Lippard (1822–1854), the author of the myth that the Liberty Bell had cracked ringing in American Independence. In his *Legends of the American Revolution* (1847) he invented wholecloth the yarn of a weather-beaten, white-haired old man ready at the clapper with 'a flaxen-haired boy with laughing eyes of summer blue' standing by to give the signal to ring forth the sound of freedom from British oppression. 'White America' took the tale to heart and believed the bell so named for that, rather than for millions of black Americans yearning for their freedom from 'White America'. Anyway, with the bell now second only to the bald-eagle in national iconography, the Wiltbank family came out of the woodwork and agitated for the return of his property, eventually agreeing to the extension of the loan for as long as the bell hung in Independence Hall. In 1984, Wiltbank heir James McCloskey tried to lay claim to the bell on the grounds that it no longer hung in Independence Hall but was on public display about a block away in its own pavillion. This, he claimed, placed the custodians in breach of the 1915 agreement therefore he wanted the bell handed over so he could melt it down, he having worked out that it would make 7 million rings, each with a crack in it, that he could sell for $39.99 a piece – nice try no cigar.

But there was someone else greatly influenced by the Liberty Bell, Charles Fey (1861–1944), inventor of the slot machine. An immigrant from Bavaria, Fey was something of a mechanical genius and built his own machines by hand, placing them in San Francisco bars of the

1890s. Knowing that many of his fellow immigrants were illiterate, he shunned numbers on the reels in favour of easily identifiable symbols – fruit. With perhaps misplaced fervour for his adoptive country, he selected the Liberty Bell as the jackpot winning line and the line of different fruits holding lesser values; a line of lemons got you nothing at all. No matter the symbols today, such machines are still called fruit-machines with Fey's company growing into Bell-Fruit and 'lemon' still used in the language for anything of no value.

POX, POX AND POX AGAIN

The white settlers invading the New World may have visited all sorts of mischief on the locals who got their own back by giving the invader syphilis in return. By the eighteenth century, the whites gave pay-back in the form of small-pox infected blankets, distributed to the Amerindians, to bring about their eradication through the first known incidence of deliberate and effective biological warfare – at least, those are two of the pox-myths attached to the opening up of America.

The myth that Columbus brought syphilis back to Europe from the New World was given wide currency by the popularity of *Candide* (1759) by Voltaire (1694–1778), whose real name was Francois-Marie Arout and 'Voltaire' an anagram of Arovet Li, the Latinised equivalent of Arout Jnr. In a classic scene designed to illustrate the naïve optimism of Pangloss, the eponymous character's tutor, while lamenting the fact that Columbus brought back 'the sickness which poisons the source of procreation', Pangloss says that this should be countered by the fact that he also brought back chocolate. But the blame aimed at the Amerindian rests on little more than the fact that the first observed and recognized outbreak occurred among French mercenaries invading the Italian port of Naples in 1495 which was a couple of years after Columbus' triumphant return to Spain. Not only is this a tad tenuous but some epidemiologists hold up examples of what they claim to be clear evidence of pre-Columbian syphilis, specifically the skeletons of thirteenth- and fourteenth-century monks of the Augustinian Friary in Hull in the northeast of England. Many of the exhumed bones bear lesions typical of such infection and the fact that they were monks should not be considered a factor in reducing the likelihood of their being so infected; *au contraire*; the ranks ecclesiastic have produced some of history's most enthusiastic horizontal-joggers; besides, what else was there to do on a rainy day in fourteenth-century Hull.

That said, after the Naples outbreak, syphilis was off around Europe like a startled gazelle and, while everyone sat around blaming each other – it was the French disease, the Italian disease, the Spanish disease, the German condition – the Italian poet-physician, Girolama Fracastoro (1553–1478) inadvertently gave name to the condition. He wrapped up his suggested cures in an instructive ditty entitled *Syphilis, or the French Disease* (1530) prompting those who had only heard of the work but never read it to think the terms interchangeable. In fact, the author meant only that the titles were alternatives to the same work. Translating from the Latin as pig-lover, Syphilis was the name of the central character, a shepherd and swine-herd who was given the new disease for his blasphemies and transgressions. Well, at least we had a name for the condition, even if it was 'pig-lover' and, as things turned out, there was a New World factor involved, albeit indirectly. The main culprit was European weather!

Professor Kristin Harper of Emory University, Atlanta, Georgia, has conducted a new study on the principles of phylogenetics (the study of evolutionary links between organisms) and has used these principles to analyse samples from around the world of the various strains of treponemes which cause syphilis and, more importantly, three other related conditions. Not only was syphilis readily identifiable as the most recently evolved member of that nasty little family but it is a kissing-cousin of a tropical disease called yaws. While this causes equally unpleasant disfigurations it is best described as a non-sexually transmitted and milder form of syphilis. It appears that Columbus' men were the conduit for syphilis but that this is not what they caught in the New World. What they brought out of America was yaws but it seems that infective learned to adapt to the cooler and drier climes of Europe where it stabilized as the syphilis pathogen and picked its new fun-time transmission route to ensure its survival. Infected with this new updated version of the pathogen, later visitors to the New World returned the nasty little spirochaete to do its work back home; show me yaws and I'll show you mine, so to speak. If Harper is right – and the lady is one smart cookie with an MPH in Global Epidemiology – then we have to rob the Amerindians of even this small revenge for what happened to them – and so to those smallpox blankets.

The entire pox-blanket myth rests on a couple of postscripts appended to authenticated letters, dating from 1763; sometimes a third source is included and it is the inclusion of this third source, among other things, which calls the whole tale into question. This last and frequently presented reference is taken wholly out of context from the diary of William Trent, commander of the Pittsburgh militia while that settlement lay under siege by the Indian Chief Pontiac, and is presented as corroboration by those wishing, for whatever reasons, to bolster up the myth with a lie. All three sources date from the Pontiac Rebellion of 1763 and the paper-trail reads as follows.

The first letter, dated 13 July 1763 and sent from the British General Henry Bouquet to General Jeffrey Amherst, presents the P.S.:

> I will try to inoculate the Indians by means of blankets that may fall in their hands, taking care however not to get the disease myself. As it is a pity to oppose good men against them, I wish we could make use of the Spaniard's Method and hunt them with English dogs, supported by Rangers, and some light horse, who would I think effectively extirpate or remove that Vermine.

In his reply to that letter, dated 16 July, Amherst also apparently resorts to a P.S. instead of addressing Bouquet's suggestion in the main body of his missive and, rather oddly, his P.S. requires a second page simply to carry the last dozen-or-so words; P.S.s are normally crammed into whatever space is left on the last sheet of the main text: 'You will do well to try to Innoculate the Indians by means of blankets, as well as to try Every other method that can serve to Extirpate this Execrable Race. I should be very glad could take Effect effect [*sic*], but England is at too great a Distance to think of that at present'. The repetition of 'effect' is the point at which the text moves to the additional page and, as was then the custom, the last word was repeated at the top of the following sheet to show the point of continuation and called the catchword, hence that term's shift to its present usage as a term referring to something on which other things hinge. On the 26th, Bouquet sends back the brief acknowledgement: 'Sir, I received yesterday your Excellency's letters of 16th with their Inclosures. The signal for Indian Messengers and all your directions will be observed.'

Now then, this author has never seen the originals of these letters, only reproductions and, even if seen would in no way be qualified to identify part or entire forgery but, using simple logic, something here smells. Had there been a plan between these two men to embark on the wholesale eradication of their Indian enemies, surely this would have taken up more detailed discussion in full letter rather than brief P.S.s nailed onto other more mundane correspondence. And that last acknowledgement of the 16th! If Bouquet really had been given the green-light to some plan to conserve manpower while inflicting casualties on the enemy like never before, surely it might have called for something more enthusiastic than 'OK; I'll give it a whirl'. Where is all the florid vehemence of before? Surely Bouquet would have lapsed to something full of 'vermine' being 'smitten and cast low by the will of God', or some such. Take away those two P.S.s and there is nothing left; that final acknowledgement sounding more like a polite indication of intended compliance with other and routine matters. Sometimes it is asserted that the following is to be found in an earlier letter of Amherst's: 'Could it not be contrived to send the Small Pox among those disaffected tribes of Indians? We must on this occasion use every stratagem in our power to reduce them.' It seems that all who have searched for this sentiment in other letters have come up empty-handed.

Apart from the problems surrounding the authenticity of the aforementioned snippets there is the problem of the medical knowledge of the day and the effectiveness of such a plan. The year 1763 lay way before the first glimmerings of mainstream acceptance of the modern germ theory; viral infection was not even considered until the late nineteenth century; in the eighteenth century it was the miasma theory which held sway. Even Florence Nightingale adhered to the miasma theory, which claimed that disease was transmitted through foul odours, and publicly lampooned anyone who said different. Not until Louis Pasteur's famous experiment of 1859 and Robert Koch's 1876 proof that anthrax was caused by a bacterium did the world change its mind and accept the germ theory so we are forced to ask how a couple of soldiers in the 1760s were 100 years advanced of mainstream medical thinking. Accepting for the moment that the P.S.s are genuine, and that Bouquet and Amherst were far-sighted medical geniuses, would it have worked? The answer to that seems to be somewhere between highly unlikely and a flat no.

The smallpox virus is extremely stable and, in ideal conditions, it can indeed survive for an alarming length of time outside the host, on such items as blankets and clothing. But exposure to sunlight and the general atmosphere greatly reduce the virus' integrity. This, coupled with the facts that the virus is only highly infectious when spread in aerosol form from coughs and sneezes and has to invade the new host through the nose, blankets from the beds of the infected would not a good vehicle make. And, speaking of blankets from such a source, it is time for William Trent's diary entry of 24 May 1763.

Trent's diary for that day does indeed include the words: 'we gave them two blankets and a handkerchief out of the smallpox hospital. I hope this will have the desired effect'. This, of course, sounds most incriminating until the reader is allowed to see the entry in its entirety. (Some punctuation has been added and unnecessary information removed to aid ease of reading):

> The Turtle's Heart, a principle warrior of the Delewares, and Mamaltee, a Chief, came within a small distance of the fort. Mr McKee went out to them and they made a speech letting us know that [Fort] Ligonier was destroyed, that a great number of Indians were coming and, that out of regard to us, they had prevailed upon the 6 Nations not to attack us but give us time to go down the country and they desired that we would set off immediately. The Commanding Officer thanked them; let them know that we had everything we wanted, that we would defend it against all the Indians in the woods … they said they would speak to their Chiefs … and returned to say they would hold fast the Chain of Friendship. Out of our regard to them, we gave them two blankets and a handkerchief out of the smallpox hospital. I hope it will have the desired effect.

So, in reading the entirety it becomes clear that 'the desired effect' was to impress the Indians with gifts of friendly intent. There is nothing to say that there were any sufferers in the unit at the time and, if there were, this well-intentioned gesture *could* have gone horribly awry. But more significantly than that, it clearly shows that educated men of the time knew nothing of such potential hazards.

While no-one can underestimate the devastating impact of the diseases carried to the New World by invading Europeans, recent genetic research seems to have come up with an answer as to why these infections went through whole populations like a dose of salts, inflicting the death tolls that they did. It seems that the fiercely defended tribal nature of Amerindian society worked against them in the disease stakes. In a parallel to the findings of Brian Sykes, the world-class geneticist based at Oxford University whose *Seven Daughters of Eve* (2001) showed just how closely we are all related, genetically, recent research in America established that all Amerindians ultimately shared common descent from a mere four women or four closely related groups of women. It is also now known that any virus caught from a member of the family hits far harder than one caught from a stranger as the bug has already figured out some or most of the genetic make up and gets smarter and more deadly with every transfer within a genetically linked group; basically the little beasts have figured out how best to by-pass or fool any of that body's defence structures. The level of interbreeding among the Amerindians, with each tribe sticking pretty much to its own, left them wide open to the ravages that were visited upon them by contact with outsiders. But there is one more American pox-tale to tell yet.

Few in the UK have even heard of the Tuskegee Experiment, a protracted 'research programme' conducted by the United States Public Health Service and one worthy of any Second World War Nazi mania. In 1932 the United States Public Health Service (US PHS) began a study of 399 African-Americans in Tuskegee, Alabama, this exercise amounting to little more than the monitors sitting back to watch how syphillis would spread from such an untreated 'sample batch' of males and how long it would take them and other infected parties to die off. Even in the America of today, any suggestion that some of these men were deliberately infected to 'bring the study up to quota' elicits howls of protest from certain quarters but the horrendously callous nature of the programme in no way rules that out; those involved obviously didn't give two hoots for their lab-rats. Deliberately infected or not, those in the sample batch were not informed of their condition, were denied any effective treatment and were fobbed off with assorted explanations for their progressively inhibiting symptoms. None of the patients were asking awkward questions as the programme was careful to focus on poor and illiterate subjects. Unbelievably, the 'experiment' was still running in 1972, when a whistle-blower called Paul Buxton got in touch with Jean Heller of Associated Press, she breaking the story in the 25 July edition of the *Washington Post*. Fred Gray, the lawyer who had defended both Martin Luther King and Rosa Parks was swiftly successful in his class-action against the US Government to secure $10 million for the survivors. (Parks, coincidentally from Tuskegee herself, is invariably hailed as a black woman who refused to vacate a white-only seat on her bus but this is not the case. She was sitting meekly in a black-only seat but, as all the white seats filled up she was told to vacate her black-only seat for a white passenger and it was at this point that she uttered her immortal 'No!')

By 1972 the full extent of the ridiculous experiment was revealed. The 'rationale' was clearly racist, an attempt to establish that white and black were 'different'. The former suffered more neurological (brain) complications upon infection while the latter exhibited more on the cardiovascular side of things. Most surprising of all, not all the monitors were white, several black doctors and technicians were fully involved and knew damned well what they were doing. All attempts from outsiders to secure treatment for those in the sample-batch were vigorously blocked by the US PHS; when certain members of the study volunteered for service in the Second World War and were identified by army induction as suffering from the condition, the US PHS intervened to prevent disclosure to said men and block any army treatment. No-one knows how many outside the experiment were infected by the 99 lab-rats but, come the close in 1972, 128 of the original batch were dead, forty of their wives infected and nineteen of their children born with the condition. The whole story make for grim reading but those interested in more detail only have to google 'Tuskegee Experiment' and then prepare for a rather unsettling read.

PRATT'S GREAT AUNTIE THAIS ONE ON

Even those who hate musicals will reluctantly confess to some knowledge of the smash-hit *The King and I* and its irksomely memorable ditties, but to be caught in Thailand with a copy of this film, or the 1999 non-musical but equally annoying remake starring Jodie Foster, will earn you a short stay in one of the country's many 'Bangkok Hiltons'. The Thais take their heritage far more seriously than do we in the West where films routinely turn history on its head with the audience not giving a damn as long as there is plenty of sex and violence to compensate for the lack of authenticity. Not so the Thais who object to this particular farrago of lies being presented to successive generations as historical fact, recorded by an English governess allegedly based in the palace during the reign of their still-venerated King Mongkut, Rama IV (1804–1868). The author of the original 'memoirs', Anna Leonowens (1831–1915), presents the king as a benighted and savage ruler, slowly brought under her calming influence, despite the odd glitch when he murders a couple of his wives, has others cast into underground dungeons, whips slaves and offers elephants to President Lincoln to help him out in the American Civil War. Oh, and of course, she has to teach him to dress in a civilized manner and use a knife and fork. No wonder the Thais are ticked off.

By the time Mongkut had ascended the throne in 1851 he was forty-seven and had spent the previous twenty-seven years on a pilgrimage around his own country, living the life of a simple monk, with no support, so that he could acquaint himself with the people he might one day be called upon to rule. He was not only extremely devout but also a voracious learner who spoke several languages. Realising the increased need to play footsie with the ever-encroaching Western powers, it was Mongkut himself who decreed a new dress-code for the court, as he was fully aware that, in Westerners' eyes, his ministers wandering aground the palace in nothing but loincloths would be taken for a bunch of primitives, even if the loincloths were made of natty silk. The reasoning behind this palace dress code was as practical as it was ancient; anyone so dressed would find it pretty difficult to enter the palace carrying a weapon; but no matter, Mongkut decreed all should clad up in full fig long before the so-called Anna Leonowens turned up in Thailand. One of his first acts was to open the doors of the Royal Harem so that any who wanted to leave and find husbands of their own were free to do so. Those who remained in the harem were welcome to stay on at the palace for as long as they cared and leave at any future time, should the mood then take them. Not content with instituting 'women's lib' in the palace he further decreed that all arranged and enforced marriage was to be banned, as it was the common practice of selling wives to pay off debts.

By 1862 the influx of Western missionaries and commercial emissaries was so increased that Mongkut thought it high time the members of the Royal Family were taught English and, to this end, he contacted his consul in Singapore, famed for its English contingent, and asked Tan Kim Ching to hunt out a suitable candidate. She should be not only well qualified and respectable but also as 'unconnected' as possible – Mongkut had no intention of hiring a spy to infiltrate his own household – and be made fully aware that the job entailed the teaching of the English language and that alone; any attempt to convert family members to Christianity or to influence their attitude towards the West in any way would invite instant dismissal.

Ching made some enquires and established that there was such a woman in town; one who seemed to keep herself very much to herself and so he invited her to interview. Unfortunately this was the woman calling herself Anna Leonowens who turned up with a false background story and a fistful of forged references which convinced Ching she might just fit the bill. It was only after she had been ensconced in the Thai palace for several weeks that Ching found out that the reason she kept herself to herself was that none of 'polite' English society would have anything to do with her as she was considered something of a black sheep but, as there had been no howls of protest from Thailand where all seemed to be going smoothly, Ching thought it best to keep his mouth shut and let sleeping dogs lie. From this point on little is known as no-one in Thailand thought her important enough to record details of her stay, no more than they would that of any other palace servant. That she stayed there for four-and-a-bit years is more than adequate proof that she did a good job but she was in no way the pivotal figure of the Thai court that she would later purport herself to have been. She did not wield any influence over Mongkut or the heir apparent, Prince Chulalongkorn, and the idea of her arguing with and invariably cowing an absolute monarch with her dictatorial, home-counties superiority is nothing short of laughable. She did not jack-boot about the palace in frilly ballgowns, altering the course of Thai history, she simply held English classes. Nor was she crouched at Mongkut's deathbed, badgering him to institute further reforms before he snuffed it – her services had been terminated in 1867 after which she returned to England and was still there in 1868 when she learned of Mongkut's death. Now feeling free to weave her fantasy, she quit London for New York where she began writing a series of increasingly elaborate 'true accounts' of her time in Thailand, including the one that caused all the trouble: *The English Governess at the Siamese Court* (1870).

Not only is this the foundation for the 'true-story' plays and films but it is also the book in which Leonowens makes all her outlandish claims within the same publication so it is on this that we shall concentrate. She begins the yarn with the same pack of lies she gave Ching to get the job in the first place; she was born

Anna Crawford in Wales in 1834, the daughter of a British Army Captain killed in the Sikh Rebellion. At fifteen she embarked on a protracted tour of the Middle East with one Revd. Percy Badger in order to escape an unwelcome marriage to a man twice her age as organized by her step-father who wanted her off his hands. Upon her return she had married Army Captain Thomas Leonowens who died on a tiger-hunt just before the family fortune was lost in the Indian Mutiny. In fact, Annie Edwards was born in India in 1831, the daughter of a cabinet maker and his Indian wife. She did indeed go on tour with the Revd. Percy Badger for the reasons stated but, with Badger's marital status being in question at the time, what she got up to with the Revd. Percy, who was also twice her age, was the subject of much gossip. Be that as it may, upon her return she married an eighteen-year-old clerk called Thomas Leon Owens, a bit of a loser who, having dragged her off to Penang where he found a job in a hotel, dropped down dead leaving Anna to head for Singapore where she was largely shunned by the English community, they knowing the truth about her.

The publication of her book, the title of which elevated her from teacher to governess, certainly made her money and something of a minor celebrity on both sides of the Atlantic, but she was soon overplaying her hand on lecture tours where she would be confronted by others who knew the land of which she spoke and who spoke its language. These people were more than a little puzzled by her assertions that Mongkut routinely threw irksome wives into dungeons beneath the palace as it was a well-known fact that the land around Bangkok was far too watery to allow excavation of any subterranean rooms, no matter their nature or purpose. There were in fact no prison-quarters at all in the palace. Those who spoke Thai were likewise shocked at her half-baked pretensions to that language which she massacred in her book and every time she tried to impress by trotting out a few garbled phrases. Another glaring hole in her presenting herself as a central figure of Mongkut's court is her complete lack of understanding of Buddhism which she consistently refers to as a religion; it is nothing of the kind. Translated from Sanskrit, 'buddha' means wisdom, awareness and understanding and, far from there being any god involved, each person following that way of life is charged with the responsibility of finding their own understanding of the nature of things to become a Buddha themselves; there is no, one, single and supreme Buddha, the world is full of them. All religions claim the immutable 'truth', demand adherents accept certain logicalities on faith alone and place control of their lives and eternal souls in the care of a supernatural being; Buddhism demands each finds their own truth and determines their own path to it. No-one enjoying even the most fleeting association with Mongkut could have failed to grasp that one essential trait in the man; it is what he lived by.

And so to the most offensive part of her yarn, as far as the Thais are concerned, and a lie made much of in her book and all stage and film versions thereof. The Princess/Concubine, Tuptim, was, according to Leonowens, personally whipped to a frazzle by Mongkut before being burnt at the stake in public for having followed her heart and trying to elope with the man of her dreams, he also meeting a suitably grisly end for his crime of passion. Not only does this run contrary to the well-documented 'standing orders' for the ladies of the harem being allowed to chose their own paths, but not one other Western observer in the city at the time – and there were many – bothers to mention such an execution. Besides, in 2001 the Thai Princess Vudhichalerm Vudhijaya (b. 1934) revealed in an interview that this same Tuptim was her grandmother and that she had, after Mongkut's death, become one of Chulalongkorn's thirty-six wives after he himself became Rama V. She also made it clear that, a Buddhist monk at heart, Mongkut was simply not capable of such behaviour.

When talking about her relationship with the prince, Leonowens would have the world believe that it was she and she alone who changed the lad from a savage chip off the old block to a modern-thinking young man who would eventually ban slavery in Thailand, some forty years after her time at the palace, and all down to her making him read *Uncle Tom's Cabin* in her class. Not only is this pure guff – remember Mongkut's strict instructions regarding her role as teacher of English and that alone – but it reveals her total lack of knowledge regarding the nature of slavery in that country. Far from the brutal reality it was in the 'civilized' West, Thai slavery, like so many Eastern institutions, was nothing like it appeared to Western eyes. The so-called 'slaves' usually entered into the state willingly in order to fund other members of their own family and could buy themselves out at any time. There were strict laws prohibiting the ill-treatment of these 'slaves' and all Western observers – the French Bishop Jean Babtiste Pallegoix (1805–1862) and the British Sir John Bowring (1792–1872) to name but two – wrote frequently on the nature of slavery in Thailand, remarking that those in such service enjoyed far better treatment and living conditions to those endured by domestic servants in Paris and London. Bowring further noted that the arrangement was so beneficial to the 'slave' that: 'whenever they are emancipated they always sell themselves again'. But, at the end of the day, slavery is slavery and, far from Leonowens' civilizing hand, aided by Harriet Beecher Stowe, it was the example of the American Civil War and its aftermath which convinced Chulalongkorn to institute a controlled programme of the deconstruction of all slavery rather than risk the upheaval he had monitored so carefully in the United States. Still persistent from the ramblings of Anna is the notion that Mongkut was so ignorant of modern weaponry and the Western industrial might that he was daft enough to write to President Abe Lincoln, offering a squadron of war-elephants to stomp all over the opposition. But something of the sort did happen; there is at least a kernel of truth to this myth. Some time before the commencement of the American Civil War, Mongkut did write to then-President James Buchanan offering the friendly gesture of a breeding herd of trained draught elephants, along with their mahouts, suggesting they might prove useful for heavy haulage in the areas not yet serviced by the railroad. By the time the letter arrived, Buchanan was replaced by Lincoln who wrote back to politely decline the offer.

Finally, the Karloff connection. Casting minds back to Anna finding solace with Percy Badger to elude the trap of an unwelcome marriage; it seems her fifteen-year-old sister, Eliza, was not so sniffy about the arrangements made for her, she happily tying the knot with Edward Pratt, a thirty-eight-year-old Anglo-Indian Civil Servant. Their son, also Edward, married one Eliza Milland, and their son, William, would go on to find international fame as monster-ghoul actor, Boris Karloff (1887–1969); well, it would have been difficult scaring people with a name like Billy Pratt. So keen to distance herself from her real roots and so great was Anna's fear of exposure to ridicule that, when some Pratt or other contacted her to say that young William would like to meet her - he no doubt anxious to capitalize on Anna's contacts to get a helping hand up the showbiz ladder – she threatened suicide if any Pratt so much as wrote to her ever again.

RED COATS AND BLACK HOPES

Although there were many major engagements fought throughout the Anglo-Zulu War of 1879, the names of Isandlwana and Rorke's Drift persist in the popular mind, mainly due to the fact that these twinned events have been so often portrayed in film that we are left with a somewhat distorted 'memory' of exactly what happened.

First came Isandlwana. The British Government had delivered an ultimatum to the Zulu Chief, Cetshwayo, on 11 December 1878, this demanding, among other things, that he disband his army within thirty days of said date under penalty of invasion. Knowing full well that this would be impossible for Cetshwayo to do within a month, even if he wanted to, and knowing equally well that the list of secondary demands would be unacceptable, the British Government and the Zulu chief were quite happy playing out their Mexican standoff when they were catapulted into conflict by the precipitous actions of General Lord Chelmsford, a blustering buffoon of a man who, without authorization, marched into Zululand on 10 January 1879 with a grand total of perhaps 5,000 regular troops and another 8,200 native irregulars and support personnel. About 3,000 of these men were delegated to the guarding of the frontier with Natal, another 2,000 sent to form a presence in the Utrecht district and, having established a supply garrison at Rorke's Drift, Chelmsford marched on with some 4,000 men to make camp at Isandlwana on 20 January. Here again, Chelmsford divided his strength, marching on leaving some 1,300 in the exposed camp where they were wiped out two days later by some 10,000 Zulu.

Victorian Britain, with its self-perception of god-given and global superiority, instinctively shrunk from facing up to the fact that 'a bunch of fuzzie-wuzzies with pointy sticks' as the Zulu were rashly dismissed by Chelmsford, had given their finest a bloody nose. Instead of admitting smug complacency and a total underestimation of the fighting capabilities of the Zulu, a cruel twist of fate had to be invented to explain such a turn of events. Modern administrations resort to similar lies when they foul up; Dunkirk was actually a victory and Singapore only fell because all the guns faced seaward and the nasty Japanese came out of the jungle behind and, in the case of Isandlwana, the 'freak' Zulu victory was explained to a relieved British public as being attributable to the new-issue Mark V ammunition boxes being too resistant to speedy opening and hidebound Quartermasters unwilling, even in the heat of battle, to release supplies of said ammunition without the properly signed paperwork. Even the centenary cinematic celebration of the battle, *Zulu Dawn* (1979) reiterates these and other misconceptions surrounding the battle.

The Mark V box was indeed a sturdy affair; what use an ammunition box that fell apart at the first bit of rough handling? Sometimes the ammo-myth is embellished with the absence of the right kind of screwdrivers to gain access to the contents but the Mark V was designed to reveal its contents by way of a sliding panel on the top; this panel was indeed secured by a single screw which could be overcome with one sharp blow from a rifle butt or a determined kick. The camp at Isandlwana held nearly half-a-million rounds of ammunition which was in abundant supply throughout the engagement; at no time did the defenders run short of ammunition or drop their rate of fire for any reason. It was Chelmsford's arrogance and folly as a commander which led to the rout.

Upon arriving at Isandlwana Chelmsford brushed aside any suggestions that he observe standard procedure with entrenchment and the forming of a laager by circling the wagons and establishing proper perimeters. Chelmsford thought his 4,000 troops – with artillery and Congreve rocket batteries – more than a match for anything the primitive Zulu could bring to the party. Unaware that the approaching Zulu army numbered upwards of 20,000, Chelmsford split his force and, heading off into the veldt with 2,500 men, left the balance of his command in the ill-established camp, now under Lt. Col Henry Pulleine, an officer more used to administrative duties than action at the sharp-end. Chelmsford's ridiculous idea was apparently to march out boldly into the Zulu heartland and invite the enemy to do battle, as if it were some sort of inter-school cricket match. His fatal misunderstanding, ignorance and underestimation of his enemy caused him to misread the contradictory incoming intelligence as to the location of the main Zulu force, thus failing to realize that he was dealing with an enemy capable of moving in armies of thousands at the staggering rate of 50 miles a day, only to rear up from the long grass to attack those thinking them yet days away. In short, the barefoot Zulu army could move further and more quickly across the African plains than a column of British cavalry. As small war-parties deliberately kept orchestrating Chelmsford's manoeuvres in the veldt, a massive Zulu impi of 20,000 was bearing down on Isandlwana.

Setting aside half the force as back-up and others positioned to cut off any British retreat, a force of perhaps 10,000 Zulu began their assault at about 12:30 p.m. and within an hour it was all but over. Pulleine had spread his men across too wide a line for them to concentrate firepower on the enemy who was soon in their midst doing what he did best – *Sigidi!*, the Zulu command to kill, a term holding for them a literal meaning of 'the song of the blade as it bites'. Disembowelled and castrated, 1,329 were left to the jackals and the vultures and, when Chelmsford got back from his misguided tour of the veldt, there was not much to bury. Even the drummer-boys had been hung up on meat-hooks with their amputated testicles stuffed in their mouths; after Isandlwana, drummer-boys were never again permitted to enter battle zones. The only survivors were some 300 native troops who, knowing better than their employers the nature of the machine heading their way, had melted into the undergrowth before the battle began, and fifty-five British troops and officers, some of whom actually made it back to Rorke's Drift. And then there is the mystery of the two officers who fled the scene of slaughter for reasons much debated.

Lt. Teignmouth Melvill and Lt. Nevill Coghill both rode away in the closing minutes, the official version of events hailing their actions as valiant efforts to save the Colours from falling into enemy hands and undertaken as the direct result of orders from Pulleine, perhaps. Not only did this account of their actions arise from anonymous sources several weeks after the battle but Pulleine is known to have been killed in the opening stages of the engagement. Also, countless witnesses said that the two men left separately, initially riding out in different directions. As Adjutant, care of the Colours certainly fell within Melvill's remit but if he was intending to run for his life, taking them with him would make a good cover-story for such actions. None of this, of course, would explain Goghill's departure. Either way, both men were killed during their attempts to cross the swollen Buffalo River and were buried on the Natal side of that watercourse. That they were killed by pursuing Zulu is highly unlikely as the impi were still busy finishing off all they could find at Isandlwana; more likely they were picked off by 'friendly' locals who had had a bit of rough handling from Chelmsford's column when it passed through their land but a few days before.

Either way, the loss at Isandlwana was deeply felt back in the UK and, perhaps determined to have no more shame attached to the event, both men were nominated for the Victoria Cross in the safe knowledge that it could not then be awarded posthumously. When such awards were made allowable, both families received the posthumous VCs in 1907. (To wax pedantic for a moment, 'posthumous' does not properly apply to such awards; originally and properly is 'postumus', meaning last-born, applying only to a child born after the death of the father. After people began the present abuse of the term the 'h' crept in through erroneous association with the humus, or soil, in which the recipient was buried). And so to Rorke's Drift.

As soon as victory at Isandlwana was guaranteed, 4,000 of the Zulus held in reserve under the leadership of Dabulamanzi kaMpande, Cetshwayo's half brother, set out in pursuit of those known to have fled but with instructions to abandon the chase at the Buffalo River and not cross into British Natal and provoke further attention from the British. The river was barely 5 miles distant and, when he got there, kaMpande could not resist crossing over to have a crack at Rorke's Drift which stood just the other side. He knew it was defended by no more than 150 troops and thought a quick victory would raise his profile, as things turned out he was lucky that Cetshwayo didn't kill him.

For its part, the supply dump had already heard of Isandlwana from absconding native irregulars so the small force had already made whatever preparations they could to receive any 'guests' that might turn up on their own doorstep. Naturally, most people's perception of what happened at Rorke's Drift is based in part on the official celebration of the event as the necessary antidote to Isandlwana and in the main from the famous 1946 film starring Michael Caine and Stanley Baker; needless to say, this latter 'source' is pretty wide of the mark, if only for the fact that most of the fighting took place in the dark.

First the minor misconceptions. The defending regiment was not Welsh but the 24th Regiment of Foot, otherwise known as the 2nd Warwickshires, which did not change its name to the South Wales Borderers until 1881. As one might expect of a regiment with its HQ so close to the Welsh border, there were quite a few Welshmen on the muster, sixteen at Rorke's Drift, but there was no 'X-Factor' sing-off with the defenders bellowing out 'Men of Harlech' in response to the Zulu war chant – apart from anything, the regimental song was 'The Warwickshire Lad'. In the opening stages of the film we are treated to Jack Hawkins' depiction of Swiss missionary Otto Witt as an over-the-hill, whisky-sodden, mealy-mouthed pacifist telling the command to abandon their posts and run for their lives before himself fleeing the scene with his pertly provocative daughter; in fact, Witt was then aged thirty and married with two small children and, far from being a pacifist railing against British intervention in Zulu affairs, it was he who had made arrangements for Rorke's Drift to be put at the army's disposal and it was he, on the morning of the attack, who had gone out scouting and, from a vantage point atop Shiyane Hill, had spotted and reported back of the presence of a large Zulu impi, still the other side of the Buffalo River. He stayed to help with the building of defences out of biscuit tins and mealie-bags before, quite rightly, leaving to ensure the safety of his own family in Oscarberg.

Similar license is taken with the depiction of most of the other characters; Chard (Stanley Baxter) and Bromhead (Caine) are presented as a pair of pukka stiff-upper-lippers whereas the real Chard was deemed lazy and inefficient and Bromhead, although a popular fop, was routinely kept away from any important duties as he was a bit of a dim-wit and almost completely deaf. Nor was there ever any dispute or debate as to who was in charge with Chard coming out the 'winner' due to his commission predating that of Bromhead by a matter of weeks; not only did Chard's commission predate that of Bromhead by years, but Chard had been left in command by the absent Major Henry Spalding so the question never arose. Having spent most of the morning listening to the gunfire from Isandlwana, Spalding decided he ought to be somewhere else – like 25 miles away in Oscarberg. His real motives only to be guessed at, he took off, ostensibly to raise reinforcements but never returned, later claiming he had been misinformed of the eradication of his force at Rorke's Drift and thought it best to stay put and help with the defence of the town in case it too was attacked. Few believed him; if reinforcement was a viable option then he should have stayed at his post and sent a junior officer instead. Basically, Spalding, Chard and Bromhead were a right trio which is why they were left in charge of a supply station which no-one for one minute thought would become a point of attack.

Moving down the ranks, Colour Sergeant Bourne, played as a 'come-along-my-lad-and-no-nonsense', by middle-aged Nigel Greene was in fact a mere twenty-three, the youngest CS in the British

Army at the time and known to one and all as The Kid. Actually, he lived until he was ninety-one, seeing out the Second World War to die in 1945, the last of the Drifters! Such license is perhaps harmless but the depiction of Private Henry Hook as a drunken malingerer caused such offence to his family that his daughter walked out of the film's premier in disgust. Hook was actually a teetotal, model soldier who had recently been awarded Good Conduct Pay; far from malingering in the hospital he and a couple of others had been sent there to defend the thirty-or-so men therein, with Hook putting up such a fight that most survived, which is more than can be said for any of the Zulu who attacked Hook's command. Rather unfairly, the 'model' soldier set in contrast to Hook, Corporal William Allen, was the real drunk of the detachment, recently busted from sergeant for repeated lapses. And one last minor point, the men did not fight in bright white pith helmets and bright red coats; standard procedure in such climes was to stain the helmet dark with tea and, in such defensive action, to abandon the red tunic in favour of a similarly stained singlet; DIY khaki, if you like; they may have been British but they were not stupid. And so to battle.

As stated, by midday they were already aware of the danger they might be in from the sound of the distant yet sustained gunfire – apart from Bromhead who exasperated one and all by announcing loudly that he could hear no gunfire – and the arrival of deserters and survivors from Isandlwana who turned up in dribs and drabs. In the film, it is Chard who takes manful control, barking orders as to how to best build defences from the supplies they were guarding whereas it was AAC James Dalton VC who took the useless pair aside and told them what they had to do. Also, while Chard and Bromhead were all for making a run for it, Dalton was the one who convinced them that they had to stay and fight as any attempt to flee would have them overtaken and annihilated by the swift-moving impi. Experienced in the likely form of the impending attack, Dalton told them exactly how best to establish their defences and apparently grew increasingly irked by Bromhead's mantra of 'I'm sorry, Old Boy, could you say that again?'. Dalton's citation for the VC says it all: 'For his conspicuous gallantry during the attack on Rorke's Drift post by the Zulu on the night [n.b.] of the 22nd January 1879 when he actively superintended the work of the defence.' With such work done all they could then do was sit back and wait for the onslaught.

The first hostile gunfire came at about 4:30 that afternoon but it is myth that these Zulu were sniping from the overlooking Oscarberg Hill with modern Martini-Henry rifles looted from Isandlwana because this impi had moved off before any such pilfering was possible; they were firing old muskets sold to the Zulu, rather ironically, by James Rorke who had established the post in 1849. Anyway, at these first shots the native irregulars and their white officers decided that it was time to go. To be fair, these men had seen what had happened at Isandlwana so no wonder their nerve went; their retreat was fired on by those without the luxury of such an option and several, including Corporal William Anderson, were brought down. And then it started; the only thing that has not and could not be exaggerated and mythologized was the savagery and scale of the onslaught and the determined response of the Warwickshires.

The small size of the post actually worked in its favour with the Zulu quickly realizing that this was not going to be any Isandlwana; although out-numbered perhaps fifty-to-one, the firepower was concentrated enough to make the Zulu pull back and have a re-think. As the next waves of attack probed here and there, Dalton morphed his defences to match or anticipate where the next strikes would fall and it is mainly due to his quick-thinking that the detachment survived at all. But the Zulu is nothing if not determined and the night attacks continued through to 2:30 the next morning with the defenders firing blind into the dark at stomach height and then concentrating on the directions from which they heard screaming. A body-shot at close range from a Martini-Henry .450 round inflicted horrific injuries, leaving an exit-wound the size of a small cereal box so even the wounded lost all interest in the proceedings and, when dawn broke, the occupants of the compound saw they were surrounded by some 400 dead and perhaps 800 wounded. What the Zulu did not know was that the defenders were at breaking point and almost out of ammunition; of their stash of 20,000 rounds, only 900 remained, so one more determined rush would have secured victory.

In the film, the Zulu return en masse to the crest of the ridge and make chanting salute to a worthy foe, in reality they simply melted away, having realized that Chelmsford and his column were advancing towards them. It was with his arrival that the atrocities began. These men had just finished cleaning up the gore at Isandlwana so some excuse can be made for their actions which were hushed up and withheld from the public domain. As the exhausted defenders took a well-earned break, the relief column strung up, shot or buried alive every last breathing Zulu. Horace Smith-Dorrien, then a lieutenant but later a general, admitted that frames intended for drying ox-hides were used as gallows to slowly strangle the wounded while others were variously dispatched or thrown into pits to be buried alive. The private journal of Lt. Col John North Crealock, held in the Royal Archives in Windsor, states that there were 351 dead Zulu and 500 wounded and it is known that no prisoners were taken.

In all, eleven VCs were awarded to the defenders of Rorke's Drift in what seems to be a political move to lionize the event to such a degree that it blanked out the memory of the business at Isandlwana, such motive strongly suspected by the British Military High Command. General Sir Garnet Wolseley objected to the 'cheapening' of the award by its being scattered like confetti on men who, in the opinion of most in the know, simply fought like wildcats to save their own skins, they having no other alternative; it was not, as he observed, a case of them volunteering to go to Rorke's Drift to lay down their lives to hold up the Zulu advance for the salvation of others. 'It is a monstrous thing', he wrote in his journal 'making heroes of those who, shut up in buildings at Rorke's [*sic*] Drift, could not bolt and fought like rats for their lives, which they could not otherwise save.' The Duke of Cambridge, Commander in Chief of the British Army, restricted himself to the wry observation that: 'We are giving the VC very freely, I think.'

SEIG HEIL COLUMBIA

The myth that the USA missed out on being a German-speaking country by only one vote is still going strong and repeated so often in print that it is doomed to longevity. But no such vote was ever taken because there was never any such proposal considered by any legislative body; what happened was this.

Heavily backed by the lobby of the so-called Pennsylvanian Dutch – such people in fact being German and their epithet a corruption of 'Deutsch' – the German contingent of Augusta, Virginia, presented to Congress on 20 March 1794 a recommendation that all laws and regulation be published in both German and English: 'for the accommodation of such German citizens in the United

States as do not understand the English language'. Unlike now, when even the lifts in town halls announce 'going up' in so many different languages that one has quit the device before the end of the recording, there was little sympathy for the request. That aside, it is clear that the move was not to replace English but to provide for all public notices and the like to be printed in both English and German for the benefit of those who could not be bothered to go bilingual. Not a popular motion, it took quite some time to limp onto the agenda; it was not even slated for discussion until 13 January 1795 and immediately proposed for adjournment. Some were of a mind to quash it there and then but others voiced that it should at least be considered. It was this vote for adjournment that went 42:41 in favour and, when the proposal was represented to Congress it was overwhelmingly rejected.

Interestingly enough, the USA has never had an official language to be challenged for its position as such; the English Language Amendment to the United States Constitution, demanding official recognition of English as the national language, has languished before Congress since 1981 and shows no signs yet of being discussed to anyone's satisfaction.

TURKEY-TROTS AND A RUM BAA-BAA

The general perception of the American Thanksgiving holds it as an unbroken tradition dating back to 1621 when the so-called Pilgrim Fathers extended the hand of friendship to the locals in gratitude for their lessons in survival and planting; Indians and settlers all enjoying their turkey, sweet potato and cranberries; not exactly. The 'tradition' of Thanksgiving on the fourth Thursday of November only dates back to 1941 when it was so decreed by Congress and, far from being some sort of inter-racial bonding ceremony, the 1621 bash was an affair of considerable tension after it was gate-crashed by about ninety curious natives who had come to see what was going on.

First, definition and a bit of the chronology; properly, a Thanksgiving (to God) was a fairly sober affair featuring religious rites and prayers, not games, races, copious amounts of beer and shooting matches spanning three days as did the 1621 knees-up. It was usually enacted after the successful conclusion of a voyage, venture or military victory and the first proper such Thanksgiving took place not at Plymouth Plantation in 1621 but fifty-six years before at what would become St Augustine in Florida. It was here that a Spanish expedition under Pedro Menendez de Aviles (1519–1574) landed on 8 September 1565 and to give thanks, they celebrated a Mass and invited a delegation of Timucua Indians to join them in a simple meal of bean soup and salt pork which was augmented by venison and seafood by the guests; a proper Thanksgiving was never marked with a gut-busting feast or over-indulgence of any kind. The next group to hold a Thanksgiving in North America and the very first to talk of it being an annual observation were the thirty-eight English settlers who, under the leadership of Captain John Woodleaf, arrived at Berkeley Hundred in Virginia on 4 December 1619, Woodleaf declaring: 'We ordaine that the day of our ships arrival at the place assigned for plantacon in the land of Virginia shall be yearly and perpetually keept holy as a day of thanksgiving to Almighty God.'

Even though he landed with a force of about 800, Menendez quickly realised the wisdom of arriving at some sort of accommodation with the numerically superior locals. This was a lesson unheeded by the Plymouth settlers who, having landed in 1620, made a complete hash of things. Upon landing, which did not involve anyone stepping ashore on the so-called Plymouth Rock, the community elected for what can only be described as a Communist system in which all laboured to the best of their individual ability, and pooled all resources, only taking back what they needed. With this running contrary to human nature, there were soon ructions with people stealing from the fields at night and the single men moaning about having to work to fill the storehouses to feed the married men's families. Although Trotsky would have been proud of them, the so-called Pilgrim Fathers soon kicked the kibbutz-kitsch into touch and shifted to a free-economy, just in time to avert total disaster. Their bacon was further saved by the assistance of Tisquantum (popularly rendered 'Squanto'), the last of the Patuxet Indians. He had been enslaved by previous expeditions, taken to Spain and was returned home in 1619 to find his people eradicated by the diseases left behind by his captors. Fluent in English, he for some reason took the newcomers under his wing and taught them how, where and when it was best to start planting; how to fish and how to make crude fertilizers to improve the crops. Basically he saved their lives which, as things turned out, prompted Indians from other tribes to kill him as a traitor in 1622.

So, having survived thanks to the misguided Squanto and various other ploys which, according to some, included the plundering of the deserted Patuxet villages, the gathering in of the abandoned harvests and a bit of grave-robbing for tools and blankets to boot, the settlers of 1620 managed to cling on. They did not however live in log cabins, these being a much later innovation introduced by Scandinavian and Germanic settlers, and they did not stomp about in black outfits with silly buckles on their hats, they wore a variety of coloured clothing, and did not brandish blunderbusses. By the time of the three-day event in question, which took place in late September or the first week in November, the previous winter had claimed forty-seven of their number, almost half, and the barley wheat and peas they had brought to plant had all failed; only Squanto's corn-fields flourished. But they resolved a celebration none-the-less; a holiday, not a Thanksgiving. They did not invite the locals to the feast and were more than a little miffed when ninety-odd of them turned up, outnumbering their fifty by nearly two to one. And most of the party-food was brought by the 'guests' which consisted of five deer, berries, lobster, duck, goose – not a turkey in sight, nor any potato of any kind – mussels and assorted fish for all; it was the settlers eating out of the Indians' grace not the other way round. But the event passed without incident and was forgotten; it was not repeated year on year and the first all-white Thanksgiving in that neck of the woods was an arrogant gathering marking an event of utter shame.

By 1637 the newcomers were fully entrenched and had struck deals and alliances calculated to set one tribe off against the other with the incentive of a scalp-bounty system – yes; scalping was introduced by the good Christians; it was unknown in the New World before their arrival. But there was still one tribe giving them trouble; the Pequot, so a combined force of settlers with Indian allies set out to finish them off at their main camp at the mouth of the Mystic River. They lay in wait until sun-up and then set fire to the long-huts, slaughtering all who tried to escape the inferno. Most of the 700 men, women and children fried alive with escapees variously hacked down by sword or shot. To quote Governor Bradford of the then Massachusetts:

Those that escaped the fire were slain with the sword; some hewed to pieces, others run through with their rapiers, so that they were quickly dispatched and very few escaped. It was conceived they thus destroyed about 400 at this time. It was a fearful sight to see them thus frying in the fire … horrible was the stink and scent thereof, but the victory seemed a sweet sacrifice, and they gave the prayers thereof to God, who had wrought so wonderfully for them, thus to enclose their enemies in their hands, and give them so speedy a victory over so proud and insulting an enemy.

And, Governor John Winthrop proclaimed: 'This day forth shall be a day of celebration and thanksgiving for subduing the Pequots.' There is in America considerable opposition to the existing fixture of Thanksgiving and its very celebration; the Hispanic element point out that 8 September (1565) should be the date of observation while the American-Indian lobby hold that the very celebration itself is a bit like asking the American Army to celebrate Little Big Horn Day. And as for the turkeys, well, they get no say in the matter at all.

For the next 100 years or so Thanksgivings were held on whim throughout the Colonies with little or no consistency of date or purpose. The first 'uniform' occasion was declared by President Washington in 1789 when he declared that the 26th of November (that year only) would be a national holiday to allow people of all denominations to spend the day in prayer and reflection on their great fortune in victory in the War of Independence (1775–1783). There was no particular significance to that date which he picked at random. President John Adams held a couple of Thanksgivings, one in 1798 and another in 1799, President Jefferson did not bother, leaving it to President James Madison to mark the close of the War of 1812 with a Thanksgiving and to hold two more in 1815, neither in the autumn. The Southern States largely shunned the occasion, they considering it an inappropriate 'nod' to Puritan bigotry. The establishment of Thanksgiving as an annual event on a specified day was the result of a long campaign mounted by the single-minded Sarah Josepha Hale (1788–1879) who badgered President Lincoln until he announced in 1863, right in the middle of the Civil War, that the last Thursday in November would thenceforth be a day of national thanksgiving and informed all that, in accordance with Hale's outline for the day, he and his family would be dining on turkey for the occasion. Just as Dickens invented the modern Christmas in his *A Christmas Carol* (1843), Hale invented the modern Thanksgiving in her *Northwood* (1827) in which she devoted an entire chapter to what she claimed constituted the 'traditional' menu of turkey and pumpkin pie. Proclaiming this to have been the meal enjoyed by the Pilgrim Fathers, cooked, no doubt, by the Pilgrim Mothers who never seem to get a mention, she likely got her notions about the turkey from a mistake in the writings of the aforementioned Governor Bradford – he of fried-Pequot fame – who recorded that turkey was a favourite of the original settlers, but he consistently used that term for the goose and sometimes for the duck. Pumpkin pie would have been an impossibility as the settlers would not have ovens for years to come. Either way, since 1863, turkeys have had little affection for American presidents.

But there were yet changes to be imposed on this 'ancient tradition'; as there can sometimes be five Thursdays in November the retail sector elected as their spokesman Fred Lazarus Jnr (1884–1973), founder of Federated Department Stores, which evolved into Macy's, he being successful in his quest to convince President Franklin D. Roosevelt in 1939 to fix Thanksgiving on the third Thursday to lengthen the run up to Christmas. The Republicans objected to his trampling on traditions dating back to the founding of 'our great nation' and the American football league was likewise hostile to the mess this made of their schedule. For the next couple of years people chose for themselves on which Thursday they observed Thanksgiving, depending on whether they were into shopping or football, FDR finally getting all parties to agree to the fourth Thursday in 1941. So, far from that day being chosen because it echoed back to something the early settlers did or did not do, Thanksgiving is pitched as a convenience for shopkeepers to better budget their Christmas stock-runs and not disrupt the football fixtures.

What of the mother of Thanksgiving, Ms Hale? It is doubtful that many readers will have heard of her but everyone in the English-speaking world will recognise her most famous quatrain concerning the antics of a certain Mary who had a little lamb. The Mary in question was Mary Sawyer (1806–1889), later Mary Tyler, of Sterling, Massachusetts, who was locally famed for her pet lamb that did indeed follow her to school, and everywhere else, for that matter. Hale, also a New Englander, gave the pair domestic and trans-Atlantic fame with her much-parodied tribute, first published in her *Poems for Our Children* (1830). No matter its banality, the rhyme soon enjoyed such ubiquity that when Edison made his first recording of the human voice in 1877 he picked the first verse of Hale's ditty as something that would be instantly recognisable throughout the English-speaking world. As for the lamb, it grew up something of a truculent maverick, dropping out of school for a life of drinking and gambolling in the local inns where it pan-handled for tots of rum, its favourite tipple; many the night it was seen staggering home, fully marinated, until one day it was no more. A cautionary tale indeed.

V-J DELAY

The general perception is that only the bombing of Hiroshima and Nagasaki brought Japan to the surrender table. It is also stated categorically in numerous sources that the occupants of both cities were forewarned by a massive leaflet-drop telling everyone to get the hell out of the area. It is also widely believed that the decision to proceed with the bombings was taken by a reluctant President Truman who had been advised from all quarters that he had no choice since the alternative was the loss of perhaps 1 million lives in the invasion of a still belligerent Japan. It is also generally accepted that Japan only considered surrender after both bombs had been dropped and that this intransigence left the Allied commanders no other alternative. All false.

Prior to the dropping of 'Little Boy' on Hiroshima and 'Fat Man' on Nagasaki the United States Air Force (USAF) had pretty much bombed Japan into the stone age; across a nine-month campaign of bombing Japanese civilians they had racked up a death toll of some 580,000 and reduced the major parts of sixty-six cities to rubble. The fire-bombing of Tokyo killed more than 140,000, this alone matching the combined death tolls inflicted by the immediate effects of both atomic devices. (The long term death toll of the drops is likely in the region of 500,000 with Hiroshima and Nagasaki still 'enjoying' ten-fold the Japanese national average of leukaemia and other cancers). None of this is any apology for Japan which was near the completion of its own atomic programme to produce similar devices; it had also committed unbelievable atrocities in every theatre of war it entered and had started the ball rolling with their sneak attack on Pearl Harbor, but the fact remains that the atomic bombings were in no way necessary in getting Japan to the negotiating table. It had in fact been asking for years; the bombs were dropped to impress another nation altogether and one seen as a potential enemy far more troublesome than Japan – Russia.

The truth is that Japan was already crippled by the close of 1943 with the civil-political powers making capitulation noises eighteen months before the drops. The army was another animal entirely and the complicated situation of having twin power-bases running the country will be examined later. The first formal offer of peace was made by Japan through the Vatican in the April of 1945 and a second through Moscow, by then in the Allied camp. Both times these approaches were rebuffed with the demand for unconditional surrender, a concept known to be alien and unacceptable to Japan which insisted on the continuing presence of the Emperor on the throne. To the enduring embarrassment of the American administration, which by then had already circulated the lie about the bombings having been reluctantly sanctioned to avoid the loss of 1 million American lives in any conventional invasion of Japan, Rear Admiral Ellis M. Zacharias, US Navy (retired) published a long and detailed account of the Japanese moves to secure peace in *Look* magazine dated 6 June 1950.

Towards the closing phases of the war, Zacharias was Chief of Staff of the 11th Naval District, based in San Diego, and as one-time Deputy Director of the Office of Naval Intelligence his particular brief was the waging of psychological war on the Japanese, through radio broadcasts and various other propaganda routes. He was also expected to keep his eyes and ears open and to keep abreast of who in Japan was in favour of suing for peace. Reporting directly to Secretary of the Navy, James Forrestal, Zacharias had soon set up certain channels of communication involving Pope Pius XII, Cardinal Fumasoni-Biondi, head of Vatican 'Intelligence', Petro Tatsuo Doi, Archbishop of Tokyo and links to the coterie surrounding the Dowager Empress in Japan, she and this circle known to be anxious for peace. As the unofficial communications through these lines intensified, the Emperor Hirohito removed the belligerent General Koiso from the office of premier and replaced him with the more dove-like Admiral Suzuki who had the specific instructions to establish peace and get Japan out of the war 'no matter how bitter the terms'. Because the Japanese 'Doves' had indicated a willingness to discuss peace terms at the Swedish Legation in Tokyo, Zacharias hatched a plan to send a submarine to Japan to establish direct contact with the Empress and her Doves and the emissary he had in mind was none other than actor Douglas Fairbanks Jnr, at the time attached to the Commander in Chief (COMINCH) at Admiral Ernest King's Washington HQ. For all his Hollywood image, Fairbanks was a highly competent officer who, after attachment to Lord Mountbatten's Commando units, set up the

United States Navy 'Beach Jumpers' units, basically commando units which went ashore in enemy territory as an advance guard to any full-scale landing. So, not only was Fairbanks a highly competent officer but also, best of all, he already knew some of the Doves, on a personal basis from pre-war contact. Despite all this and the door being held open in Tokyo, the idea was dismissed by Washington as 'so much Buck Rogers crap'.

Undeterred, Zacharias formulated a plan to use the highest-ranking Japanese officer in American hands, General Hiroshi Oshima, he the Japanese Ambassador to Germany who had been found hiding in the southern reaches of that country by the advancing Allies. Basically, the idea was to arrange a supervised meeting with Admiral Suzuki on some remote island and give him something concrete to take back to the Emperor. But, as soon as the basics of the plan were mooted, Oshima was whisked out of their grasp and 'buried' somewhere until after the drops. When Archbishop Doi communicated through the Vatican yet another desperate plea for peace, this time direct from Hirohito, this too was burked by Washington with the State Department muttering some fluff about their doubts that the American public 'might never approve of a peace negotiated with the help of the Roman Catholic Church'. Forced to the inevitable conclusion that perhaps Washington simply did not want peace but an overwhelming military victory, Zacharias decided to take matters into his own hands.

On 21 July 1945, with Truman safely out of the way at the infamous Potsdam Conference where the fate of Hiroshima and Nagasaki was sealed, Zacharias made a broadcast through diplomatic channels to Japan without telling the President, the State Department or the Joint Chiefs. Hirohito was told in plain language that it was either complete destruction followed by a dictated peace or an 'unconditional surrender with its attendant benefits as laid down in the Atlantic Charter'. As Zacharias himself put it: 'the hornets' nest was stirred' with all and sundry screaming for his head. But, in the midst of the ensuing political storm: 'Tokyo broadcast the first answer to my announcement. It was, in effect, an open invitation to begin surrender negotiations on the terms we had proposed.' To continue in Zacharias' own words:

> But though we gained a victory, it was soon to be cancelled out by
> the Potsdam Declaration and the way it was handled. Instead of being

a diplomatic instrument, transmitted through regular diplomatic channels and giving the Japanese a chance to answer, it was put out on the radio as a propaganda instrument pure and simple. The whole manoeuvre, in fact, completely disregarded all essential psychological factors dealing with Japan.

It [the official American reply to the Japanese offer of talks] was drafted in the presence of the Russians as they stood poised to enter the Far Eastern War, convinced that Japan could not accept it in the time limit set. It was offered in the shadow of the A-bomb, ready to be released over a city whose population had not been forewarned as other cities to be bombed by the Air Force had been forewarned before. The Potsdam Declaration, in short, wrecked everything we had been working for to prevent further bloodshed and insure our post-war strategic position. Just when the Japanese were ready to capitulate, we went ahead and introduced the world to the most devastating weapon it had ever seen and, in effect, gave the go-ahead to Russia to swarm all over Eastern Asia. We now know that, without those extreme measures, Japan would have quit by September 15.

And it wasn't only Zacharias who thought the bombing unnecessary; this was also the opinion of Admirals Leahy and King, and Generals Eisenhower and LeMay. Einstein spoke of having 'put dynamite in the hands of children' and even Oppenheimer thought it brutally pointless to drop the bombs on 'an essentially defeated enemy'. There were indeed warning leaflets dropped on the devastated cities, but three days after the event which is how they survived to be touted as exhibits. The American newspapers, at the behest of the administration, trumpeted headlines claiming there to have been no fall-out in the target areas which were 'clean' and any post-drop footage of the target areas showing anything but the structural devastation was impounded. Ninety-five per cent of the dead and 'survivors' were women, children and other non-combatants, and no-one back home wanted anyone seeing people staggering around with all their hair and half their skin missing. While it is true that Hiroshima did have an outlying and important army base, the bomb was targeted on the city centre. There was a later myth, circulated by the anti-bomb lobby, which tried to promote the belief that nothing would grow in the two drop-zones for years after, but the opposite is true. Within days the ruins were covered with all sorts of fresh growth because the radiation had zapped all the bugs, insects and other elements hostile to vegetation which was then free to run rampant; a rather drastic solution to a greenfly problem but there it is.

In the months immediately following the drops there was no need of justification as the American public were, according to contemporary polls, consistently 85–90 per cent in favour of the action; only later, when awkward questions were asked, did Truman's camp come up with all the saving-of-a-million-lives guff, McGeorge Bundy, who popularised the figure through speeches he wrote for Secretary of War Henry Stimson, later admitted that he had simply plucked the figure out of the air as the sort of number the American public would be able to relate to. In 1946, the United States Strategic Bombing Survey stated that:

> Even without the atomic bombing attacks air supremacy over Japan could have exerted sufficient pressure to bring about the unconditional surrender and obviate the need for invasion. Based on a detailed investigation of all the facts, and supported by the testimony of the surviving Japanese leaders involved, it is the Survey's opinion that ... Japan would have surrendered even if the atomic bombs had not been dropped, even if Russia had not entered the war and even if no invasion had been planned or contemplated.

The National Archives in Washington holds countless documents detailing the fact that America was well aware of Japan making overtures of peace 'even if the terms were hard' from 1943 onwards and that Henry Stimson told Truman that he was fearful that the US Air Force would have Japan so bombed-out that the new weapon would not be able to show its strength. Stimson himself would later admit that: 'no effort was made, and none was seriously considered, to achieve surrender merely in order not to have to use the bomb' and that his foreign policy colleagues were eager 'to browbeat the Russians with the bomb held rather ostentatiously on our hip'. General Leslie Groves, director of the Manhattan Project that made the bomb, testified: 'There was never any illusion on my part that Russia was our enemy, and that the project was conducted on that basis.' As Churchill himself points out in Volume 12 of his *Memoirs of the Second World War*, the Japanese Navy had been virtually eradicated and the air-defences were so weak that, by the spring of 1945, the American B29s were flying missions with impunity. As highlighted by the following exchanges and observations, the decision to drop the bombs had nothing to do with any desire to hasten the end of the war with Japan. Leo Szilard of the Manhattan Project team recalled that when he expressed his concerns over use of the bomb against a civilian target to Secretary of State James Byrnes: 'he did not claim that it was necessary to use the bomb to win the war. His idea was that the possession and use of the bomb would make Russia more controllable.' The Chief of General Staff, Admiral Leahy reckoned that: 'The Japanese were already beaten and ready to capitulate. The use of this barbaric weapon made no material contribution to our fight against Japan.' Eisenhower thought pretty much the same.

All this considered it is hard to dismiss the lobby maintaining that the Americans dropped the bombs simply because they wanted to, ignoring anything the Japanese said or did to make this politically unacceptable. Virtually everyone in America was then still seething at the very mention of Pearl Harbor and the horrors of Guam, Okinawa and Iwo Jima, to mention but a few of the names of the battles with the Japanese in the Pacific, which still provoke an emotional response in America today. Historians may banter the rights, wrongs and reasons for the bombings to this day, each lobby armed to the teeth with quotes and statistics, but none take into account the most powerful motivation for dropping the bomb – apart from making it clear to the Russians that America could blow the snow off their boots any time they chose – human nature. Whatever the uniform, there are still warriors underneath and warriors have a natural inclination to use any new toy at their disposal. In short, there would have been an overwhelming curiosity to see just what this new bomb could do; if they only wanted to scare the Japanese into submission why not drop it on an already bombed-out city or an uninhabited island? Give any group of boys/men a dangerous firework and, sooner or later, one of them will put a match to it; the prevailing sentiment in America of 'well, you started it' was as broadly represented in the upper echelons of the Armed Forces and the administration as it was throughout the rest of American society. Basically, America dropped the bombs on Japan because they wanted to hurt them while scaring the bejabbers out of the Russians but, most of all, they were just itching to see what such a device could do to a populated target.

The nuts-and-bolts of the bombing are well known; Brigadier Paul Tibbets (1915–2007) painted up the nose-cone of his B-29 with his mother's name, Enola Gay, a touching gesture which prompts arched eyebrows among psychologists to this day, and took off from Tinian Island in the Marianas to drop 'Little Boy' on Hiroshima on 6 August 1945, 8.15 a.m. local time. Squadron Commander Charles W. Sweeney, at the controls of another B-29, nicknamed Bockscar, took off on the 9th to bomb Kokura, a city which had a lucky escape due to bad weather and cloud cover. Swapping to his secondary target, Sweeney headed for Nagasaki, this last-minute diversion serving to highlight the lie of warning leaflets as no-one knew for sure which city would be hit, even after the planes had taken off. In 1976, Tibbets would take the controls of a restored B-29 at the Texas Air Show in Harlingen to conduct a re-enactment of the drop, complete with a mushroom cloud put up by conventional explosives on the ground, and all to the wild enthusiasm of the crowd. When the US Government had to apologize on his behalf to the Japanese, Tibbets said he couldn't understand what all the fuss was about and that, given the same circumstances, he would do it all again for real. He was ordered to refrain from making any further comment to the press.

Prior to the bombings Japan had been sent a final ultimatum – still not mentioning what the Americans had in waiting in the wings – and it was at this point that Japan shot itself in the foot with its unfathomable language. In their reply, the Japanese acknowledged the Potsdam Declaration and the conditions offered there but unfortunately used the word '*mokusatsu*' which can either mean to ignore or to refrain from making comment at the time – to take it under consideration and reply later, if you like. Washington chose to understand this as 'ignore' and set things in motion. After Nagasaki, the Japanese picked their words with a little more care and the war was over, bar one last-minute glitch. As mentioned before, Japan was a country led by the twin power-bases of the military and the civilian administration and it must be said that the army was not best pleased at the notion of surrender; there most certainly was a small element determined to fight to the last man standing. It is not much known that after Hirohito recorded his capitulation speech, a handful of junior officers attacked the Imperial Palace and tried to capture the recording and beg the Emperor to change his mind. They were confronted by senior officers who told the rebels that their promises of compliance had been given to the Emperor and they could not go back on their word so, after much wailing and gnashing of teeth, the rebels committed suicide and the Japanese acceptance of surrender was broadcast.

WALL STREET SHUFFLE

At the time of writing, much is being made of the imagined similarity between the prevailing economic recession and the Wall Street Crash of October 1929 when, as modern-day journalists and commentators would still have us believe, those responsible for that implosion of the market did the decent thing and flung themselves to the pavements, hundreds of feet below their luxury offices. Such myths were born then and are sustained now by a 'the bastards deserved it' mentality among those who lost homes, pensions and savings by tail-coating the roller-coaster rush for a quick buck. Just as most of those responsible for the current disaster are 'cushioned' against the fall-out of their own folly, the vast majority of those responsible for the 1929 disaster remained removed and unmoved by the devastation they had wrought.

Basically, people just loved the idea of fat-cat bankers getting their comeuppance; leading comedians such as Eddie Cantor and Will Rogers joked about executives pulling rank to jump the queues for the highest ledges, of hotels having two rates, one for sleeping and another for jumping and speculators selling space for bodies in the East River. Even Winston Churchill, in New York at the time, got in on the act, presenting letters to the *Daily Telegraph* recounting nights' sleep lost on account of financiers converting themselves to pavement-pizzas outside his hotel. The British tabloids ran daily and lurid accounts of pedestrians picking their way through corpses or being killed by plummeting stockbrokers. But all was base pandering to the mobs' lust for vengeance; no-one ever went broke by telling the people what they wanted to hear. In an attempt to quash the myth, the Medical Examiner's Office of New York announced that there had in fact been fewer suicides in the last quarter of 1929 than there had been in the corresponding period in 1928 and more in-depth analysis of statistics allowed J.K. Galbraith in his *The Great Crash:1929* (1954) to reveal that the suicide rate in the USA had been steadily climbing from 14 per 100,000 population to 17 per 100,000 in 1934 with, rather puzzlingly, a significant 'dip' across the tail end of 1929 and the first quarter of 1930. Between the opening refrains of the Crash on Black Thursday (24 October) and the end of the year only four of the 100 or so actual or attempted suicides in New York could be linked to the Crash and, of those, only two occurred on Wall Street; both these were indeed jumpers; the first was Hulda

Borowski, a simple clerk in a brokerage who leapt on 5 November and the second a Mr G.E. Cutler, head of a produce company who, for reasons unknown, flung himself from the window of his lawyer's Wall Street offices on 16 November. So, both Wall Street-related but neither a banker nor a financier.

The latest suicide figures for the USA show an increase to just under 23.7 per 100,000 population while Sweden, historically believed something of a world-leader in the self-topping tables, only manages 28.5 per 100,000, way behind Germany, Japan and, surprisingly, New Zealand. World leader is plucky little Lithuania with an impressive 87.4 per 100,000 rushing rudely unannounced into the presence of their maker every year; Russia comes a close second with 86.6 per 100,000 pop.

WICKED WITCH OF THE LEFT

Read the following quotation and ponder the author:

> We are Socialists; we are enemies of today's capitalistic economic system for the exploitation of the economically weak, with its unfair salaries, with its unseemly evaluation of a human being according to wealth and property instead of responsibility and performance, and we are determined to destroy this system under all conditions.

Point 9 of the manifesto of this speaker's political party stated that: 'All citizens shall have equal rights and duties'; Point 11 demanded 'The abolition of incomes unearned by work and the breaking of the slaver of interest'; Point 13 called for 'the nationalization of all businesses which have formed into corporations or trusts'; Point 14 demanded 'Profit-sharing in large industrial enterprises' and Point 18 called for 'The ruthless prosecution of those whose activities are injurious to the common interest. Common criminals, usurers, profiteers etc. must be punished with death, whatever their race or creed'. This chap also pronounced that: 'There is more that binds us to Bolshevism than separates us from it. There is, above all, genuine revolutionary feeling, which is alive everywhere in Russia … I have always made allowance for this circumstance and have given orders that former Communists are to be admitted to the Party at once. The petit bourgeois Social Democrat will never make a National Socialist but the Communists always will.' Thus speaks Adolf Hitler, a lefty through and through. Poor old Hitler;

no-one wants him in their tent: vegetarians do not like to include him in their roll of honour which is fine because it is myth that he so abstained; anti-smoking campaigners blanch at mention of the fact that Hitler was the first national leader to denounce smoking as anti-social and harmful and so banned it from all public buildings. It was also *verboten* in the Luftwaffe and the SS, so the image of the sneering Nazi with a cigarette holder is well wide of the mark. In addition, the left-wing always rear up in horror at the slightest hint that Hitler belongs in their camp, pointing to his anti-Semitic fervour as if it were some sort of right-wing marker – try telling that to the Jews who suffered widespread atrocities under Stalin. Even the man who coined 'anti-Semitic' was a hard-line lefty. Wilhelm Marr (1819–1904) 'invented' the term for his *The Way to Victory of the German Spirit over the Jewish Spirit* (1880) in which he blamed all the ills of his country on the Jews. Actually, Marr's coinage is a bit cockeyed; the Semitic peoples are predominantly Arab and only such Jews as hail from the Middle East can be included in that category. At the end of the day, the Jews are no more a race than are the Catholics; German/Hungarian/Russian/American Jews are not Semites, they are, for example, Russians who adhere to a particular belief-system; there is no such thing as 'Jewish blood' any more than there is 'Protestant blood'; it simply does not exist unless someone chooses to believe that it does, and that is when things get dangerous. But consistency was never Marr's strong suit; his first three wives were Jewish.

The famous Marxist historian, Eric Hobsbawm, witnessed Hitler's rise to power in the 1930s and was so struck by the similarity between Hitler's mob and the Communists that he wrote: 'If I had been German and not a Jew, I could see I might have become a Nazi.' It is not necessary here to over-egg the pudding with example after example and quote upon quote; those wishing to dig deeper into Hitler's left-wing credentials should google 'Hitler was a Socialist' and then select the *jonjayray.tripod.com* option which will take you to a fine, thirty-odd page article absolutely heaving with clarifying detail. The same argument can be made for Mussolini, raised by his dyed-in-the-wool Socialist parents who christened him after the left-wing Mexican revolutionary, Benito Juarez. Described in numerous police reports as a dangerous 'revolutionary Socialist' he established his left-wing Fascist Party and laid out its doctrines and principles with the help of Margherita Sarfatti (1880–1961), a hard-line, left-of-centre Socialist who only quit the Fascist Party she co-founded – and Mussolini's bed – when he started to play footsie with Hitler. Initially, Sarfatti was awash with admiration for Hitler and his Nazi doctrines too, but when the anti-Semitic element loomed too large for her to ignore she thought it wise for her, as a Jewess, to quit the scene. So, when present-day left-wing elements bandy 'Nazi' and 'Fascist' as insults for their political 'opposites', this is very much pot-and-kettle. Even today in Britain the confusion continues; Lord Tebbitt has repeatedly described the 'right-wing' British Nationalist Party (BNP) as 'Labour with racism and the BNP itself frequently acknowledges its ranks to be continually swelled by disaffected Labour and other left-wing voters, not those from the right. Anyone today wishing to hear Fascist rhetoric of the 'hang 'em, shoot 'em, flog 'em, deport 'em' variety only needs to visit any working-class pub, packed to the rafters with staunch 'left-wing' Labour voters, to think themselves in the Germany of the 1930s.

And what of Hitler the warlock, obsessed with the occult and astrology, constantly sending forth task forces to find the Spear of Destiny, the Arc of the Covenant, or whatever. This may make for jolly romps of the Indiana Jones genre but this too is rubbish; Hitler was openly scornful of all such mumbo-jumbo. In fact, under his regime, clairvoyants, astrologers, freemasons, spiritualists and assorted ouija-whackos were subject to legal proscription and persecution. The assertions that the Nazi regime had its roots in the occult is as wrong as it is still ongoing; since the 1950s there has grown a veritable industry founded on the idiotic notion that Hitler & co were a bunch of warlocks, or whatever, and that all their symbols and paraphernalia were drawn from the dark arts. Proponents of this nonsense insist, among other things, that the swastika, originally a good-luck solar symbol, was turned anti-clockwise by the Nazis to proclaim their satanic purpose but this is simply not so; the Nazi swastika always presented a clockwise rotation. Sure, the Nazis made great use of evocative signs and symbols but only because they knew that the bulk of the people could readily identify with them and because they united the mob. True, they made use of the ravings of that old charlatan, Nostradamus; even dropping thousands of leaflets over Europe presenting distorted versions of the original verses to 'prove' the Nazi cause, but then the British did exactly the same without attracting the slightest suggestion that Churchill too was into the occult.

Neither Hitler nor Churchill believed in such nonsense but were both acutely aware that an awful lot of people did – and still do; there is not a regional or national newspaper or women's magazine or similar sold in the UK without a horoscope page, Harry Potter is a hero and on Hallowe'en, or All Saints' Eve, the churches are empty while half the nation runs around dressed up as devils and vampires – should we designate the UK an occult nation? No, the really scary thing about Hitler was not that he was guided by some malevolent force/occult agenda, nor even that he was mad – which he wasn't – the really terrifying thing about Hitler was that he was a rather mundane little man and frighteningly human. (Any reader who wants to have a peek at the Nazi camp-guard in all of us only has to google 'The Milgram Experiment', conducted to coincide with the war-crimes trial of Adolf Eichmann, which proved that about three quarters of us are quite happy to kill innocent parties if instructed to do so within an apparent structure or official sanction).

As stated, all the Nazi-occult rubbish started in the 1950s, not built on any reality but on the machinations of a couple of con-men out for a fast buck during the war. In pre-war Germany, Goebbels began to explore the possibilities of using astrology and the writings of Nostradamus as a psychological weapon. As early as 1937 he established Section Six of the Reich Security Office and put it under the control of an opportunistic astrologer called Karl Ernst Krafft (1900–1945). It was Krafft who penned all of the bogus pro-German Nostradamus leaflets which, among others, were dropped all over France just before the invasion. Although Krafft boasted of being Hitler's personal astrologer he neither met him nor conducted any 'readings' or forecasts for him. When the Nazis realized towards the end of the war that Krafft was hedging his bets by working both sides of the astrological fence, cheerfully predicting success to anti-Hitler factions, they locked him up in the Lehrterstrasse Prison before shipping him out to Buchenwald Concentration Camp for gassing, he dying of typhus en route in his cattle truck. Bet he never saw that one coming!

Anyway, knowing of Krafft's involvement with the Nazi regime, another con-man, Louis de Wohl (1903–1961) managed to worm his way into British Intelligence by suggesting that if Hitler was being guided by an astrologer then he, Wohl, could figure out what Krafft was likely to be telling Hitler and thus second-guess what his decisions would likely be. Given the rank of captain and attached

to the Department of Psychological Warfare – SO2, Propaganda
Section, it was Wohl who knocked up *Nostradamus Predicts the Course
of the War*, the British booklet that was dropped in its thousands all
over Europe. In a memo to his case-officer, Lt. Col Gilbert Lennox,
and his Head of Department, Sir Charles Hambro (he of the banking
dynasty) Wohl wrote that by mirroring what he knew of Krafft's
methods he could predict Hitler's long-term strategy:

> The system, according to which Hitler is advised, is universal, and,
> being mathematical, has nothing whatsoever to do with clairvoyance
> or mystic matters. Checking up on the events of the past, I found
> that all major enterprises of Hitler since he came to power have been
> undertaken under "good aspects". Hitler's famous "divine intuition"
> is in reality simply knowledge about planetary tendencies. This
> opens, of course, many possibilities from the psychological point of
> view. An attack made against Hitler at a time when he knows that
> his aspects are bad will certainly find him prone to some amount of
> defeatism. To force his hand then would be a definite advantage for us.

To say that no-one believed in Wohl's ability to deliver would be
to swing the pendulum too far the other way. Polls in both the UK
and the USA are fairly consistent in showing that about 40 per cent
of the populations actually believe their destinies to be governed by
glittering balls of plasma and spheres of rock millions of miles out in
space so, take any group of, say, doctors, accountants, taxi-drivers or
even intelligence officers, and a healthy proportion will be believers.
But Wohl was not hired because his handlers believed he had such
skills; they hired him because of their misplaced belief in the myth
that *Hitler* believed in such. In fact Lennox refused to circulate any
of what he deemed to be Wohl's 'pseudo-science' in case anyone *did*
believe it and started taking decisions based thereon. The Director of
Naval Intelligence, Admiral John Godfrey, although not a believer in
astrology, certainly thought that Wohl might prove invaluable if he
could figure out what Krafft was supposedly telling Hitler; having
re-examined some of Hitler's erratic decisions and actions Godfrey
was convinced that something or someone other than sanity was
directing the little chap and that could well be some star-gazer. But
it soon became apparent to all that Hitler needed no help from
anyone in the silly-decision department and that Wohl was nothing

but a cheap opportunist. The whole silly affair is best summed up by Professor Christopher Andrew PhD of Cambridge University who in February 2003 accepted the post of Official Historian of the Security Service and is due to release his official history of MI5. Andrew highlights a wealth of evidence clarifying that Hitler thought that astrology and all-such was pure nonsense: 'but the belief that he did pay attention to horoscopes entered the corporate mind of the Joint Intelligence Chiefs.'

The only prominent leader of any Western nation to be guided by astrology was not Hitler but Ronald Reagan (1911–2004), 40th President of the United States of America. Throughout their Hollywood years of the 1950s and '60s Ronald and Nancy let 'celebrity' star-gazer Carroll Richter influence their career-decisions and it then mattered little if a couple of B-movie stars allowed such a 'guru' to run their lives. But when the Reagans were in the White House it was regarded as altogether more sinister that another astrologer, Jan Quigley, was always on hand to issue 'guidance'. Naturally this was a PR disaster ('disaster' itself being a word that means 'against the stars') waiting to happen and, eventually, the White House did have to issue an acknowledgement on 3 May 1988 to the effect that the Reagans paid heed to the advice of Ms Quigley when it came to the President's schedule and so forth.

In the UK, there remains on the statue books the provision for burning at the stake for treason anyone who casts the horoscope of any of the presiding royal family. In previous and obviously more enlightened times, this provision was deemed a sensible precaution in case such shenanigans were employed by any usurper wishing to prepare for a coup on the day fate decreed that the monarch would die. The first to risk such condign punishment was Arthur Christiansen (1904–1963) entertainments editor of *The Sunday Express* who commissioned R.H. Naylor (1889–1952) to cast not only the horoscope of the newly born Princess Margaret (1930–2002) but also that of the rest of the royal family. Despite pressure from a few wags demanding their public execution, readers can see from their dates that no such action was taken.

BIBLIOGRAPHY

Anderson, Terry L. and Peter J. Hill, *The Not So Wild, Wild West: Property Rights on the Frontier* (Stanford Economics & Finance), Stanford University Press, 2004

Carnes, Mark C. *Past Imperfect: History According to the Movies*, Cassell Illustrated, 1996

Cawthorne, Nigel, *Sex Lives of the Kings and Queens of England: From Henry VIII to the Present Day*, Prion Books, 1996

Chambers Biographical Dictionary, Chambers, 1988

Encyclopaedia Americana (International Edition)

Encyclopaedia Britannica, 12th edn, 15th edn, Encyclopaedia Britannica Inc.

Goldman, Lawrence (ed.), *Oxford Dictionary of National Biography*, OUP, 2009

Hutton, Ronald, *The Triumph of the Moon: A History of Modern Pagan Witchcraft*, OUP, 1999

Ingstad, Helge and Anne Stine Ingstad, *Viking Discovery of America: The Excavation of a Norse Settlement in Anse Aux Meadows*, Facts on File, 2001

Jones, Terry, *Terry Jones' Medieval Lives*, BBC Books, 2004

Krech III, Shepard, *The Ecological Indian: Myth and History*, W. W. Norton & Co., 2000

Loewen, James W., *Lies Across America: What Our Historic Sites Get Wrong*, New Press, 1999

Lord, Walter, *A Night to Remember*, Henry Holt & Co, 1955

McKinsey, C. Dennis, *The Encyclopaedia of Biblical Errancy*, Prometheus Books, 1995

Purvis, Thomas L., *A Dictionary of American History*, Blackwell, 1997

Shenkman, Richard, *Legends, Lies & Cherished Myths of World History*, Harper Paperbacks, 1994

Takaki, Ronald, *Hiroshima: Why America Dropped the Bomb*, Little, Brown and Co, 1996

Uglow, Jennifer (ed. & compiler). *The Macmillan Dictionary of Women's Biography*, 2nd edn, Macmillan, 1989

Wilkins, Robert, *The Fireside book of Deadly Diseases*, Robert Hale, 1994

INDEX